AF700283

Finance Fictions

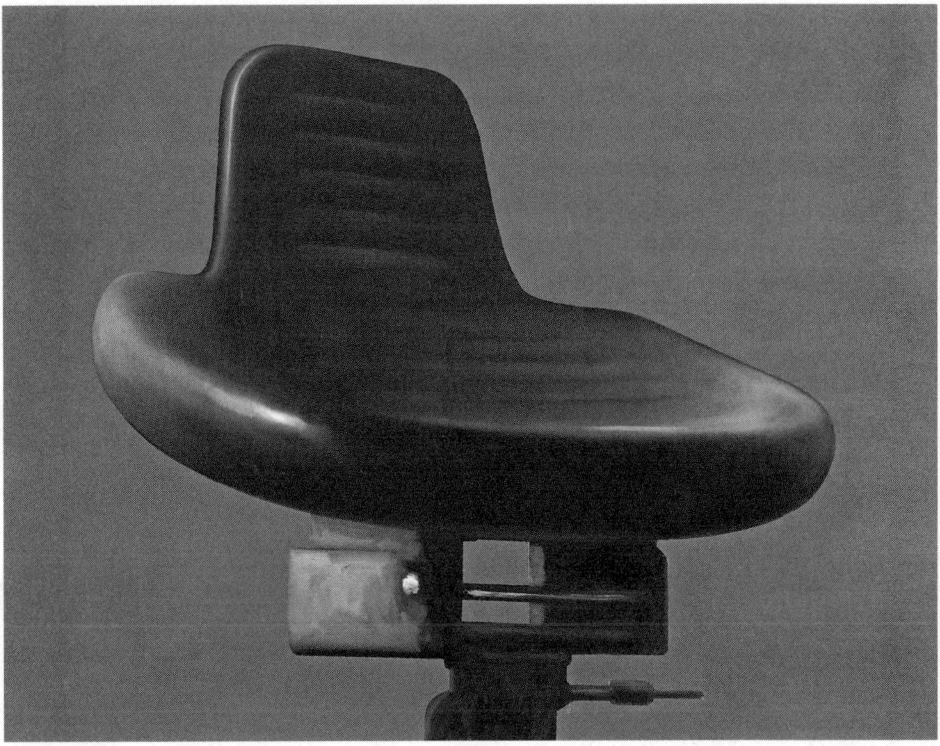

Finance Fictions

Realism and Psychosis in a Time of Economic Crisis

Arne De Boever

FORDHAM UNIVERSITY PRESS
NEW YORK 2018

Frontispiece: Asmund Havsteen-Mikkelsen, *Directing the Economy* (2011). 100×130, oil on canvas.

Copyright © 2018 Fordham Univvty Press

All rights reserved. No part of this publication may be reproduced, stored in a retrieval system, or transmitted in any form or by any means—electronic, mechanical, photocopy, recording, or any other—except for brief quotations in printed reviews, without the prior permission of the publisher.

Fordham University Press gratefully acknowledges financial assistance and support provided for the publication of this book by the California Institute of the Arts and by the Institute's School of Critical Studies.

Fordham University Press has no responsibility for the persistence or accuracy of URLs for external or third-party Internet websites referred to in this publication and does not guarantee that any content on such websites is, or will remain, accurate or appropriate.

Fordham University Press also publishes its books in a variety of electronic formats. Some content that appears in print may not be available in electronic books.

Visit us online at www.fordhampress.com.

Library of Congress Cataloging-in-Publication Data available online at https://catalog.loc.gov.

Printed in the United States of America

20 19 18   5 4 3 2 1

First edition

CONTENTS

It is all there in Plato (427–348 BCE*), down to the details of the hunched shoulders, the flickering screens, and the myopia.*

—J. M. COETZEE, letter to Paul Auster

In a deep sense, money is not. It exists empirically, but it is not essentially there at all. All money is what the French call escroquerie, swindling, it is a virtual or at best conceptual object. It is, in the strictest Platonic definitional sense (forget Baudrillard), a simulacrum, namely, something that materializes as an absence, an image for something that doesn't exist. Money is delusionary and faith in money is a form of collective psychosis. In the godless wasteland of global capitalism, money is our only metaphysics, our only onto-theo-logy, the only transcendent substance in which we truly must have faith. It is this faith that we celebrate, we venerate in commodity fetishism.

—SIMON CRITCHLEY AND TOM MCCARTHY

An artwork can remind you of the fact that the human construction of fictions and not some inevitable natural process is what determines experience to a large degree, you know?

—BEN LERNER, interview with Karl Smith

. . . feel the presence of absent human beings.

—BRIAN HOLMES, "Information's Metropolis"

. . . how everything turns away
quite leisurely from the disaster . . .

—W. H. AUDEN, "The Fall of Icarus"

Introduction

> He had recently found himself reading an article on the Web about hedge funds, absorbed in this subject as thoroughly as if it were *literature*, thinking about his own money as he kept reading, wondering whether he should invest with the charismatic guy who was being profiled—and he caught himself doing this and was shocked. He'd been lulled and snared by the pulsing screen and the promise of money begetting more money. It happened to people all the time; it had happened to him.
>
> —MEG WOLITZER, *The Interestings*[1]

Terror and Finance

If the images of the September 11 terror attacks—of the collapsing Twin Towers—are still with us today, that may be in part because they can be read as the prophetic announcement of the event that triggered this book: the economic collapse of 2008 and the state of economic crisis that it opened up. After all, it was not just the Twin Towers but the World Trade Center that collapsed on 9/11, and the images of the towers falling were arguably an uncanny anticipation of what was to come: not so much the war on terror, but the economic war between the 99 percent and the 1 percent that was produced in the aftermath of the financial crisis.

That very shift from 9/11 to the 2008 financial crisis has featured prominently in a number of contemporary novels. The best example is perhaps Don DeLillo's *Cosmopolis*.[2] Set in 2001, just before the September 11 attacks, but published in 2003 (it was DeLillo's first novel after the attacks), the novel's description of the young financier Eric Packer's self-destructive drive through New York (a "death drive" that Michael Naas has analyzed as an autoimmune reaction against Packer's fortified life)[3] suggests there is a connection between an economy driven by people like Packer (a speculator who trades foreign currencies, in particular the yen) and the attack on the World Trade Center.[4] Jacques Derrida—and Naas is one of the best Derrida scholars writing today—already proposed in a conversation with Giovanna Borradori that the September 11 attacks could be read as an autoimmune reaction against "fortress USA,"[5] drawing out all the more starkly the absurdity of the US government's response to the attacks: more fortification.[6] Packer is a figure of that narrative of sovereignty—a narrative of bodily immunity that is emphasized, in DeLillo's novel, by the storyline about Packer's "asymmetrical prostate."[7] The asymmetrical prostate (pro-state?) poses a potential threat: what to do about it? Packer, throughout the novel, seems to be in search of such threats and their potentially fatal consequences in a desperate attempt to encounter something—anything—real.

But this 9/11 narrative of sovereignty is tied to the novel's concern with the economy. In addition to being a figure of sovereignty, Packer is also a currency speculator, and there too he is on a crash course, as his currency analyst Michael Chin attempts to point out. Packer, however, does not back down: he appears to be in search of the crash—the book is structured, after all, around his attempt to "get a haircut," which is financial slang for suffering major losses. Packer's motivation appears to be that in such a loss, he will encounter something—anything—real. And he will indeed find this real at the very end of the novel, in his murderer "Benno Levin" (a portmanteau of "bin-Laden" and "nine eleven"? "Bin-Eleven?"), one of Packer's disgruntled former employees who through his erratic behavior seems to qualify as a representative of the real.

Looking over Packer's dead body, Levin reveals that he wanted "his pocket money for its personal qualities, not its value so much. I wanted its intimacy and touch, his touch, the stain of his personal dirt. I wanted to rub the bills over my face to remind me why I shot him."[8] If money, for the currency trader, is an immaterial tool for the generation of value—the art of money-making, as Packer's chief of theory, Vija Kinski, calls it—Levin breaks it out of that logic and turns it into a fetish of the material and the real: "intimacy," "touch," "stain," "dirt," "rubbing." That's exactly what

Packer desires: something real. Levin's "material" money, outside of the sphere of economic value, is presented as the antidote to a situation in which, as Kinski explains: "All wealth has become wealth for its own sake. There's no other kind of enormous wealth. Money has lost its narrative quality the way painting did once upon a time. Money is talking to itself."[9] Such non-narrative, self-referential money exists only on "screens," which Kinski "loves": "The glow of cyber-capital. So radiant and seductive. I understand none of it."[10] This goes beyond money as the mere flow of information: "We are not witnessing the flow of information so much," Packer muses, as "pure spectacle, or information made sacred, ritually unreadable. The small monitors of the office, home and car become a kind of idolatry here, where crowds might gather in astonishment."[11]

Kinski, as opposed to Chin, advises Packer *not* to divert from the financial crash course he is on: whereas Chin, the currency analyst, still believes in the ability to foresee the market—to trace it, analyze it, and predict it—Kinski, the chief of theory, thinks "it's all random phenomena": "[I]n the end you're dealing with a system that's out of control. Hysteria at high speeds, day to day, minute to minute. People in free societies don't have to fear the pathology of the state. We create our own frenzy, our own mass convulsions, driven by thinking machines that we have no final authority over. The frenzy is barely noticeable most of the time. It's simply how we live."[12] Packer will side with Kinski, who doesn't seem to give theory a particularly good rap: understanding nothing about cyber-capital—or so she claims—she gives up all authority over it, as if the market were a text whose author (in a distinguished theoretical tradition) is dead, with the text wandering the globe like one of Frankenstein's monsters and us passively exposed to its whims.

DeLillo's novel was visionary, a novel published in 2003 about the crash of 2008. It is also, however, and just as emphatically, a "pre-9/11 novel"[13]—about sovereignty, its limits and limitations—and it is up to readers to pursue the connections and differences between both.

The shift from 2001 to 2008 can also be read into the even earlier case of David Fincher's *Fight Club* (Fox, 1999), a faithful adaption of Chuck Palahniuk's novel by the same title. The novel came out in 1996, the film in 1999, so at first sight it does not seem like they can be used as examples in this context. And yet, that is precisely what the ending of Fincher's film—which is different from the novel's ending—enables us to propose when it is viewed

Collapsing towers in David Fincher's *Fight Club*.

again after the September 11 attacks. Whereas Palahniuk's novel about a psychotic recall campaign coordinator for a major car company ends either "in heaven"[14] or—more likely, given the mention of the "rubber-soled shoes" and the fact that the narrator can receive mail there and make telephone calls[15]—in a hospital or asylum, the film ends by showing the collapse of various credit card company buildings: they have been bombed by the narrator's alter ego, Tyler Durden, and his revolutionary group Project Mayhem.

If in 1999, one could perhaps still behold this attack in sympathy with Durden and his crew, who are fighting consumerist capitalism throughout the novel and by their bombing seek to erase debt, that subject position became much more complicated after the September 11 attacks, which featured a collapse of towers that was, from an aesthetic point of view, strikingly similar to the collapse of towers shown at the end of Fincher's film.[16]

Politically, there may have been a connection as well, given that the September 11 attacks had the World Trade Center as their main target. But it seemed impossible, at least at first, to make that connection. Seeing the film again, however, in the aftermath of the 2008 economic crash, and then also in the context of the rise of the Occupy Wall Street movement and the economic war between the 1 percent and the 99 percent, those affects are likely to have shifted once more, with Durden potentially reappearing—as the September 11 window is closing—as a hero in today's economic crisis.

Sam Esmail's *Mr. Robot* (USA Network, 2015)—a TV series about Elliot Alderson, a cybersecurity engineer by day and activist hacker by night who brings down the world financial system in an attempt to erase debt—makes this for now final rereading of *Fight Club* explicit through its general indebtedness to Fincher's film. In the ninth episode of the show's first season, when it becomes clear beyond doubt that Elliot suffers from psychosis and that a major character in the show (Elliot's father) was a hallucination, Esmail puts Maxence Cyrin's piano cover of The Pixies' "Where is My Mind?" to images of Elliot accepting responsibility for the revolution that, unwittingly, he has been creating—a clear reference to the ending of Fincher's *Fight Club*, which has the original Pixies song playing over images of the collapsing credit card company towers.

The song's title "Where is my mind?"—which came to resonate with the end of the Cold War shortly after it came out (on The Pixies' *Surfer Rosa* album, in 1988)—of course marks the importance of psychosis in both *Fight Club* and *Mr. Robot*, a state of mind that (as I will discuss both in this introduction and in the following chapters) is intimately connected to financialization. Indeed, it is Elliot's father—a hallucination—who explains some twenty minutes before the end of season 1, episode 1 that the money by which his son is governed is not real: "Money hasn't been real since we got off the gold standard," he lectures. Sounding very much like Vija Kinski in *Cosmopolis*, he adds that money has "become something virtual, software, the operating system of the world." It's probably no coincidence that the scene is followed by images of Elliot walking through the New York City subway system, with Neil Diamond's rendition of "If You Go Away" (an English-language cover of the Belgian singer Jacques Brel's stunningly beautiful "Ne Me Quitte Pas"): the Neil Diamond version is from 1971, the very year when "we got off the gold standard." One has to imagine "Diamond" addressing "gold" here, as one precious material to another: "If you go away . . ."

Post-2008 culture has established the link to 9/11 as well: think, for example, of that memorable moment in Adam McKay's *The Big Short* (Paramount, 2015), when Ryan Gosling's character Jared Vennett presents a modern mortgage bond "Jenga" tower made up of blocks representing tranches of flawed mortgages, with Vennett starting to take some of the blocks out—to mimic the effect, for example, of homeowners defaulting on their mortgage payments after the increase of their adjustable interest rates kicks in—until of course the tower comes crashing down. "That's

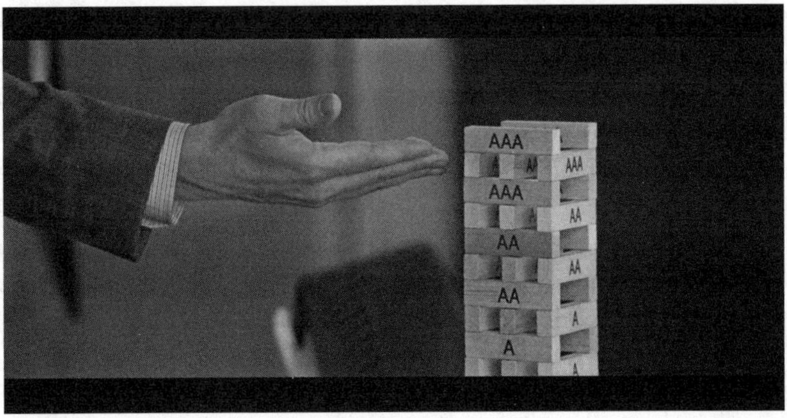

Jenga tower in Adam McKay's *The Big Short.*

America's housing market," he concludes, looking into the immediate future—but viewers had also already seen that collapsing financial tower before: in 2001.[17]

In other words, there is a chronology of finance and terror at work in my multiple readings of *Fight Club*—one that's evident in DeLillo's *Cosmopolis* and McKay's *The Big Short* as well—that deserves to be considered in the context of any investigation of cultural representations of the 2008 financial crisis. Put the finance *before* the September 11 attacks (as in DeLillo, or *Fight Club* before 9/11), and you create the suggestion that the contemporary economic situation was quite simply inviting the attacks. Treat the financial crisis *after* the September 11 attacks (*Fight Club* after 9/11), and you may defuse the reader's anger toward the financiers responsible for it.

Something like that risks to happen in Cristina Alger's novel *The Darlings*, which was based on the Madoff investment scandal, and credited as one of the first to deal with the 2008 crash.[18] Alger, whose book I will return to at the end of chapter 1, reverses the chronology of finance and terror that can be found in *Cosmopolis*, with some of the criminal financiers whose stories she recounts nostalgically looking back at their lives before the attacks. The effects of this are complex: it humanizes the financiers and makes the reader sympathize with them.[19] More concretely, the relation to September 11 risks to prevent one of the characters who is in a position to expose financial corruption from actually doing so, creating the provocative suggestion that the trauma of the collapse of the World Trade Center may have softened our collective response to the excesses of Wall Street. They already took a big hit then; should we really go after them *again*? Fly into their buildings all over again? Become terrorists of a kind?

There are, of course, other options: some of the force of Jess Walter's *The Zero* (2006) comes from its discussion of the post-9/11 speculative real estate market (a "young stock analyst wanted us to make an option offer on a hedge for a potential studio in a proposed rehab on some regrade land possibly slated for rezoning down in BPC"[20]) next to negotiations with a lawyer earlier on in the novel about the valuation of a human life that was lost in the terror attacks. For one of the novel's characters, a real estate broker who lost both her husband and her sister in the attacks, her job stops making sense. She is troubled in particular by the amounts of money involved (they far exceed the state's valuation of a human life) and the immaterial "air"-like[21] nature of real estate speculation (as opposed to the real, material loss of a human life) and she breaks down at the office several months after the attacks. Finance comes after terror here, but Walter uses the devastating affect of 9/11 to go after post-9/11 speculative finance.[22]

Consider also, as two final examples in this context, Mohsin Hamid's *The Reluctant Fundamentalist* (2008), which treats finance before the September 11 attacks but complicates the situation by having its protagonist—a young Pakistani who is very successful in New York's corporate finance world—become a target of racism and Islamophobia after the attacks, thus making him revisit the dubious ethics of his employment and gradually pushing him into his titular role of "reluctant fundamentalist," the position from where the novel is narrated.[23] The narrative voice of Hamid's financial 9/11 novel resonates, I would suggest, with that of Teddy Wayne's novel *Kapitoil* (2010), which traces the pre-9/11 rise and fall of another Muslim immigrant, Karim Issar, who works as quant for a New York–based financial firm and designs an algorithm that can predict fluctuations in oil prices. While Wayne's novel mostly takes on the automated and dehumanized financial world and was received (after its publication in 2010) in light of the 2008 crisis, it is worth noting that Wayne himself has characterized it as a pre-9/11 novel, thus tying together the terrorist attacks with the collapse of the financial markets—a connection that, as I indicated, already lay inscribed in the 9/11 event.

Finance Fictions

While this book will turn out to have taken place in the shadow of the 9/11 events, with my conclusion returning to those events to theorize the politics of some of the economic transformations that I discuss, my focus will be on the 2008 financial crisis, and on how novels—mostly Anglo-American novels, but I will look beyond that as well—have captured the new economic reality that contemporary finance has produced.[24] As my title suggests, I will be looking specifically at the *finance* economy, that is, at an economic system in which the commodity that is central to Karl Marx's theory of capital—a theory in which M (money), through the production and sale of C (commodity), leads to M' (money that is worth more money)[25]—has been replaced by complex financial strategies and instruments such as portfolio insurance, collateralized debt obligations (CDOs), or credit default swaps (CDSs).[26] This is no longer an economic system in which the workers face the owners of the means of production; it is no longer a system that is organized around material labor, even if such economic systems also continue in addition to the financial one. By contrast, finance names a digitized economy of algorithms that trade immaterial constructs, often at frequencies too high for human beings or even computers to observe. As Randy Martin has pointed out, the usefulness of finance's "commodities," if they can still be called that, is based merely on the fact that they allow for further exchange.[27] Exchange—or more precisely, circulation—is the only need of the body or the mind that, as commodities, they satisfy. If workers still exist in this new form of capitalism (much human labor has of course been replaced by bots), they are often performing cognitive, immaterial labor and often pride themselves on what some have analyzed as an "artistic" sensibility that makes them creative, flexible, and adaptable to the whims of the contemporary economic regime.[28] With their savings, mutual funds investments, or retirement accounts exposed to the risks of the digitized market, these cognitive laborers are the new proletariat or cognitariat whose livelihood is being traded for the benefit of so-called trader scalpers (short-term traders with no real investments in the market) whose algorithms help them to become rich fast.[29]

There is a particular economic and technological side to this that I will address in my chapters and that involves—though in a way that's more complicated than Elliot Alderson's father in *Mr. Robot* suggests—the Nixon administration's decision in 1971, in response to the rising cost of the Vietnam war, to unilaterally abolish the gold standard, thus ending the Bretton Woods system of international exchange which had been in place since after World War II and pegged all currencies to the dollar (which was pegged to gold). This threw the economy into a state of crisis that is commonly referred to as the "Nixon shock."[30] While finance is obviously much older than the 1970s—Fredric Jameson points out that it was used in a book title as early as 1910 and Arjun Appadurai traces the origins of derivatives (central to the financial era) back much further even[31]—it is a point of general agreement that Nixon's abolition of the gold standard marked the beginning of an era of unbridled economic speculation (high-risk financial action) that is at the origin of our economic situation today. In his essay "Culture and Finance Capital," however, Jameson also warns for the false suggestion of solidity and tangibility that risks to come with the reference to the gold standard, as if before the gold standard money somehow held actual, material value.[32] Felix Martin and David Graeber among others have undermined those kinds of materialist accounts—commodity theories of money—that trace money back to societies of exchange in which, as the story generally goes, people started using money as a substitute for the valuable material goods that they were trading, with precious metals such as gold or silver standing in for the value of, for example, cattle.[33]

The abolition of the gold standard fits in that story as an example of how sovereigns over time hollowed out the actual, material value of money (leading to the fiat theory of money, a theory of money that is valuable by sovereign fiat rather than as commodity), creating the impression that there was a time—the good old days—when money was actually worth something. Scholars such as Martin and Graeber have shown that this is a false genealogy: money has no actual, material value. It is a social relation that originates in transferable credit (Martin) or debt (Graeber) (the credit theory of money), and gold and ultimately the gold standard simply created the *illusion* of money's actual, material value. That materialist approach to money is ultimately no more than an aberrant episode in the history of money theory, one that we are unfortunately still suffering from today; in reality, money has always been "speculative," a symbolic or tokenistic representation of credit or debt, and in that sense the complex financial products—ultimately no more than glowing green symbols—that are traded on the economic markets today are perhaps less troubling than they seem.[34] As Graeber puts it in *Debt*: "What we now call virtual money came first."[35] From commodity theory, to fiat theory, to the credit/debt theory of money: as Ole Bjerg has demonstrated, none ultimately provides a full philosophical theory of money, as they all need to take recourse to each other to be philosophically coherent. This leads Bjerg to present money as a "dirty" philosophical object: something that "never exists in any theoretically pure form." Money's "fundamental constitution . . . is somehow *unknowable*."[36]

However, and even taking into account analyses such as Martin's or Graeber's, the Nixon shock still remains a key moment in recent financial history because in a sense it restored money to its speculative origins, setting free the speculative potential it harbors to an unprecedented degree. There is no doubt, even in view of Martin's or Graeber's corrective narratives, that the economy is more speculative today than it was before the 1970s, even if that does not mean that it was not speculative before. While the reference to the Nixon shock should not bring the false suggestion of solidity and tangibility for which Jameson already warned us, that caveat should also not take away from the fact that speculation has clearly intensified in the economy since the 1970s. *Finance Fictions* inscribes itself into that intensification,[37] and most of the materials that I will be looking at date from after the 1970s—my "economic" understanding of "the contemporary" in this book begins there, with the September 11 attacks standing somewhere in the middle between that moment and the time of my writing. This is also the history of the creation of the complex financial instruments that I have already mentioned and the rise to dominance (since 2000, but especially after 2008) of a subset of automated trading, high-frequency trading.

While "finance" thus receives a specific definition, philosophical understanding, and also history in this book, *Finance Fictions* is not immune to what Leigh Claire La Berge has characterized as finance's "representational dominance" in studies of literature and the economy[38]—to finance's eclipse in representations of the economy of other aspects of the economy. As La Berge points out, this appears to be endemic to the field (it might in fact be a key aspect of financialization) and some of its central objects of study.

Although Tom Wolfe's *The Bonfire of the Vanities*, for example, became famous because of the stock market crash of 1987, the "financial" part of the novel in fact deals with the bonds market, a difference that has gone largely unnoticed. To a certain extent, I too will contribute to that confusion by moving across financial markets and eliding differences that some may think should have been more carefully assessed—and should have been mobilized as integral parts of the argument. And yet, while not all of the economy adds up to finance, and while not all markets are stock markets, I am also suggesting that finance—as a general term that contends with that other general term, the economy—reveals something already present in capital, something that is also at the core of money, that is intimately related to the tension between psychosis and realism that I will show to be prominent in the financial fiction genre. If finance therefore attains a representational dominance in this book, it is in part as a concept that enables us to reveal that core.

The consequences of the Nixon shock for human beings were multiple, but I focus on one in particular that is brought up in the novels I look at: increased psychosis. Put simply, over and over again the novels I look at contain the suggestion that the economy—money, but in particular finance—renders human beings psychotic. By this, I mean (following the standard Freudian definition) that money and in particular the speculative operations of finance make human beings disavow existing reality, sometimes in combination with the substitution of another reality for the existing one. This theme was already lurking in some of the examples that I gave earlier: Eric Packer in DeLillo's *Cosmopolis* seeks to destroy the fortified reality in which he lives because it is a psychotic construction—supported by money—that removes him from actual reality. Eric's autoimmune response seeks to break through this psychotic situation—interestingly, in part through his currency speculation—as part of a desperate search for the real: a real that will arrive, perhaps predictably, at the end of the novel in the form of Eric's death.

Fincher's *Fight Club* effectively uses its medium—the difference between literature and film—to translate Palahniuk's psychotic tale to the screen: Tyler Durden, the narrator's alter ego—referred to in the novel as "a projection," "a dissociative personality disorder," "a psychogenic fugue state," "my hallucination," "a separate personality," "just like Tony Perkins' mother in

Psycho" (more on that last reference in chapter 2)[39]—is at various moments briefly spliced into Fincher's film, in the same way that pornographic images are spliced into the family films that Durden is showing during his job as a projectionist. Those splicings emphasize Durden's psychosis, the fact that the film's narrator has been rendered psychotic by the financialized world in which he lives.

But it would be equally important to note—and perhaps even more important given the fact that Durden's attack goes against credit card companies—the creative side of Durden's psychosis in this situation: Durden, like Packer, mobilizes the psychosis that finance has produced in him *against* finance—a creative reappropriation of finance's pathologizing condition in the service of the destruction of finance. It is in that sense that the film's final, murderous (suicidal?) struggle between ego and alter ego needs to be understood: as the autoimmune response of a system—finance/the narrator—against itself.

Interestingly, one of the most notable instances of Durden's creative splicing occurs in the film's closing scene, where Fincher inserts a pornographic image of a penis into the footage of the collapsing towers. There is an obvious connection here with castration, the attack on phallocentric power and the "big swinging dick" culture (see chapter 4 and my conclusion) that still dominate the trading world. Indeed, and in spite of the focus on male subjectivity that tends to come with the territory of finance, much of the criticism of the connection between sovereignty and finance that I develop in the following chapters can be read as a feminist criticism of a masculinist immunity strategy that ends up producing precisely the opposite of what it aspires to.[40]

It would be important to insist on psychosis rather than neurosis in this context.[41] According to Freud, who was much more interested in neurosis than psychosis, a psychotic person (1) disavows reality and (2) substitutes another reality for it (3) in the service of an Id that has gotten out of control. Psychosis is to be contrasted with neurosis on these counts: the neurotic will (3) repress the Id (1) in favor of a reality (2) that is in tension with the Id.[42] This means, as MOMA's curator Klaus Biesenbach points out in a text about the artist Douglas Gordon (see chapter 2), that "the diagnostic border between neurosis and psychosis occurs when the patient can no longer cover up his symptoms, when the inner voice or paranoid plot within him takes over and rules his daily behaviors."[43] *Fight Club*—as well as several other finance novels, including (as I will show in chapter 1) the supposedly "realist" *Bonfire of the Vanities*—dramatizes this situation. The neurotic does not break with existing reality but neurotically confirms it—the neurotic breaks, rather, with him- or herself. The psychotic, on the other hand, totalizes him- or herself, leaving existing reality behind.

The question of the awareness of one's doing is, from the clinical point of view, a big issue in this context, and one that has been marked by the difference between psychosis—which is considered irrational and comes with a hallucinatory dimension—and psychopathy, where affected individuals know what they are doing and why they are doing it. The difference can bring some nuance for example to the conversation about Bret Easton Ellis's *American Psycho* (chapter 2), which arguably chronicles a shift from psychopathy to psychosis. However, I will not mobilize that distinction here. Instead, I will use the term *psychosis* in a more general fashion to reveal what I consider to be the key affliction of our particular economic moment: with the abolition of the gold standard, the creation of complex financial instruments, the rise of high-frequency trading, and the unbridled intensification of speculative economic practices, we have moved from an era in which neurosis was the dominant affliction into an era in which psychosis has become prevalent.[44] While the capitalist era, and Marx's theory of capital, can largely be confined to the neurotic paradigm, illustrated by the centrality of the actual, material commodity to Marx's theory (isn't Marxism—with its insistence on, for example, the conditions of production—arguably a neurotic philosophy and politics, confirming reality against attempts to disavow it?), it nevertheless already contained elements of psychosis that, today, have gotten out of control. From the fetishism of the commodity (a particular form of neurosis that enables the reality of a thing and its phantasy to coexist) of the first volume of *Capital*[45] to the "fictitious capital" in the third volume that has been defined as "value, in the form of credit, shares, debt, speculation and various forms of paper money, above and beyond what can be realized in the form of commodities,"[46] Marx was already on the track of the ultimately psychotic, reality-disavowing effects of money, capital, and (ultimately) finance.

Part of the historical confluence that must be considered in this context is the ways in which this intensified psychosis of finance has linked up, in the late twentieth and the twenty-first centuries, with technological developments in digital culture that have produced a hypermediatized environment that has been characterized as psychotic.[47] The psychotic culture of finance thus connects to psychotic digital culture, creating the particular situation of digitized finance that is responsible for example for the market crash of 2010.[48] *Finance Fictions* is ultimately interested in the role of the novel in that situation. This requires different kinds of assessments: what is the role of psychosis in the finance novel, how does the novel as a work of fiction relate to it? What is the role of the digital in the finance novel? Finally, and related to both of the previous, what is the role of finance in the finance novel? How does the novel relate to contemporary finance? Can it represent it? How?

I will be interested, first of all, in marking the novel's role as a fiction in relation to the psychosis that characterizes contemporary digital and financial culture. Although the novel, as a fictional genre, shares some elements with psychosis—as fictional constructs, all novels can be said to disavow existing reality and to substitute another reality for it—fiction nevertheless takes up an attenuated position in relation to full-blown psychosis in the sense that a full-blown psychotic novel would probably be illegible because it would destroy entirely the possibility of a relationality between the reader and the reality represented in the novel. In other words, although all fictions are arguably psychotic, there is a degree of realism in fiction that makes it different, still, from psychosis.

By saying this, I do not mean to mark a stark borderline between reality/realism and psychosis (and there is a way in which both terms will continuously be looping back to each other throughout this book): indeed, we must consider the possibility (in my discussion of *American Psycho*, in particular; but also in my reading of *The Fear Index* in chapter 3) that the "psychotic" reality may ultimately be more real than actual reality, that it may accomplish a higher form of realism—especially when it comes to writing digital and financial culture—than ordinary realism. This is why, I think, Antonio Scurati uses the term "psychotic realism" in another but not unrelated context to name novels that describe our contemporary hypermediatized situation.[49] While the novel can thus be said to bring a degree of realism to psychosis, it is nevertheless also important to insist on the question of degree: a novel, after all, always also remains a fiction, and thus it always also maintains a degree of what could be called "psychosis" in relation to, say, the dry, actual reality that—in relation to the psychotic loss of reality—it can be said to write. Fiction mediates, in other words, between psychosis and realism and the novel's position at this crossroads between the disavowal of reality and the affirmation of it will come to play a crucial role in the following chapters.

As media studies and digital studies approaches to the novel as well as some of the debates about the digital humanities illustrate, the novel's relation to digital culture is complicated—and developing as I write—and I doubt that I will be able to address it in a satisfactory way. As some of my other work has made clear, I think the novel—specifically the realist novel, a form that (as I suggest in chapter 3) includes both realist and psychotic elements—should be assessed within a history of other media (life-drawing, photography, silent film, color film, 3-D film) that have sought to write life in its most intimate details.[50] When it comes to writing life in the digitized era, I am particularly interested in the project of novel writing in the information society—how do novelists deal with the wealth of information that is currently available to them as they are writing a novel? How do contemporary novels reflect the expansiveness of the information era?[51]—which operates at a speed that is generally considered to be at odds with the novel (traditionally understood as a slow genre), and is often driven by nonhuman agents (also a big no-no for the novel). Is it possible to write a novel of the high-speed information society governed by algorithmic agents? "Realism" is thought to have an affinity with "the gold standard" through its referentiality. If the new gold standard (established in the 1970s) is information—if the gold standard has been replaced by "the information standard," as Walter Wriston has suggested[52]—what is its equivalent literary aesthetic? Some experiments have pushed into those directions: science fiction has experimented with nonhuman narrators[53]; the form of the novel has been morphing into a collection of intricately connected short stories, thus possibly returning to the serialized form as which it originated.[54] Tweet fiction is formatted perfectly for the contemporary age.[55] The rising popularity of television series over feature films is arguably also an indication of those developments.[56]

I single out these elements—information, speed, nonhuman agency—because they are crucial for digitized finance as well, and in fact some of the transformations that the novel has undergone in recent years could also be read as financializations of the novel form, looping back to the serialized novel's origins in capitalism but also going beyond that into new modes that are shaped by a different technological and dromological situation.[57]

In the following chapters, and following other work in this field,[58] I consider "realism" as one possible name for the battle field where some of those tensions I have mentioned are played out.[59] The field is, obviously, vast and I will drastically shrink it down in view of the discussion that has occurred around realism in readings of the financial fiction genre and in view of the philosophical argument about the reality of contemporary finance that I want to pursue. I consider realism's program at its most basic, and some might say vulgar, to be to give an account of the world. Some would insist on a realism of subjective experience instead. After that, it all depends: some would fill in those programs by a call for descriptive detail—the more the better; others by a call for *some* detail: here, it is the careful choice of detail that accomplishes the realist aspiration. Others yet might argue for as few details as possible—for only such a minimalist description can encompass it all. Those positions arguably have come into their own in view of the fact that realism is essentially an impossible aesthetic: a text will never be able to give an account of the world (internal or external), if to give an account of the world ultimately means to overcome the difference between the self, the world, and their representation. There is an ontological gap—evoked, for example, in Jorge Luis Borges's story "On Exactitude in Science"—that persists.

One could be tempted, following Ben Lerner's discussion in *The Hatred of Poetry* (see chapter 6), to speak of a "virtual realism" in this context, that is, of a realism that inevitably always holds back from its ultimate aspiration—that can always only write the gap between the world and its representation. Perhaps that is part of the reason why realism, like poetry (though not to the same extent), has also attracted a good number of haters. Modernism and postmodernism, rather than marking a break with realism, should be considered as aesthetic intensifications of realism's essential virtuality, its impossibility: the fact that it wants to give an account of the world, but can't. Realism would, then, in the words of Anna Kornbluh, need to be understood precisely "not as the determined reflection of established reality, but as the over-determined representation of unsolvable dilemmas that disrupt the integration of reality."[60] Realism doesn't just give an account of the world but "makes a world while highlighting the artifice of its making" and it is "as fiction," Kornbluh argues, as "the creation of excessive, aberrant, counter-factual realities—and not as documentary evidence—that realist literature is also able to think the conditions of fictitious capital."[61] One thing is for sure: after postmodernism, contemporary literature and literary criticism are invested in realism once again and part of what I want to explore is the nexus between that revival of literary realism and the revival of the finance novel.

My suggestion is that the finance novel is a site where those core issues of realism become particularly exposed. The finance novel is caught up, I want to show, between a psychotic approach to finance that draws out finance's—and by extension money's—psychotic effects on human beings as well as what I understand to be money's historical, psychotic core; and a realist approach to finance that would seek to move away from psychosis in order to focus, in a vulgarly realist manner, on the technical details of finance (the "what" and the "how" of finance). While the recent history of the finance novel shows a promising development from psychosis to realism in this context, "realism" is confronted with a fundamental issue here because it seeks to give an account of what essentially defies narration and even representation. While this seems to pose an inevitable problem to what could be called the cut-and-dry realism of a journalistic finance novelist such as Tom Wolfe, who insists novelists should become better reporters if they want to tame the financial beast—in chapter 4 I argue that today's finance marks an ontological difference to Wolfe's epistemological approach—that is likely not so much the case for more capacious understandings of realism, which would recognize that realism has always been aware of its impossible or virtual project. Like Lerner, who in his discussion of the virtual poem develops close readings of poems in which poets, as he sees it, mobilize poetic techniques that seem to consciously set their writings aside from the poem that they set out to produce, one would then have to distinguish similar techniques in contemporary realisms as well, techniques that would consciously set aside their descriptive project from the reality they seek to capture. That is part of what I seek to do, and it will involve taking realism outside of the straightjacket in which it is caught in order to restore it to the looser fit of its origins. This also requires, in chapters 5 and 6, the assessment of the relation of realism to financialization—the consideration of the possibility of a complicity between the logic of realism and that of financialization.

Today's digitized financial reality of high-speed algorithmic trading ultimately pushes the realist novel in this book outside of its neurotic, reality-affirming framework—importantly, not into a full-blown psychotic fiction but toward a realist account of psychotic finance. For the thinking part, I will rely in chapter 4 on recent philosophical developments in speculative realism that have been picked up in a so-called market philosophy: philosophical reflections about the financial markets. My aim is, however, to tie the philosophical conclusions that are reached in such reflections to an ongoing conversation about literary realism and specifically its relation to finance, in order to show—following a Jamesonian trajectory,[62] but going beyond postmodernism—that the kind of realism that has been proposed to capture finance is hopelessly outdated: instead, we need another kind of writing. Traces of such a writing can already be found in some classic examples of the finance fiction genre, even if it takes a certain kind of reading to tease it out. But I will also discuss, at the end of chapter 4, some more experimental, and in some cases conceptual, forms of writing that accomplish a destruction of the novel in their (in my view, successful) attempt to write finance.

That will leave us with the question of the novel's compatibility with finance: if the novel, at the point when it writes finance, is seen to self-destruct, this might reveal an essential, unbridgeable gap between the one and the other that, on the one hand, could deem the novel to be completely irrelevant as a literary form in the era of digitized, high-frequency trading; on the other hand, it could also present the novel as a last resort in the ever-expanding process of financialization, a battleground on which the tensions involved in that process are played out—in some cases with the destruction of finance or of the novel as a consequence.[63] Finally, there is also a more perverse reading of this "destruction" that I will consider: the realist novel's reluctance to properly write finance which may be read as a financialization of realism itself—as a drawing out of realism's financial logic of deriving its value from the promise of a reality that it cannot deliver. The realist novel would become, according to this reading, a financial instrument, ideal for speculation, prone to the booms and busts of finance.

As far as my focus on the novel goes, it is my interest in realism that has pushed me there. The novel seemed to be the obvious place to look in order to find a realism of finance. By that I do not mean to suggest that the novel is the only place to look if one wants to think through finance and literature. As a matter of fact, it is precisely the limits to realism that finance poses that (in addition to adjusting a narrow understanding of realism) open up my discussion of novels onto experimental writing and poetry. The difference can be marked by what I call, in chapter 4, a shift from a descriptive toward a performative or also conceptual realism that manages to write finance otherwise. Those are certainly also traits that the novel can take on, techniques that the novel can mobilize, to write finance. But when it comes to the program of a vulgar kind of financial realism, namely, to give an account of finance, I would imagine that the novel is still the best place to look. And what I found there was an essential impossibility to deliver such an account, an impossibility that—much more generally—resonates with realism's essential virtuality, the impossibility of its project. That applies, of course, to anything that's up for representation; but finance marks this impossibility with an intensity of its own.

I have, at several moments in this introduction, evoked Marx and it would probably be helpful to mark, however minimally, this project's relation to Marxism. In its desire for a realist representation of finance (against what I would characterize, after Bernard Stiegler, as our "proletarianization" in relation to finance[64]), this project is arguably a Marxist one, in the sense that it expects the so-called finance novel to have something to say about finance. That means that if the finance novel ends up privileging psychosis over finance, it can be criticized from a Marxist point of view, for leaving the reality of finance by the wayside. But the book also challenges a certain kind of Marxist response to this, namely, the call for finance novels that would in turn drop psychosis and focus on finance alone: that would forget about a key aspect of finance, capital, and money—one that Marx was already on the track of with the fetishism of the commodity and fictitious capital. In fact, the cut-and-dry realism that a certain kind of Marxism might want to aspire to in this context decidedly will not be able to capture the reality of finance today, in the same way that it wasn't able to capture capital (fictitious capital in particular; the fetishism of the commodity as well), or do justice to money's immaterial origins. This gestures at the centrality of fiction to my position.

Some of those negotiations within realism and Marxism can be evoked through a reconsideration of the title of Joseph Vogl's book *The Spectre of Capital.*[65] Vogl borrows his title from DeLillo's *Cosmopolis*, which includes the line: "A SPECTER IS HAUNTING THE WORLD—THE SPECTER OF CAPITALISM."[66] That line is of course in turn a reference to "The Communist Manifesto," which opens with: "A spectre is haunting Europe—the spectre of Communism."[67] To understand the full impact of that line in the context of *Finance Fictions*, one must understand how it operates in the manifesto. What Marx and Engels point out is that communism is evoked as a specter, or ghost, in order to frighten the Europeans. Their project in the manifesto is to de-spectralize communism: to show its concrete demands (which they list in their text), to show that it is anything but a ghost. Vogl pursues a similar project with capitalism, which he argues (after DeLillo) is made into a specter today. Vogl thinks we should de-spectralize it: understand it, reveal its concrete operations and demands. Only then will we be in a strong position to confront it. While I largely agree with Vogl—indeed, my pursuit of a "financial realism" in this book should be read along similar lines—my discussion of speculative realism in chapter 4 will also indicate a holding on to what I understand to be an essentially spectral element of contemporary finance and its elements: the complex financial products that it trades, the speed of its algorithmic trading, and so on. One cannot give up the ghost in the discussion of the contemporary economy: a more peculiar realism is required. In that sense, I may be closer, then, to Jacques Derrida's *Specters of Marx* (1994), which shows that capitalism cannot be thought without the specter.[68]

Finally, a note about scope and methodology. I consider this to be first and foremost an American studies project, in the sense that my focus is mostly on US cultural production, the US economy, and the US stock markets. That said, the project is also more internationalist in scope and includes discussions of novels from the United Kingdom, France, and Germany; much of its philosophical apparatus is drawn from continental Europe, in particular France. My suggestion is that those sources of continental thought, in particular of market philosophy,[69] can help us think the reality of the stock markets today. I therefore look at finance and finance fiction mostly from a Euro-US perspective. Within this perspective's limitations, I do not develop strong comparativist claims about US fiction versus French fiction, for example; I understand, of course, that the United States and France play different roles in the world economy, but the reason I turn to the French novelist Michel Houellebecq in chapter 5 is quite simply because his entire oeuvre engages the related questions of economic issues and realist representation that I also engage in this book. In part also because of its connections to Bret Easton Ellis's work, and especially to Ben Lerner's *10:04*, Houellebecq's oeuvre seemed like a good place to turn for the specific concerns I wanted to push in the book's closing chapters.

When I turn to Sebald in my conclusion, that too does not come with a strong comparativist claim, although it is worth noting how Sebald's own emigration from Germany after World War II is connected to the country's economic *Wiederaufbau*, which eclipsed a deeper, psychological reconstruction. In Sebald's case as well, we are dealing with an author interested in realism, and while he is not a finance novelist, Sebald puts his finger on a political logic that can, in part, travel into the economic realm and help explain—up to a certain limit, as I will discuss—what we see going on in the stock markets today. I understand it is counterintuitive to talk about Sebald in the context of a conversation about algorithmic, high-frequency trading (one of Sebald's former students reports that he never wrote an e-mail and refused to have a PC installed in his office[70]), but his work can help explain some of the motivation behind both the what and the how of contemporary markets.

To say that I am limited to Euro-US perspective is also to say that the picture I offer is hardly complete. But my guess is that some of what I say will be able to travel outside of that immediate sphere of investigation; it could, for example, travel to China and be mobilized in the context of the story of "The Fall of Xu Xiang," as Alex Palmer engagingly told it in the *New York Times* magazine. Palmer mentions in his piece about the fall of a hedge fund king "a series of Hong Kong gangland movies about stock-market geniuses" that was apparently inspired by Xu Xiang's having become "the subject of a heated dispute between two powerful Shanghai gangsters."[71] *Finance Fictions* could also have looked at K. D.'s novel *Headless*, and weighed in more heavily on offshore banking and the Panama Papers—it could have flung itself further off the Euro-US shores to investigate how financiers in the United States and Europe use exotic locations as tax havens to conceal their wealth. And one doesn't necessarily have to look that far to expand my scope: what about those millions of people whose homes were foreclosed due to the housing market crash of 2008? Shouldn't their stories have received some attention here? Why focus on the financiers—who are the perpetrators in this situation—once again? Doesn't the book at large suffer from the same issues that Wolfe's *Bonfire of the Vanities* suffers from—that it once again privileges the perspective it sets out to criticize? If financialization has, as Brian Holmes in a remarkable essay about Chicago and global finance has suggested,[72] two sides—foreclosed homes and high-speed traders—then this book clearly comes down on the high-speed trading side.[73] Why?

My goal is first and foremost to deproletarianize myself in relation to the contemporary finance economy. Quite simply, I wanted to understand better how it works. That involved familiarizing myself both with the *what* of contemporary trading, the complex financial products that are being traded, and the *how* of contemporary trading, the high-frequency algorithmic trading that dominates stock markets today. Taken together, the what and the how provide insight into the content and the form of contemporary markets, which in their turn together have created what one could consider to be a "living" entity whose being poses some challenges to those who seek to give a realist-materialist account of it. I became particularly interested in how literary or visual representations might be able to realistically account for contemporary finance, which seemed to pose a real challenge to those who try to de-spectralize it. That problem does not pose itself in the same way with foreclosed homes, which are part of the "traditional" content of realism: that is in fact, what realism would focus on—not the high-speed trading side of finance's coin. Part of what I have learned from reading Marx is that one must pay careful attention to the economy—one must try to understand it, which includes (in my view) not merely an economic but also a philosophical and political understanding—in order to be able to act effectively in relation to it. Proletarianization happens not only when someone loses their home, but also when people feel they no longer understand how "the economy" works: like politics, which increasingly seems inseparable from it, it is left to the specialists to "manage"—but in the meantime our salaries are dwindling, our benefits are cut, our retirement funds collapse, our debts soar, and our homes are taken away from us. This is one of the reasons why the work of Scott Patterson and Michael Lewis, two key sources for this book, is important: because it sets out to explain, from the economic side, what is going on. It *can* be done. And literature can participate in this process. Patterson and Lewis in fact make literature participate in it—their works have a literary flair and include literary references.

It is easier, of course, for literature not to engage and to leave finance to the economists. But part of my position is that doing so would mean to irresponsibly hollow out the finance novel and leave literature in some kind of passive relation to the economy—whereas truly, my title is meant to reveal literature's essential connection to today's markets, and even to the origin of money. There is a fictitiousness that lies at the origin of our economies that has become forgotten, but that today—in the era of virtual money—has returned with full force. For that reason, it seems crucially important to think through finance in fiction, to give real content to the genre that calls itself finance fiction.

ONE

Revisiting *The Bonfire of the Vanities*

Tom Wolfe's Realisms

Although Tom Wolfe's *The Bonfire of the Vanities* is now considered a classic finance novel, it actually has very little finance in it. At first sight, the financial part of the novel can be reduced to the chapter about the Giscard, a gold-backed bond that the novel's protagonist, bondsman Sherman McCoy, is interested in.[1] Some might say that such a focus on bonds (rather than stocks) already draws the supposed financial focus of the novel into question; certainly, the fact that the bond is gold-backed seems to throw Sherman back into a time before 1971, when (as I discuss in the introduction) the Nixon administration unilaterally abandoned the gold standard and the financial era took off. If "gold" calls up a certain referentiality—that is, the materiality of precious metal backing up the financial instrument of the bond—then Sherman's interest in a gold-backed bond could be seen as a misguided and even comical attachment to "realism" at a time when the economy has abandoned it.

Indeed, much of the novel's (nonfinancial) drama revolves around that problematic of realism, specifically around the question of what really happened to Sherman McCoy on that fateful night when, on his way back from JFK airport where he picked up his girlfriend Maria Ruskin, he ended up in the South Bronx and his car hit a young African American named Henry Lamb. In this case too, Sherman presents himself as a realist who struggles to steer clear from the various stories that the journalists and the politicians seek to spin about him. Wolfe continues the humor in this case as well: as I will discuss in detail later on, there is something comical about Sherman's use of the Black Power salute at the end of the novel to mark his distance not only from Wall Street and Park Avenue where he used to live with his wife and daughter, but also from the various mediatic and political forces that risk to consume him.

In fact, we know from a manifesto that Wolfe published in 1989, two years after *Bonfire* came out, that realism was a central concern for Wolfe when he wrote his book. Titled "Stalking the Billion-Footed Beast," the manifesto reveals that *Bonfire* was conceived not as a finance novel but as a big-city novel in which Wolfe sought to capture the entirety of New York City between the novel's covers. However, the humor that Wolfe brings to Sherman's attachment to realism—his misguided interest in a gold-backed bond; his absurd use of the Black Power salute—is absent from Wolfe's own claim to realism. It's not that "Stalking" is not funny; it has all the hallmarks of Wolfe's other writing. But the humor is not directed at the project of realism itself. Instead, Wolfe defends the realism of what he calls "the new social novel,"[2] arguing that novelists should engage in reporting and documentation if they want to capture a reality that, in its outrageousness—a Park Avenue man using the Black Panther salute—exceeds what we think of as realistic. The manifesto is a plea for novelists to bring the "billion-footed beast" of reality to terms in an era when creative writing traded in realism for postmodernism.

While Wolfe expresses admiration for certain antirealist experiments in writing, his manifesto reads like a spirited plea against the abandonment of realism and the rise of postmodernism—a plea that, even when considered only from the perspective of the historical account it offers, can be tied to the rise of finance. Indeed, Wolfe dates postmodernism's take-over of reality in the early 1970s: that is when realism's eclipse by postmodernism was pretty much complete.[3] What's interesting, of course, given that *Bonfire* was received as a finance novel, is that the early 1970s also mark the time when the gold standard is abolished, and finance takes off. Wolfe's plea for a literary realism in this context could very well be tied to Sherman's interest in the gold-backed bond; his interest in realism, in bringing the "billion-footed beast of reality" to terms,[4] could very well be tied to Sherman's insistence to tell what *really* happened in the Bronx. Those connections appear to be strengthened by the fact that when *Bonfire* was first published as serialized installments in *Rolling Stone* magazine, the story's protagonist was not a bondsman but a writer, emphasizing the link between Sherman and Wolfe. However, none of the humor that is directed at Sherman's realism appears to be directed at Wolfe's; whereas Sherman's realism is presented in *Bonfire* in the mode of satire, Wolfe's realism takes the form of a manifesto. It is presented with so much conviction in fact that Michelle Chihara, in a recent review of two scholarly books about finance and literature, can refer to it as "big swinging dick realism,"[5] thus characterizing Wolfe's brand of realism with a moniker that was used on the Salomon Brothers trading floor (where some of the research for Wolfe's novel was done). Chihara thus brings the satire of realism that pervades Wolfe's novel to his manifesto and its bombastic program.

Given that *Bonfire* is considered not only a classic finance novel but a classic of financial realism, it seems odd that realism would appear to be a target of *Bonfire*'s satire. If anything, that would reveal *Bonfire* to have some affinity with the very postmodernism that Wolfe in his manifesto attacks (and Leigh Claire La Berge has pointed out that "there is something wonderfully postmodern about Wolfe's project"[6]). On the other hand, if realism is the target of Wolfe's "postmodern" satire, then it would also seem odd that the manifesto would defend it so seriously—that in the manifesto it would seem free from satire altogether. In this chapter, I will pursue the first point, namely the status of realism in Wolfe's novel and in particular the novel's postmodern aspects and how they are related to finance. While Wolfe's manifesto will play a role in this, I will defer an in-depth engagement with the manifesto—and a serious pursuit of the limits of the manifesto that Chihara's satire begins to expose—to chapter 4. My goal is to show that although *Bonfire* has become known as a classic work of financial realism, its central drama is ultimately one of psychosis that mobilizes the tension between realism and postmodernism, turning the novel's realism into a higher-level aesthetic that is able to account for the very struggles in which it is caught up. In response to the psychotic situation it records, *Bonfire*'s project, then, is not to reassert reality; it is not to tell us what *really* happened to Sherman in the South Bronx. The novel's realism seeks to give a realistic account of how that reality became caught up in its various representations, and it is that postmodern fracturing of reality that the novel's realism captures.

This can be tied back to finance and to the realism of the gold standard: what *Bonfire*'s particular brand of realism accomplishes is not a return to the gold standard—a return that the shiny, gold-colored cover of my edition of the novel evokes; the novel looks like a brick of gold, not all that different from Kenneth Goldsmith's work of conceptual writing, *Capital* (2015), which also seeks to write the totality of New York City and of course takes on realism in its experimentation.[7] The novel's project, rather, is a realistic representation of the various narratives that have been spun about gold. As I suggested in my introduction and will explore in more detail in chapter 2, that kind of realism is essential to the understanding of postmodern, psychotic finance and its relation to what I have characterized as the "immaterial" origins of money in debt and transferable credit. In other words, if *Bonfire* is a finance novel, it is not so much as an instance of "big swinging dick realism," but as a peculiar postmodern take on realism that manages to turn the tension between realism and postmodernism into a key feature of finance.

Postmodern Realism

Bonfire chronicles the fall of the "fabled bondsman" Sherman McCoy, a self-dubbed "master of the universe." This now famous phrase, which links Sherman's work in finance to power and the cosmos, comes to Sherman "one fine day, in a fit of euphoria, after he had picked up the telephone and taken an order for zero-coupon bonds that had brought him a $50,000 commission, *just like that*. . . . On Wall Street he and a few others . . . had become precisely that . . . Masters of the Universe. There was . . . no limit whatsoever!"[8] Resident of a multimillion dollar apartment on Park Avenue, and working in the bond-trading room at the investment-banking firm of Pierce and Pierce, Sherman wonders where "all of this astonishing new money [comes] from" (58)—and indeed, when asked at various points in the novel what he does for a living, he appears to have some difficulty explaining how it is that you can make money from bonds.

Pierce and Pierce's executive officer, Eugene Lopwitz, offers this explanation: "In the Lopwitz analysis, they had Lyndon Johnson to thank. Ever so quietly, the U.S. had started printing money by the billions to finance the war in Vietnam. Before anyone, even Johnson, knew what was happening, a worldwide inflation had begun. Everyone woke up to it when the Arabs suddenly jacked up oil prices in the early 1970s. In no time, markets of all sorts became heaving crap-shoots: gold, silver, copper, currencies, bank certificates, corporate notes—even bonds" (58–59). The Democratic Johnson, who stepped in as president when John F. Kennedy was shot, would be succeeded by Republican Richard Nixon, whose decision to unilaterally abolish the gold standard immediately followed and intensified these developments. By the 1980s, when *Bonfire* is set, the "heaving crap-shoot" days of the early 1970s are over: "experienced salesmen such as [Sherman] were all at once much in demand" in a bond market that "had caught fire" (59). And whereas Sherman, when he was just starting out on Wall Street, "had *enjoyed* telling [his wife] Judy that while he worked *on* Wall Street, he was not *of* Wall Street and was only *using* Wall Street" (70), "this was a new era": "This was a new Wall Street!" (71). And Sherman has very much become a part of it.[9]

However, what Sherman perceives as "mastery" (even though "he had never so much as whispered this phrase ['Master of the Universe'] to a living soul" (11)) is about to collapse. His marriage to Judy will come apart because of his affair with the "'foxy' brunette" Maria Ruskin (502), wife of Arthur Ruskin, a Jew who has made a fortune chartering planes to fly Muslims to Mecca for the *hadj*. By the end of the novel, Arthur will be dead, and the "heiress of the Ruskin air-charter fortune" will be married to a young Italian painter she's been seeing throughout the novel (683). In addition to these personal disasters—and probably partly in relation to them as well, as Sherman's boss Lopwitz suggests—Pierce and Pierce's top bondsman will lose several million dollars on a deal he has been working on involving a "gold-backed bond" (52), the Giscard. Whereas Sherman, at the beginning of the novel, confidently asserts that he has become a part of Wall Street, the novel will end with him insisting that he is not: "I have nothing to do with Wall Street and Park Avenue" (682), he tells reporters who are still following his case. If he can still think of himself as a master of the universe in the novel's opening pages, he has become the universe's excrement by the novel's end—"an abject creature" (477), something closer to the actually existing masters of the universe: "a set of lurid, rapacious plastic dolls that his otherwise perfect daughter liked to play with" (11). No master but a toy.[10]

Sherman's story is a classic tale of hubris, as one might read it in the newspapers. As such, any of its elements—the end of Sherman's marriage, the end of his affair, his bonds deal gone sour—could probably have been overcome. However, it's not these elements, or even their particular interplay, that do Sherman in: what kills him—or nearly kills him; what turns him into a creature—is an event that occurs early on in the novel, in a chapter titled "King of the Jungle."[11] In it, Sherman drives his black, two-seat sports roadster Mercedes to JFK Airport to pick up Maria. On their way back, the couple miss the off-ramp to Manhattan and end up in the Bronx. What happens then appears to be the following: finding their way back to the ramp to the expressway, they have to stop because something has been thrown "off the guardrail of the ramp" and is "lying in the road, blocking the way" (86). When Sherman gets out to remove it—it's a wheel—he is approached by two young black men. One of them—the big one, Roland Auburn—asks if he needs some help; Sherman is nervous and suspects that the situation is a set-up (this appears to be confirmed by other versions of the story that are included in the novel later on). Meanwhile, Maria has taken the wheel of the car and is urging Sherman to get in. When they take off in a rush trying to get away from those whom they perceive to be their assailants, the car fishtails, hits the other young man—Henry Lamb—and knocks him over. Thanks to Sherman's navigating, they ultimately manage to get out of the Bronx; but the memory of the situation they were in persists.

Sherman thinks they "ought to report this to the police" (92)—by reporting it, they will protect themselves against any follow-up. Maria disagrees: what would they tell the police? That "Mrs. Arthur Ruskin of Fifth Avenue and Mr. Sherman McCoy of Park Avenue happened to be having a nocturnal *tête-à-tête* when they missed the Manhattan off-ramp from the Triborough Bridge and got into a little scrape in the Bronx"? (94). "I'm gonna tell *you* what happened," she tells Sherman. "I'm from South Carolina, and I'm gonna tell you in plain English. Two niggers tried to kill us, and we got away. Two niggers tried to kill us in the jungle, and we got outta the jungle, and we're still breathing, and that's that" (94). Sherman—master of the universe, and king of the jungle—heroically got himself and his girlfriend out of this mess. With that—with the explicit language and the metaphor of the jungle—the racial, and racist dimension of this event is foregrounded: it will also determine how the event will be spun by both the media and politics, and it will dominate Wolfe's novel (and the criticisms it has received) as well.

As information—and most of the time, misinformation—about the event gets out, Sherman is construed as the face of evil, racist, upper-class white privilege, while Henry Lamb, the young man he hit, comes to stand in for good but poor and discriminated-against black people. *Bonfire*, which may start out as a finance novel, thus quickly becomes a novel about race and class in New York City. And with that, the phrase "master of the universe" that is launched in the opening pages of the novel to describe the influence of Wall Street begins to apply elsewhere—specifically in the realms of the media (focused in the novel around the *City Light* journalist Peter Fallow) and of politics (focused on the Harlem Reverend Reginald Bacon and the Bronx District Attorney Abe Weiss and his assistant, Larry Kramer).

Key to *Bonfire* is what happened in the South Bronx. The novel recounts different versions of it as well as the motivations behind those constructions. Given that the novel never fully clears up what actually happened—indeed, there may not have been a clear motivation for Auburn and Lamb's actions; in other words, there may not have been much to clear up other than the fact that Sherman and his girlfriend panicked and hit Lamb with Sherman's car[12]—*Bonfire*'s project seems to lie elsewhere: in the realist description of how the different versions of reality that circulate in the novel come about. As such, *Bonfire* can be characterized as a realist novel with a postmodern touch.

Consider, for example, how Henry Lamb is construed in the newspaper. The story about what happened in the South Bronx comes to the journalist Peter Fallow through Albert Vogel, "an American lawyer whose specialty was unpopular political causes" (209). The African American Reverend

Bacon called Vogel to ask his advice about the Lamb situation (Henry's mother, Annie Lamb, used to work for Bacon and turned to him to discuss her son's accident—she didn't want to go to the police because of parking tickets she's received and hasn't paid), and Vogel turns the story over to Fallow to get the media involved. The aim is to "shake up this fucking city" (216). Fallow realizes almost immediately that "he was being used" (217). Indeed, Bacon wants to see this story run not so much out of concern for Henry and Annie Lamb—although I'm happy to grant him this as part of his motivation—but to "embarrass the Mayor" (223), and to challenge specifically the Bronx District Attorney Abe Weiss. Meanwhile Fallow, whose journalistic career is at an all-time low due to his heavy drinking, realizes that this story could show to his employer that he is actually working on something. In short: Vogel wants to shake up the city, Bacon is after the mayor and Abe Weiss, and Fallow wants to rescue his career.

Whatever is going on here has very little to do with Henry Lamb. This becomes increasingly clear when Fallow is doing his research on Lamb. Calling up Mr. Rifkind, one of Henry's old teachers, he twists and turns Rifkind's words to try to construe Henry as "an honor student." What Rifkind actually says is: "[A]t Colonel Jacob Ruppert High School, an honor student is somebody who attends class, isn't disruptive, tries to learn, and does all right at reading and arithmetic" (228). Says Fallow: "Well, let's use that standard. By that standard, is Henry Lamb an honor student?" Rifkind: "By that standard, yes." When the article is reproduced in the novel, one sees to what extent Rifkind's words are manipulated to construe Henry as a saintly figure. Bacon will follow up by organizing demonstrations, all in careful coordination with the media, both print and TV. Again, one senses that *Bonfire*'s point is not so much to offer the truth about Henry Lamb; instead, the novel is interested in why and how different versions of that truth get construed. If that is a realist project, it is a realism that has learned a lesson or two from the postmodernism that by the time of Wolfe's writing has eclipsed it.

That claim must be considered in light of Wolfe's famous manifesto for "the new social novel," titled "Stalking the Billion-Footed Beast." Published in 1989, the manifesto lays out an aesthetic that Wolfe already realized in his previous novels, including *Bonfire*, which (as he notes) was published in October 1987 and hit the shelves "a week before the Wall Street crash."[13]

In the manifesto, Wolfe seizes the opportunity of this novel's success—the fact that so many called the book "prophetic"[14]—to make the case for the realist novel. As Wolfe sees it, contemporary American novelists have given up on the attempt to try and represent reality in their works. Well aware that "the imagination of the novelist is powerless before what he knows he's going to read in tomorrow morning's newspaper"—he means that reality outdoes fiction in its outrageousness—novelists have drawn from this "the wrong conclusion": "The answer is not to leave the rude beast, the material, also known as life around us, to the journalists but to do what journalists do, or are supposed to do, which is to wrestle the beast and bring it to terms."[15] The manifesto ends on this polemic note: novelists have to "wrestle the beast" and "love the battle"[16]; they must "capture the beast" like he has in both his fiction and his journalism.[17] American novelists need "the spirit to go along for that wild ride."[18]

As I already indicated, *Bonfire* was written serially, "for *Rolling Stone*": in Wolfe's account, he was "producing a chapter every two weeks with a gun at my temple."[19] The manifesto reveals that it was not written as a finance novel; indeed, the serialized version did not have a financier but a writer as its main character. As the manifesto explains, *Bonfire* is Wolfe's big, ambitious, New York City novel. The manifesto begins with a discussion of the attempt to write "a novel about this astonishing metropolis, a big novel, cramming as much of New York City between covers as you could."[20] As Wolfe's manifesto explains, Wolfe had for a long time been waiting for someone to write such a big city novel—but it seemed the novelists who dare to take on such a project "no longer existed."[21] There are no more novelists who would write "the big novels of the racial clashes, the hippie movement, the New Left, the Wall Street boom, the sexual revolution, the war in Vietnam."[22] Instead, the realistic novel—"a slice of life, a cross section, that provided a true and powerful picture of individuals and society—as long as the bourgeois order and the old class system were firmly in place"[23]—was dead. With the disappearance of that order, the genre also passed. And Wolfe regrets that very much: he characterizes reality as a feast that is spread out before every writer, and yet no writer seems willing to plunge into it. By the early 1970s, as he points out, modernism and especially postmodernism have entirely taken over from realism. He quotes Philip Roth (in 1961): "'The actuality is continually outdoing our talents, and the culture tosses up figures daily that are the envy of any novelist.'"[24] Wolfe mentions new types of novels that have arrived: the "Puppet-Master novels," for example, which "were in love with the theory that the novel was, first and foremost, a literary game, words on a page being manipulated by an author."[25] The grand conclusion to which they lead is that in the end, the author was just making it up as he went along.

For Wolfe, there's something deeply wrong with all of this. In his view, "the future of the fictional novel would be in a highly detailed realism based on reporting, a realism more thorough than any currently being attempted, a realism that would portray the individual in intimate and inextricable relation to the society around him."[26] Novelists shouldn't draw back in panic when faced with today's society: "American society today is no more nor less chaotic, random, discontinuous, or absurd than Russian society or French society or British society a hundred years ago, no matter how convenient it might be for a writer to think so. It is merely more varied and complicated and harder to define."[27] In short, there's no reason to panic; instead, one must report! He exhorts novelists to apply themselves to "documentation."[28] That's how, in the manifesto, we get to *Bonfire*, which appears to be based on such reporting and aims to capture the city in its entirety—it realizes his case for realism.

However, *Bonfire*'s claim to a democratic realism turned out to be an issue: critics argued that although "capturing the city in its entirety" might be the novel's aspiration, *Bonfire* in fact does not at all succeed in this. Indeed, some have argued that the novel, told almost entirely from a white perspective and leaving the comatose black young man Henry Lamb largely out of consideration, is racist and ends up, in its attempt to speak for all, privileging the voice of the wealthy white man once again (and rendering the poor black man mute).[29] Wolfe has an explanation for this—the novel grew organically out of environments he was quite close to—but that doesn't solve the problem, of course. So that's where, in the view of many critics, we end up: with a realist novel based on reporting that claims to represent the entire city but fails in troubling ways.

Now, one thing that must be asked when considering Wolfe's own retrospective analysis of *Bonfire*'s project, is whether his manifesto correctly assesses what the novel is doing. Is *Bonfire* indeed as programmatically realist as Wolfe suggests? Can it be inscribed in the opposition between realism and postmodernism that Wolfe develops in his manifesto? Is it allied with realism within that opposition? As I already indicated, I disagree with Wolfe's presentation of his own novel, which (in my view) delivers a peculiar kind of realism that has been informed by postmodernism. Such a reading can be backed up with the satire of realism that Wolfe's novel—unlike his manifesto—delivers: in *Bonfire*, it is Sherman who is associated with realism—the gold-backed bond; the story of what really happened in the Bronx—and uses (preposterously) the Black Power salute (more on this in a moment) to mark his distance from Wall Street, Park Avenue, and the various fabricated stories in which his life has become caught up. *Bonfire*'s realism is more sophisticated than Sherman's in that it does not present a return to the gold standard nor a concern with what actually happened in the Bronx but offers a higher-level, second-order realism that gives an account of the various narratives that are spun about reality. That amounts to a realism with a postmodern touch that also affects the realism of a gold standard to which Sherman is still attached.

A Clenched-Fist Salute

> Pierce & Pierce only know how to handle one kind of capital. They don't understand the steam. They can't handle the steam.
>
> *Reverend Bacon, in* Bonfire of the Vanities *(537)*

To draw this out further, let me focus on one instance in the novel where realism seems to become the target of Wolfe's satire (itself delivered as part of a realistic program)—namely, Sherman's use of the Black Power salute in the novel's final pages. *Bonfire* ends with an epilogue that supposedly reproduces an article from the Metropolitan News section of the *New York Times*. Published one year after the tumultuous courtroom hearing with which the novel ends, it includes a reference to a "gesture" whose "meaning . . . was unclear" (683). "At one point," the courtroom reporter notes, "Mr. McCoy looked toward his wife, smiled slightly, and raised his left hand in a clenched-fist salute. The meaning of this gesture was unclear. Mrs. McCoy refused to speak to reporters" (683). However, readers of the novel know where this gesture originates. Earlier on in the novel, when Sherman (alone at their

Park Avenue residence) is speaking over the phone to his wife who has moved with their daughter to their house in Southampton, he recalls the time "when we used to live in the Village," and specifically "the way I used to go off to work." "When I first started working for Pierce & Pierce," he says, "I used to give you the raised left fist when I left the apartment, the Black Power salute. . . . It was supposed to say that yes, I was going to work on Wall Street, but my heart and soul would never belong to it. I would use it and rebel and break with it. You remember all that?" (640–41). Judy remembers but the "memory . . . is not alive. . . . All our memories of that time have been terribly abused" (641). Sherman's point though is surprising: "Well, now I've broken with Wall Street. Or Wall Street's broken with me. I know it's not the same thing, but in an odd way I feel liberated" (641).

One year after the novel's final courtroom hearing—many more, of course, were to follow—he seems to be insisting on this rupture. When "asked by reporters to comment on the contrast between his Wall Street and Park Avenue background and his current situation, Mr. McCoy yelled out, 'I have nothing to do with Wall Street and Park Avenue'" (682). Sherman's downfall appears to have liberated him from Wall Street, thus realizing the freedom he held dear when he was young—and that he used to mark, in those days, by appropriating the Black Power salute. Given that the Black Panthers' Ten Point Program—mentioned by Wolfe in his literary manifesto—starts with "We Want Freedom," Sherman's use of the salute to mark the fact that his heart and soul would never belong to Wall Street (and, later on, that he no longer belongs to it) may make some kind of sense. It may mark, indeed, Sherman's attachment to a reality that would be free from the stories that are spun about it. But of course, it mostly *doesn't*: it's hard, in fact, *not* to read the mini-plot about the Black Power salute (which punctuates the novel's beginning, middle, and end) as anything but satire.

Sherman's use of the gesture recalls Wolfe's text "Radical Chic," published in *New York Magazine* in 1970, which satirizes a party at Leonard Bernstein's where the Black Panthers were the guests of honor.[30] Wolfe's account includes toward the end a rendering of how the Bernsteins, in the aftermath of the party, quickly became the object of criticism: the *New York Times*, which published two noncritical accounts of the party, followed up with an editorial that attacks the Bernsteins' "romanticization" of the Panthers and deems it "an affront to the majority of Black Americans."[31] The party creates, according to the editorial, "one more distortion of the Negro [*sic*] image. Responsible black leadership is not likely to cheer as the Beautiful People [i.e., New York's Park Avenue elite] create a new myth that Black Panther is beautiful."[32] Things got even worse for the Bernsteins when Black Power groups turned out to be voicing "support for the Arabs against Israel,"[33] ultimately forcing Bernstein to distance himself from Black Panther politics while insisting nevertheless that it has a place in democratic culture. Sherman's use of the Black Power salute echoes the Bernsteins' Black Panther party: Wolfe puts New York's cultural elite and their romanticization of the Panthers to ridicule once again.

In this case too, "realism" is an issue, as evidenced by the fact that in Wolfe's account of "Lenny's Party," the Black Panthers are hailed by the other invitees at the party as "real": "they're *real*, these Black Panthers . . . who actually put their lives on the line . . . [with] real Afros . . . these are real men."[34] Following the language of the *Times*, one would have to suggest that the Black Panthers are "romanticized" here as "real." Wolfe's project in this case is not to block that romanticization with an actual account of the Black Panthers; he doesn't seek to offer a "real real" as opposed to the "romanticized real" of the Park Avenue elite. On the contrary: his realism seeks to show the outrageousness of the fact that the Black Panthers truly were the guests of honor at this party at the Bernsteins. Again, as far as realism goes, this has what La Berge characterizes as a "wonderfully postmodern" touch to it. If Sherman's use of the Black Power salute seems outrageous, Wolfe's account of the Bernsteins' party shows that one should actually reconsider that assessment: catachrestic things like this *were actually happening at the time*. There is a way, then, in which the Black Panthers are caught up in the tension between realism and postmodernism that characterizes Wolfe's novel and structures his manifesto.

If I have suggested that this tension is also related to the financial history of the time, with Nixon's abolition of the gold standard emerging as a postmodern attack on the referential real of precious metal, it is worth pointing out that this connection can be established in the case of "Radical Chic" as well. Published in 1970—right around the time when Wolfe in his manifesto dates postmodernism's eclipse of realism; and one year before Nixon's abolition of the gold standard—"Radical Chic" is the account of a fundraiser where the Park Avenue elite is asked to write out checks in support of the Black Panther Party. Those checks, even if they are only paper, seem to also have an aura of reality associated with them: Wolfe's text repeats several times that, because they are made out to the Black Panthers, the checks are not tax deductible—and that seems to increase their realness, the realness of their gift (a donation is even more of a donation if it cannot be deducted from one's taxes; the impossibility of deducting it somehow seems to make the donation more real).[35] And indeed, it seems to be that concern with the real, which surrounds not only the Panthers in Wolfe's text but also the checks that are made out to them, ultimately haunts the project of the fundraiser.

For what actual projects will the money from the fundraiser support? As one girl in Wolfe's text asks: "Besides the breakfast program . . . do you have any other community programs, and what are they like?"[36] Donald Cox starts answering the question, but Wolfe notes that "soon he is talking about a Panther demand that police be required to live in the community they patrol."[37] The girl will later ask the same question again: "What other community programs are there? We want to do something, but what can we do?"[38] Instead of answering, Cox talks about the breakfast program—which she wanted to get beyond in the first place—and about how churches are "clos[ing] the door in our faces" when the Panthers come "to use their kitchens, to feed hot breakfasts to hungry children." The girl will ultimately receive an answer from "a black named Rick Haynes, president of Management Formation Inc., an organization promoting black capitalism":[39]

> Well, I suggest that she forget about going into *the black community*. I suggest that she think about the white community. Like the *Wall Street Journal*—the *Wall Street Journal* just printed an article about the Black Panthers, and they came to the shocking conclusion—for them—that a majority of the black community supports the Black Panthers. Well, I suggest that this lovely young lady get somebody like her *daddy*, who just might have a little more *pull* than she does, to call up the *Wall Street Journal* and congratulate them when they write it straight like that. Just call up and say, We like that. The name of the game is to use the media, because the media have been using us.[40]

We don't seem get one step beyond where we were when the girl initially asked her question. What is going on here? Why do the Panthers seem to have such trouble naming the concrete community programs in which the money from the fundraiser would be invested? What do we learn from the answers that are being provided?

One could argue that one possible answer to those questions is delivered in the much later *Bonfire*, where the African American Reverend Bacon, who collects funds to support the revival of Harlem, offers a theory of what he calls "the capitalism of the future" (155). Consider how Bacon, who is about to be informed about the Henry Lamb situation by Lamb's mother, Annie, talks about money given in support of concrete projects in Harlem to two young, white men from the Episcopal Church. They have come to question Bacon about some $350,000 in funds they committed to the creation of the Little Shepherd Day Care Center. Their aim is to retrieve it because "there are people with prison records on the board of directors" of the center (148). Bacon, understandably, will have none of it. First, because he thinks that wanting to contribute to the renaissance of Harlem while objecting to people having prison records is an example of "old colonialism" (149): "if you're saying, 'You can't participate in the rebirth of Harlem, because we gave up on you as soon as you got a record' . . . then you're not talking about the rebirth of Harlem" (149). Second, and more importantly for my purposes, it appears that all of the money that the church donated has been "committed" even though nothing has been built (152)—even though no architectural plans have been designed. Bacon considers the money to be a direct investment in Harlem, even though it might not lead to the center that his donors had in mind.

To understand this, one has to appreciate what one might call Bacon's power theory of economics: "I'm gonna tell you something," Bacon begins (sounding a little like Maria Ruskin in the aftermath of the accident in the South Bronx), "I'm gonna tell you something about capitalism north of Ninety-sixth Street. Why do you people think you're investing all this money . . . in a day-care center in Harlem?" (153). Bacon's answer:

> You're investing in *steam* control. . . . It's a capital investment. It's a very good one. You know what capital is? You think it's something you own, don't you. You think it's factories and machines and buildings and land and things you can sell and stocks and money and banks and corporations. You think it's something you own, because you always owned it. . . . But you are mistaken. Capital is controlling things. Controlling things. You want land in Kansas? You want to exercise your white deed of property? First you got to control Kansas . . . see . . . Controlling things. (154)

Immediately after this discussion we get to the "boiler room" metaphor, which is close to the factories and machines that Bacon lists in the passage I just quoted—but it is used here to describe something quite different: "I don't suppose you ever worked in a boiler room. I worked in a boiler room. People *own* the boilers, but that don't do 'em a bit of good unless they know how to control the *steam* . . . see . . . If you can't *control* . . . the steam, then it's Powder Valley for you and your whole gang" (154). What the two young white men from the Episcopal Church are investing in, according to Bacon, is steam control. "So what I'm telling you," Bacon concludes, "is, you best be waking up. You're practicing the capitalism of the future, and you don't even know it. You're not investing in a day-care center for the children of Harlem. You're investing in the souls . . . the *souls* . . . of the people who've been in Harlem too long to look at it like children any longer, people who've grown up with a righteous anger in their hearts and a righteous *steam* building up in their souls, ready to blow" (155).

As a lecture about capitalism, Bacon's speech is fascinating. If capitalism, as per Karl Marx's classic account, is defined by the M-C-M' (money—commodity—money worth more money) formula, which shows how money can be transformed into money that is worth more through the buying and selling of the intermediary of the commodity,[41] Bacon offers a theory of capitalism that takes the commodity—the Little Shepherd Daycare Center building—out of it. In "the capitalism of the future" money doesn't buy commodities but souls: it invests in the souls of the people, atones their "righteous anger," and prevents the steam that has been building up within them from blowing. That capitalism is not about what you own: it is about how you can control the people's anger. Bacon's capitalism of the future is a technique of government—an anger-defusing politics. From a certain perspective, this is a "day care" of a kind: not for children (like the Little Shepherd Daycare Center) but for angry adults. It's a daycare that's not housed in a building that someone can own but one that is diffusely spread out through the Harlem community. Specifically, "white" capitalism of the future seeks to be the "shepherd" that keeps angry black people under control; and Bacon, as its facilitator, reveals that its qualification as "white" is not entirely correct—in that sense, Bacon recalls Rick Haynes, who promotes black capitalism in "Radical Chic." When the girl at the "Party at Lenny's" is asking about concrete projects into which the Park Avenue elite's money will be invested, one could imagine (although 1970 is no doubt a bit early to do so) an answer informed by Bacon's theory: the checks are deposits into Harlem steam control.

A couple of things are worth noting. First, if one accepts Bacon's theory as a theory of capitalism, it should be pointed out that Bacon understands capitalism politically, as a technique of government that works on the people's revolutionary affect (specifically, their anger). By making financial deposits into what one could perhaps call (with loose reference to Peter Sloterdijk's work) the "rage bank" (rather than the boiler room),[42] white people are able to keep black people's anger contained.[43] It is Bacon who runs Harlem's anger bank; sometimes, he will let the anger out, to rattle its white investors—but he knows that is a risky game, because he is not certain that he will be able to rein in the anger again.

The financial government of souls is referred to in Bacon's speech as a "capitalism of the future." At first sight, the phrase seems to be a mere temporal designation, referring to a kind of capitalism that will come *after* the capitalism that we have now. Upon closer consideration, however, Bacon is also theorizing a capitalism that seeks to make a claim *on* the future: that deposits money now with an eye on future yield, namely the control of popular anger. As such, those capital investments have something of the speculative to them: they seek to manage a future risk, to obtain a hold on contingency. They are, more precisely, financial investments—"capitalism of the future" refers to the "finance" that, as explained in the introduction, comes after capitalism. The steam control that Bacon promises in return—his management of popular anger in Harlem; the peace that is the surplus value return of the commodityless financial investment—can be described as fictitious: for it is not something that Bacon actually owns. It is Bacon's promise, he is supposed to be good for it, one is supposed to believe—to give credit (from the Latin verb *credere*, "to believe")—to the reverend on that count. But when push comes to shove, as it does in Wolfe's novel, it would of course be vain for Bacon to think that he can control all the righteous anger in Harlem: like Sherman McCoy, Bacon is no master of the universe either, and if Bacon can be read as a black version of McCoy, *Bonfire* exposes the vanity of Bacon's illusions of grandeur just as it does with McCoy's. If Bacon directs the anger bank, *Bonfire* brings us the moment when the bank cannot provide the return it promised on future capitalism's investments.

What "Radical Chic" and *Bonfire* might be showing us, I have suggested, are not only the ways in which the Park Avenue elite romanticizes Black Power and thus brings the radical into the chic. Precisely around the crucial date of 1971, they might also be showing us something about the neoliberalization and, as I suggested earlier on, financialization of Black Power—the way in which the chic is brought into the radical. Wolfe's "Radical Chic" does not develop that angle, in my view—its setting is firmly on Park Avenue (although it gives a speaking role to Rick Haynes, who promotes black capitalism). The later *Bonfire*, on the other hand, accomplishes this through the figure of Reverend Bacon, a character for which Wolfe was criticized. "From the start," as Wolfe notes in "Stalking the Billion-Footed Beast," "there was a certain amount of grumbling, some of it not very nice, about my depiction of Reverend Bacon. He was a grotesque caricature of a black activist, grotesque or worse."[44] "Worse" is probably a silent evocation of the charge of racism, which Wolfe incurred for his novel. But Wolfe points out that just three months later, Reverend Al Sharpton appears in the newspaper "having his long Byronic hair coiffed at a beauty parlor in Brooklyn." The reporters thought they were going to catch him in a bad situation, but in fact Sharpton welcomes their presence: "Come on in, boys, and bring your cameras. I want you to see how . . . a real man . . . gets his hair done."[45] Sharpton was so "flamboyant," as Wolfe points out, "the grumbling about Reverend Bacon swung around 180 degrees. Now I heard people complain, This poor fellow Wolfe, he has no imagination. Here, on the front page of every newspaper, are the real goods"[46]—and Reverend Bacon hardly comes close. In other words, and to repeat the familiar point: reality exceeds what the realist novelist can deliver. The connection between Reverend Bacon and financial neoliberalization that *Bonfire* sets up has become only more pressing since then, as the work of Lester Spence on "the neoliberal turn in black politics" has shown.[47]

To read Wolfe's *Bonfire* thus leads to a web of related issues that all go back to the early 1970s: realism's eclipse by postmodernism; the origins of finance and neoliberal government; the neoliberalization of Black Power. If we go by Wolfe's manifesto, which takes it up for realism and mentions the 1960s and the civil rights movement as a key inspiration for the realist aesthetic, one might situate Wolfe on the other side of finance and with a Black Panther Party that would steer clear from its financialization and neoliberalization. However, *Bonfire*'s satire of Sherman's outdated interest in a gold-backed bond as well as his "radical chic" use of the Black Power salute draws such a positioning into question. Wolfe's "postmodern" realism is not about a return to the referentiality or materiality that a gold-standard realism—including one of the Black Panthers—might claim to offer. Instead, Wolfe offers a realism that writes the struggles in which such realism, and everything that is associated with it in *Bonfire* (the economy; Black Power), is caught up.

A Psychotic Tale

As such, Wolfe's realism does not only have a wonderfully postmodern touch—there is also something of the psychotic to it, if psychosis can be defined as the disavowal of existing reality and the substitution of another reality for it. *Bonfire* itself, of course, is not producing this psychosis—although some may argue it is through its privileging of the upper class, white perspective; but its central drama revolves around a psychotic situation where the existing reality of Sherman McCoy's life as well as that of the life of Henry Lamb (as I indicated earlier) are being denied by the media and political forces that substitute another reality for it. By that, I do not want to suggest that Sherman and Henry are somehow caught up in the *same* problem—that would be a radical chic gesture that Wolfe (in "Radical Chic") is quick to expose. When, in response to Donald Cox's account of his experience of racism, Leonard Bernstein points out that "most of the people in this room have had a problem about being unwanted," Wolfe interjects by suggesting psychology and psychoanalysis are being used here to universalize the racist experience so that it includes everyone: "One way or another we all feel insecure, right?"[48] I'm not trying to say that Sherman's and Henry's situations are the same; but there are, to be sure, elements of psychosis to both: neither one's reality corresponds to the reality that is being written for them.

This is so because Sherman and Henry are caught in the nets of the media and political power players that, each in their own way, seem to think they master the universe. I have already discussed Reverend Bacon. Consider also, for example, Bacon's opponent in *Bonfire*, Richard "Abe" Weiss, the Bronx District Attorney. A media man himself (101), his Machiavellian concern is to maintain power over his district—and that concern is challenged when Bacon accuses him of moving too slowly on the Lamb case. The charge, summarized under the slogan "Weiss justice = white justice," is that white people receive a very different treatment from Abe's court than black people. And so the entire Sherman McCoy case becomes a means, for Abe, to prove that this is not so. Abe wants a show arrest on Park Avenue, but Sherman's lawyer is able to prevent him from going through with it; once in the Bronx, procedure is followed to the letter, making Sherman wait in the rain, stripping him of his clothes and possessions. He does not just not get a preferential treatment—his treatment appears to be worse than other people's. Evidently, Sherman is being used by Abe to make a point. Sherman is powerless against these political machinations that in fact intervene—as his lawyer points out—with the law.

And Sherman's lawyer is by no means the only one who thinks this is the case: Judge Myron "Mike" Kovitsky also raises serious questions in the novel's closing, courtroom scene about the objectivity of Sherman's arraignment. Kovitsky's target in this scene is one of Weiss's assistants, Larry Kramer. Kramer is married and has a newborn child, but he is also starting an affair in the novel with Shelley Thomas, a woman who was on the jury for a case in which he was involved. His desire for Shelley influences his performance in the courts: he goes after the accused in the case for which Shelley is on the jury with ridiculous furor, to impress Shelley (131). Shelley also influences how he pleads in the McCoy case: he wants to emerge from the case as the "hero" of black Harlem, as the prosecutor who is on the people's side—but this skews the objectivity of his judgment. *Bonfire* suggests that Kramer "lights up his witness" (425); after his courtroom presentation of Roland Auburn, the novel notes that "Charles Dickens . . . couldn't have done it any better" (625). As Kovitsky points out during the final courtroom scene of the novel, Kramer is also "play[ing] to the mob" (671): in a previous courtroom scene, he waved a petition in the judge's face, and this time too he tries to use the people's will to influence the judge's decision. But as Kovitsky correctly indicates, it's not the angry mob that should decide Sherman's fate—that should be left up to the judge, who should examine the evidence and decide blindly, irrespective of the "steam" that has gotten out of control. This proves to be nearly impossible in this situation—

Bacon's steam has gotten so much out of control that it risks interfering with the legal process altogether. Indeed, it seems at the very end of the book that the case will be decided against Sherman, even if he is not guilty of what he is being charged with. I would characterize this as a psychotic situation in which the real world is being replaced with another one, produced by the media and politics, and Sherman's life is consumed by uncontrollable forces.

At this point, and to give some relief to the fraught link between Sherman and Henry on this count, I want to suggest a comparison that, like Sherman's use of the Black Power salute, might appear to be a stretch: what if we imagine *Bonfire of the Vanities* as a rewriting of Richard Wright's *Native Son*, set on Wall Street, and with Sherman McCoy in the role of Bigger Thomas? Readers of *Bonfire* may recognize, in *Native Son*, the psychotic problematic that I have hinted at. When Bigger in the immediate aftermath of the disappearance of Mary Dalton (whom he has murdered) is asked about what happened on the night when she was last seen, he has a meaningful realization in this context: "They wanted him to draw the picture and he would draw it like he wanted it. He was trembling with excitement. In the past had they not always drawn the picture for him? He could tell them anything he wanted and what could they do about it?"[49] This—being autonomous, making your own reality rather than having your reality be made for you—becomes a key element during his trial later on: his lawyer argues that after killing Mary, Bigger "felt that he was free for the first time in his life."[50] Society doesn't allow him to be free: it writes his reality for him. It is the psychosis of racism, the novel suggests, that Bigger targeted with his actions. For once, Bigger felt that he could act for himself. The prosecution questions the attempt to make us see this as "an act of creation,"[51] but from the perspective of the psychosis of racism, it is: in the aftermath of his murder, Bigger asserts his reality against the one that is being written for him.

But what to make of that resonance, what to make of that reference to one of the twentieth century's great novels about race in the United States in a novel about the vanities of a rich, white finance man? Is it merely satirical? (Look at how the white, rich finance man imagines himself as a version of Bigger! Radical chic!) Does it then merely underline the difference between Sherman and Bigger, with Bigger arriving at a kind of enlightened, realist insight into the limits of his power while Sherman comically holds on to a basic sense of reality and mastery? Or do we have a shared tragedy of two individuals who, to be sure, have done a bad thing, but have gotten caught up in the psychotic creations of the media and the politicians who write the reality of their lives for them? The differences between Sherman and Bigger are obvious. But what about the tragedy of self-determination—a tale of psychosis—that also ties them together? Ultimately, *Bonfire* revolves around this problematic of psychosis, which is intimately tied to the problematic of realism and, more generally, that of writing.

Terror, Writing, and Finance

> Nothing we have is real.
>
> *Cristina Alger,* The Darlings[52]

In closing, I would like to give a political articulation to this constellation of issues, following on but different from the economicopolitical reading that I already provided. In a chapter of his book *Art Power,* titled "Art at War," Boris Groys observes: "Don DeLillo writes in his novel *Mao II* that terrorists and writers are engaged in a zero-sum game: by radically negating that which exists, both wish to create a narrative that would be capable of capturing society's imagination—and thereby altering society. In this sense, terrorists and writers are rivals—and, as DeLillo notes, nowadays the writer is beaten hands down because today's media use the terrorists' acts to create a powerful narrative with which no writer can contend."[53] If the context of this passage is clearly the post–September 11 moment of contemporary history, it must be updated into the era of economic terror, to draw out the ways in which today's finance men (and it's mostly men, really) are writing the world and thereby fit within the psychotic game of negation/creation that Groys presents. Although Wolfe focuses more on the media and politics in his novel, that was of course part and parcel of what *Bonfire* brought home to us, even if its key point was also radically opposed to this: it is vain, the novel appeared to be saying, to think that one masters the universe—whether one is a finance man, a journalist, or a politician. Strangely though, when it comes to writing, Wolfe appears to be rather vain himself, calling for a social realism in the novel that would be able to tame—through a journalistic method—the billion-footed beast of reality.

Of course, what he had in mind was not the psychotic rewriting of reality that Groys (after DeLillo) is interested in, but a meticulous description of reality in all of its complexity. It is Wolfe's antidote for the reality-disavowing and reality-substituting activities of some writers and also terrorists (as per DeLillo).

Today—and the passing of time has made the context in which Wolfe was making those statements resonate even more[54]—that antidote stands in tension with the writing of finance itself, the way it is negating/creating the world. Cristina Alger, whose novel *The Darlings* can be situated in the history of the realist finance novel that Wolfe marks out,[55] makes this the focus of her tightly plotted book, which is largely told from the perspective of its main players—various members of the Darlings family, as well as some other key figures. Based on the Madoff investment scandal, the novel exposes the fake performance of Delphic Capital, and specifically Reis Capital Management (RCM): over Thanksgiving weekend in 2008, it is revealed that the value RCM is generating is a lie, "an illusion."[56] Alger's realist novel exposes the psychotic world of finance.

What's gone unnoticed in the reviews Alger's novel has received is the fact that Alger constructs this realist exposure of psychotic finance as a meditation on fiction and on finance's aspiration to rewrite the world—its aspiration *to fiction* (used as a verb). The novel exposes the lawyer Sol Penzell's attempt to rewrite—with the financier Carter Darling's approval—reality in order to save Carter. The plan of Penzell, who is a specialist in "extralegal deal brokering,"[57] is intricate: on the side of Delphic Capital, they will blame everything on Carter's flamboyant partner Alain and emphasize that Carter had no oversight, and therefore carries no responsibility; with the Securities and Exchange Commission (SEC), they will implicate an investigator as having been bribed not to go after Carter's firm—this is to save Carter's girlfriend Jane, who works at the SEC and has been using her clout there to protect Carter. To make all of this happen, however, Sol needs to ask his secretary to set up backdated wire transfers for offshore money, deposited into accounts that can be traced to the investigator at the SEC whom he wants to accuse of having been bribed. There is one catch in this elaborate fiction that will ultimately make it fall apart: to set up the wire transfers, Sol implicates (although without consulting him) Carter's son-in-law Paul, who is the moral center of Alger's novel. It's this move that makes Sol's secretary, as well as Paul and his wife, Carter's daughter Merrill, stand up against Sol and Carter and go to the SEC.

This is the finance men's plot, and it is also the plot of Alger's novel: finance and fiction seem to coincide to the extent that they become indistinguishable. Alger's novel thus begins to reflect, in Wolfe's footsteps, on the extent to which contemporary finance men are fictioning reality. A realist novel about contemporary finance, it actually further develops the wonderfully postmodern element that Leigh Claire La Berge has distinguished in Wolfe's novel.

All of this obviously connects to the financial fictioning that triggers Alger's novel, namely the Ponzi scheme that Morty Reis set up. Indeed, RCM has all the usual characteristics of a Ponzi scheme operation: highly secretive, it guarantees its investors a consistent return, regardless of market performance. If clients want to be paid out, the money comes from new investments rather than from money earned on the market; many clients, however, don't ask for their money to be paid out and keep it invested in the scheme, where it seems to continue generating consistent returns. In reality, of course, those returns are nonexistent. Such schemes usually end when their operator vanishes with all the investments; or when the scheme collapses due to market pressure, or investments slow down. In 2008, when the market was under pressure, it was revealed that Bernard Madoff, former NASDAQ chairman, had been running such a Ponzi scheme (he claims the scheme had been going on since the 1990s but investigators suggest that the fraudulent activity goes back to the 1970s). RCM is modeled after Madoff's unregistered hedge fund; *The Darlings* explores the fallout of its collapse.

There is an infamous quote recorded by the journalist Ron Suskind in a 2004 interview with an aide of George W. Bush, believed to be Karl Rove, that captures very well the idea of a finance that is not only *fictitious* but that also actively *fictions*. Here is how Suskind renders it:

> The aide said that guys like me [i.e., journalists] were "in what we call the reality-based community," which he defined as people who "believe that situations emerge from your judicious study of discernible reality. . . . That's not the way the world really works anymore," he continued. "We're in an empire now, and when we act, we create our own reality. And while you're studying that reality—judiciously, as you will—we'll act again, creating other

> new realities, which you can study too, and that's how things will sort out. We're history's actors . . . and you, all of you, will be left just to study what we do."[58]

If this quote captures perfectly the creative, inventive, indeed fictive exceptionalist politics of the Bush regime, today, after Tom Wolfe's novel and read in the context of a novel like Alger's, the quote seems to capture the present *psychotic* (as Franco "Bifo" Berardi in a discussion of the above quote has pointed out[59]) financial regime, which *makes* the reality that journalists are left to describe.

Put simply, today's financiers are close to fiction writers—and to terrorists, as DeLillo might have it. They are rivals in the psychotic, radical negation of what exists, and the substitution of another reality for it. One can see why realism, and even the Wolfian tie of realist fiction to journalism, gains importance again in such a situation.

However, there is something that such an understanding of finance as an acting fiction, as something that fictions a world into being, seems to misrepresent, and that is the strong sense of "agency" that one finds in the quotation above. *We act*, the Bush aide claims; *we create* our own reality—you, journalists, are left to study it. Part of the question, however, is how much of that agency is left when it comes to finance: the *New York Times* reported in late January 2016 that the last human-occupied seats at the New York Stock Exchange had been sold to a computerized trading firm, making the "high-frequency takeover of the New York Stock Exchange . . . essentially complete." Noting that on the stock market floor "most prices are generated by algorithms that determine when to buy and sell," the article adds that "humans are generally present to monitor the computers and to step in if anything goes wrong, as has happened on several occasions in recent years."[60] This is clearly not the view of power that the Bush aide projects. The fact that finance *fictions* (as a verb) would then have to be taken quite literally, as referring not to the human agents doing the fictioning but to finance itself—trading algorithms, for example—having agency in this context, with humans being "left to study" what those algorithms do: To monitor, and step in if something goes wrong. Another way to put this is that algorithms are no longer merely the tools of the contemporary trader; they have taken the place of the contemporary trader and need to be considered as agents in their own right.

Although Wolfe and Alger clearly appreciate the fictioning power of the media, politics, and finance, and although both invite their readers to think that fictioning power in relation to the practice of the creative writer and in particular to the project of realism, neither one ultimately thinks the fictioning power of finance itself. That is to say, neither one considers the ways in which finance, outside of the human agent, has come to generate realities that humans are simply left to study. As Mark Greif in a review of DeLillo's *Cosmopolis* points out, this shift is doing "something weird to experience"[61]—a weirdness that, while it draws into question traditional realism, at the same time intensifies our need for it.

TWO

Psychotic Realism in (*American*) *Psycho*

> People who suffer from their desire are neurotic; people who suffer from no longer having any desire are psychotic. It's a worldwide phenomenon, at a massive scale, and it's compensated by hyperconsumption. The more this addictive consumption makes up for the loss of desire, the more it supports this loss.
>
> —BERNARD STIEGLER, *interview with Frédéric Neyrat*[1]

Return to Psychosis

Although Bret Easton Ellis's novel *American Psycho* is generally considered to follow in the footsteps of Tom Wolfe's *The Bonfire of the Vanities*—Ellis wrote it in the wake of the 1987 stock market crash and the novel explicitly references Wolfe's novel on several counts—its graphic and surreal, psychotic first-person narration is also considered to mark a stark difference from Wolfe's social realism. My attempt in the previous chapter was to show how the theme of psychosis, which takes center stage in *American Psycho*, already lay contained in the realist *Bonfire*. Generally, of course, that interest in psychosis is thought to have come from another one of *American Psycho*'s intertexts: Alfred Hitchcock's film *Psycho* (from 1960), itself based on Robert Bloch's novel *Psycho* (from 1959). Ellis's genius, some have suggested, is that he reimagined the story of Norman Bates on Wall Street—in other words, that he added the economic setting to the psychotic tale of Bloch's novel and Hitchcock's film. At the same time, it was a stroke of genius as well to take that theme of psychosis to Wall Street—that is, in turn, what he added to Wolfe's novel. Now, in the same way that the theme of psychosis already lies contained in Wolfe's novel, *American Psycho*'s interest in finance already lies contained in Hitchcock's film and Bloch's novel. I would like to explore that interest in detail so as to be able to better assess both the role of psychosis and the relation between psychosis and realism in Ellis's novel.

At first sight, *American Psycho* tells us very little about finance.[2] Instead, the novel is focused entirely on psychosis, which the novel suggests is a superstructural, psychic effect of an economic system that itself remains largely implicit in the novel as the material substructure of Patrick Bateman's psychic affliction. Ellis's novel reads as a protracted description of the symptoms while it never really gets into the causes. The novel is all sickness, but offers no diagnosis nor cure ("THIS IS NOT AN EXIT," as its closing line, referencing an existentialist drama,[3] indicates). As a finance novel, then, *American Psycho* arguably fails: its focus on psychosis leaves finance out of the picture. I want to show, however, that the focus on psychosis in the novel's first-person narrative—a narrative that, since it is told from the point of view of a psychotic, is obviously itself psychotic—in fact does tell us something about the effects of finance on human beings. *American Psycho*'s intertexts will help us uncover this. And finance's connection to psychosis is even more intimate than this: I will also provide a theoretical discussion that lays bare how finance itself is arguably an intensified psychotic form of money. Indeed, money itself is psychotic, as recent revisionist accounts of its history can help us understand.[4] This will enable me to recuperate what critics have characterized as *American Psycho*'s "grotesque" and "carnivalesque"[5] focus on psychosis in the chapter's final section as what I call (after Antonio Scurati) a psychotic realism.[6] Such a realism prophetically anticipates aspects of what I present, in chapters 3 and 4, to be the "speculative" mindset required to think and ultimately write the reality of the economy today.

Money in Psycho

Of course, when it comes to the "psycho" that is referred to in the title of Alfred Hitchcock's notorious film, the first candidate that comes to mind is Norman Bates. And indeed, *Psycho* seeks to provide insight into the mind of this psychotic murderer (a character that was inspired by the real-life story of the psychotic murderer Ed Gein,[7] also the inspiration for *The Texas Chainsaw Massacre* (now in 3-D!) and *The Silence of the Lambs*).[8] However, this attribution—the identification of Norman as the murderer—is also destabilized by the novel's central theme of psychosis.

As Mary (Marion in Hitchcock's version) Crane's lover Sam Loomis reports in Bloch's novel: "[Bates is] a multiple personality with at least three facets. There was *Norman*, the little boy who needed his mother and hated anything or anyone who came between him and her. Then, *Norma*, the mother, who could not be allowed to die. The third aspect might be called *Normal*—the adult Norman Bates, who had to go through the daily routine of living, and conceal the existence of the other personalities from the world. Of course, the three weren't entirely distinct entities, and each contained elements of the other."[9] So who is responsible for the murders here? Sam's diagnosis is striking: "Mother killed [Mary]," he insists to Lila, Mary's sister. "*Norma* killed your sister. There's no way of finding out the actual situation, but [the doctor] is sure that whenever a crisis arose, *Norma* became the dominant personality. Bates would start drinking, then black out while *she* took over. During the blackout, of course, he'd dressed up in her clothing. Afterward he'd hide her image away, because in his mind she was the real murderer and had to be protected."[10] So it appears that Norma, and not Norman, is the murderer.[11]

The final chapter of the novel adds another layer of complexity to this situation. There, it becomes clear that Norma has taken over Norman, and that she blames everything on Norman:

> The bad man had really committed the murders and then he tried to blame it on her.
>
> *Mother killed them.* That's what he said, but it was a lie. . . . Why, she wouldn't even harm a fly . . . [12]

Norman Bates's psychotic gaze in Alfred Hitchcock's *Psycho*.

So Norman *is* the murderer after all . . . at least if you can believe Norma. Hitchcock captures this final destabilizing moment with a psychotic shot in which mother's dead, dried-up skull flickers briefly over Norman's face.

While all of this is interesting, it is also obvious: it doesn't take much of a reader to draw out *Psycho*'s psychotic deconstruction of responsibility. What fascinates me more is the conclusion that Mary's sister Lila draws from it: now that she understands—now that she can "almost understand," as she puts it—she realizes that "we're all not quite as sane as we pretend to be."[13] I think that is the *real* conclusion of Bloch's novel; certainly, the novel insists on this again and again. It comes up, first, when Mary is having a lengthy conversation with Norman after she has arrived at Bates Motel. When Mary suggests in response to something Norman has said about his mother that his mother may not be well in the head and should perhaps be put in an "institution,"[14] Norman responds furiously, shouting, "*She's not crazy*!"[15] However, he himself adjusts this resonant "no" at the end of that same paragraph in which it appears: "But who are you to say a person should be put away? *I think perhaps all of us go a little crazy at times* [emphasis mine]."[16]

Mary recalls this final suggestion of *generalized psychosis* later on in the novel, now applying it to her own situation. And it is here, I want to suggest, that things get really interesting. It is worth recalling, although strangely many critics don't, that Mary in the film steals $40,000 from her boss Mr. Lowery:

Marion Crane's psychotic gaze in *Psycho.*

> Yes. It was true. All of us go a little crazy at times. Just as she'd gone crazy, yesterday afternoon, when she saw the money on the desk.
>
> And she'd been crazy ever since, she *must* have been crazy, to think that she could get away with what she planned. It had all seemed like a dream come true, and that's what it was. A dream. A *crazy* dream. She knew it, now.[17]

Here we get to the overlooked part of *Psycho*, namely its economic dimension. Critics have tended to forget about the money in *Psycho*, probably because Norman Bates doesn't know about it. The money disappears, unseen, with Mary's body in the trunk of her car, and into the swamp where Norman dumps the car and the body. But it is through the money that we understand that there is more than one psycho in *Psycho*: Norman/Norma are only the extreme, clinical case; Mary too is a little psychotic[18]—more precisely, she turns psychotic when she sees the $40,000 at her boss's office.[19] And *all of us can turn a little psycho*, the novel suggests, when we are dealing with money.[20]

Hitchcock draws this out nicely in what is probably—after the psychotic shot of Norman Bates that I mentioned earlier on—the most psychotic scene in the film: Marion's drive to Bates motel, during which she is projecting—voicing—imaginary conversations about her theft in her head. The voiceover, in combination with Janet Leigh's facial expressions, are truly uncanny and should be compared, I would suggest, to Norman Bates's facial expression at the end of Hitchcock's film.[21] However, it takes some attentive reading and viewing—and reading and viewing for the money—to uncover all of this.

Put briefly, I am trying to suggest, that *Psycho*, and by extension *American Psycho*, show us something about the effects of finance on human beings. If *Psycho*'s central theme is that money renders all human beings psychotic, one would have to recognize (and I will lay bare the history of this in the following section) that this has only intensified with money's transformation into finance.

Sacha Gervasi, whose recent film *Hitchcock* (Fox, 2012) chronicles the making of *Psycho* and the stress it put on Hitchcock and his relation to his wife Alma Reville, certainly seems to have gotten the point (even if it also seems to have made him get creative with some of the facts): indeed, Gervasi's movie reveals money to be the key cause of that stress. Due to a lack of studio support, it suggests, Hitchcock had to take out a mortgage on his own house to be able to finance the film—a fact that Hitchcock scholar Patrick McGilligan has said to be false.[22] In Gervasi's reconstruction of the shower scene, *Hitchcock* has (in what McGilligan claims is another fictional scene) Hitchcock take over from Anthony Perkins (as mother), showing Perkins how the stabbing should be done. At this point, Gervasi focalizes through Hitchcock, and shows what Hitchcock is supposedly seeing when he is stabbing away at Janet Leigh: all those who are related to his money troubles. Every time we were seeing that classic scene of psychosis, in which a woman is being stabbed to death, we were actually *also* seeing Hitchcock stabbing away at his money troubles. It is hard to imagine a tighter connection between psychosis and money.

From Money to Finance

> —Money . . . ? in a voice that rustled.
> —Paper, yes.
> —And we'd never seen it. Paper money.
> —We never saw paper money until we came east.
> —It looked so strange the first time we saw it. Lifeless.
> —You couldn't believe it was worth a thing.[23]
>
> *William Gaddis*, J R

> "Phoenix. Janet Leigh was from Phoenix. . . ." I stall, then continue. "She got stabbed in the shower. Disappointing scene." I pause. "Blood looked fake."[24]
>
> *Bret Easton Ellis,* American Psycho

Although the economic theme and its link to psychosis might thus be what ties *Psycho* and *American Psycho* together, it is important to note from both a historical and philosophical point of view the difference between money and finance in this context, or (in other words) the different historical, economic situations in *Psycho* (from 1959/1960) and *American Psycho* (from 1991). This is one of those cases to which I alluded in the introduction, where what Leigh Claire La Berge calls the "representational dominance" of finance should be questioned.[25] For *Psycho* is not about finance but about money—money that will be used, in fact, to acquire real estate.

In this context, it is worth recalling how money is described in Bloch's novel:

> She [Mary Crane] had been standing in Mr. Lowery's office when old Tommy Cassidy hauled out that big green bundle of bills and put them down on the desk. Thirty-six Federal Reserve notes bearing the picture of the fat man who looked like a wholesale grocer, and eight more carrying the face of the man who looked like an undertaker. But the wholesale grocer was Grover Cleveland and the undertaker was William McKinley. And thirty-six thousands and eight five-hundreds added up to forty thousand dollars.

Marion looking at paper money in *Psycho*.

> Tommy Cassidy had put them down just like *that*, fanning them casually as he announced that he was closing the deal and buying a house as his daughter's wedding present.[26]

One paragraph later, Mary's boss, Mr. Lowery, is described as "scooping up" the money.

Money, even if it is paper money (rather than coins), is stunningly material in this passage. It comes in a "big, green bundle"; it has faces on it that look like the faces of "fat wholesale grocers" and "undertakers"; it can be "fanned"; you use it to buy real estate; you can "scoop it up" (try doing that with a derivative!).

And yet, the effect this money has on Mary is strangely immaterial: it propels her into what she will later analyze as madness—into a crazy, psychotic dream. I have already mentioned that in his representation of the paper envelope full of money lying on Marion's bed, or of the money folded into a newspaper lying on Marion's beside table, Hitchcock makes the money that is emphatically and materially present here—and, I should note, present as "paper" (an envelope, a newspaper), as something that, materially, is of little value—zing with an immaterial, symbolic, even fetishistic energy that explains its psychotic effect on people. Clearly, this is no ordinary paper.

Bloch and especially Hitchcock thus draw out paper money's peculiar position at the crossroads of the material and the symbolic, a reality that has only become more intensified as money has morphed through time from its

Paper money in envelope in *Psycho*.

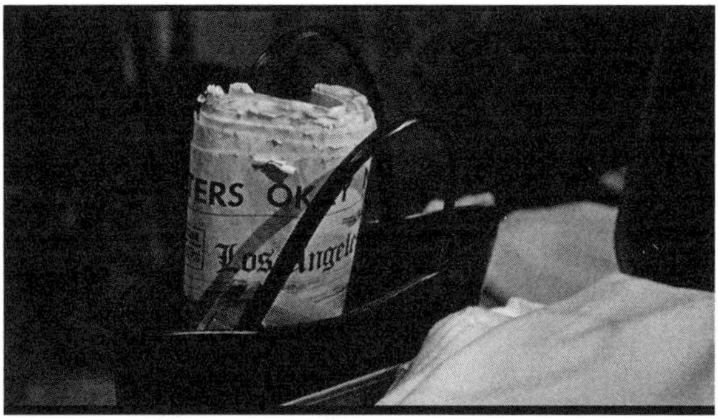

Newspaper in *Psycho*.

Paper money and newspaper in *Psycho*.

Paper money in newspaper in *Psycho*.

paper form into its digitized existence today in the form of, for example, bitcoin.[27] With this intensification, which spans economic history from *Psycho* to *American Psycho* and beyond, also comes the intensification of money's psychotic effects.

One perhaps more engaging way to present this historical development could be (and my consideration of it was partly triggered by Gus van Sant's dreadful attempt to reshoot Hitchcock's *Psycho* scene by scene in 1998, but with different actors and in color): What would Bloch's novel or Hitchcock's film look like if they were remade today? My suggestion would be that any genuine remake of these works would need to involve the contemporary world of finance to be successful: the money that renders Mary and Marion psychotic would need to become financialized. While Bret Easton Ellis's novel *American Psycho* certainly seems to have understood this, finance unfortunately plays even less of a role in that novel than money does in Bloch and Hitchcock, with psychosis being the novel's major theme. In chapter 3, I will discuss an example of a more successful—a less psychotic, more financial—contemporary rewrite of *Psycho*.

For now, I will pursue the historicoeconomic dimension of the "remake" question: what happened in economic history between 1959, when *Psycho* was published, and 1991, when *American Psycho* was published? How did money and the economy change during the thirty years that separate those two novels from each other? Needless to say, I cannot survey all of the economic developments in this time period. In anticipation of the philosophical argument that I lay out in chapter 4, I focus only on those that seem significant in light of what I intend to say then.

As I indicated in my introduction, a key moment of economic history was the year 1971, when Nixon because of the high cost of the Vietnam War abolished the "gold standard"—thus ending the post–World War 2 Bretton Woods system of international financial exchange, propelling the world financial system into "shock." If money had arguably always been symbolic, this change realized a more extreme version of money's symbolic value, opening up an era of unprecedented speculation. In 1971—which is incidentally a date that is inscribed in the opening sentences of *American Psycho*[28]—those who did not know it already (or who had forgotten that their self-created illusions are illusions, to echo Friedrich Nietzsche) discovered the truth about money. Whereas previously, there was still gold backing up paper, from 1971 onward paper was merely paper—*Monopoly* money.[29] Capitalism thus became what four contemporary German thinkers in a recent publication call "divine capitalism" (*göttlicher Kapitalismus*)[30]: *god* is dead (Nietzsche again) yet human beings continued to live as if he were still with us.[31] Isn't it the same with *gold*, one might ask? From such a perspective, the recent collapse of the financial market and the bailout of the banks in both the United States and in Europe further expose the performative nature of money and of the economy at large: the collapse shows that the wealth of the banks was not real. A particular cruel irony is that the bailout, with taxpayer dollars, seems to have made it real *ex post facto*. This could be described as a case of what Anna Kornbluh has called "realizing capital"; Kornbluh points out, following John Vernon, that there is a realist aesthetic that underwrites such a realization, going all the way back to the gold standard and the idea that paper money refers to actual gold that backs it up.[32] Of course, the final twist in this theologicoeconomic tale is that god never existed in the first place, in the same way that—as Felix Martin and David Graeber, among others, have shown—gold never really backed up the value of money in the first place. Such a realism was always already fictitious. Let me explain this further.

The key moment in the becoming-symbolic or becoming-divine of capital—the so-called Nixon shock—fits neatly in a hackneyed narrative about money that has been told again and again, but that has recently been drawn into question. Consider the history of money as summarized by Adam Smith (to give just one example) in his 1776 classic *The Wealth of Nations*.[33] In the chapter "Of the Origin and Use of Money," Smith suggests that whereas cattle used to be the "common instrument of commerce,"[34] and people would pay for a commodity with cattle (he also mentions salt, shells, dried cod, tobacco, sugar, and hides as other such instruments), people began giving preference to metals because they were more practical (losing them did not come with a loss of commodities; they were easier to carry around; their value could be more precisely determined). Of course, these metals also had to be weighed and assayed (one needed to know how much bronze there was in a particular piece of metal, for example) and this too was a cumbersome process. Sovereigns took it upon themselves to attach a public stamp to pieces of metal that had been weighed and assayed to guarantee their value. This made the process of exchange—now no longer through cattle or unauthorized pieces of metal but through "mints"[35]—much easier. However, sovereigns being who they are (as Smith points out), they started "abusing the confidence of their subjects" by decreasing the value of the metals while still attaching their stamp of approval to them[36]—which means that a mint was worth what it said it was "in appearance only,"[37] Smith writes. It is at this point, one could argue, with the shift to the appearance of value and thus the fetishization of money as a commodity (for money is of course itself a commodity that can be bought and sold), that money becomes performance—marking the intensification of its psychotic effects that will culminate in *American Psycho.*

The problem with this particular narrative—which already combines the commodity and fiat theories of money mentioned in the introduction and which can be found in Smith and many other philosophers—is that it is wrong. Building on the work of other scholars in the field, Felix Martin has convincingly demonstrated in *Money: The Unauthorized Biography—From Coinage to Cryptocurrencies* that money never had any actual, material value—value that would be based in cattle, for example.[38] Instead, our economic system originates in credit, more specifically in transferable credit. The idea is simple: say you performed a service for someone, this service would be recorded in an "I owe you" note. If the credit of the one owing you was good, that meant you could transfer that "I owe you" to another, third party, in exchange for a service they can deliver. Your credit was then transferred to them, revealing money to be a social relation rather than a "thing" of "material" value. When it comes to actual currencies, for example "the dollar," Martin points out—again building on other research that's been done in this field—that there is no such thing as an actual, material dollar. A dollar is simply an agreed-upon but ultimately arbitrary unit of measurement like a kilo—but there is no such thing as an actual, material "dollar's" worth of gold, for example. All of these values are social relations rather than objective truths. Shifting the focus from credit to debt, the anarchist anthropologist David Graeber has challenged the traditional narrative about money's material origins along similar lines in *Debt: The First 5,000 Years.*[39] Martin and Graeber deliver a credit/debt theory of money that brings an important corrective to both the commodity and fiat theories of money even though it fails to operate independently from them (as Ole Bjerg has shown[40]).

While these corrective approaches are thus tremendously important, and necessary to understand the reality of the economic today—which is not so much an aberration as an extreme development of money's immaterial origins in transferable credit or debt—I do not think they undermine the historical point I am trying to make with respect to finance's tie to psychosis, namely, that the psychotic effect of money on human beings has intensified over time, with money's development into finance, and in the context of a misconstrued philosophy of money that posited money as an actual, material value. The difference that Martin and Graeber add to this account, however, is that this development is not a development into something new but marks in fact a return to money's immaterial origins, revealing—in a strange turn of argument—that money's intensified psychotic effect today is in fact a piercing through to a more correct understanding of money. The point is not, in this intensified psychotic situation, to reinforce the material value of money over and against immaterial financial instruments of today's economy; rather, it is to see money for what it is—something with no inherent value, a mere token or symbol for an underlying social relation of credit or debt. It is only by moving through that realization that financial psychosis can in any way be addressed; any simplistic opposition of the psychotic to the real is, in this context, doomed to fail—for there never was any real to begin with.

Taking all of that into account (and thus with a certain suspicion about approaches to money that pitch the material against the symbolic), it is worth considering that some have suggested J. L. Austin's category of the performative can be mobilized to describe the psychotic economic culture in which we have landed:[41] someone *declares* that "this piece of paper is worth $100," and the performative declaration makes it *true* (the fiat theory of money). It gives a wholly different ring to the notion of the "performance economy" as we know it from economic theory.[42] Christian Marazzi, for example, discusses this idea in *Capital and Language*; Bernard Stiegler also mentions it in *For a New Critique of Political Economy*.[43] However, Marazzi as well as other thinkers such as Franco "Bifo" Berardi (to whom I will return in chapter 3) have taken the argument even further. While Marazzi thinks that the notion of the performative is useful to capture the truth about the contemporary economic situation, he argues that the nature of contemporary finance capital is reflected not merely in performative utterances but in *all* utterances, and in *language as such*. Capital, Marazzi and other like-minded thinkers argue, has become linguistic: it refers to nothing other than itself (the notion of the sign that circulates here does not include an external referent but is limited by the signifier-signified relation). Whereas capital, in Karl Marx's useful formula (taken up again by thinkers such as Marazzi and Berardi), comes about through the M-C-M' cycle, where—importantly—money (M) leads to "money which is worth more money" (M') via the intermediary of the commodity (C),[44] in the world of *finance* capital M leads to M' *without* the intermediary of the commodity. What is traded in the so-called post-Fordist era are no longer commodities, or goods, but complex financial products such as derivatives—immaterial constructs that even professionals have some difficulty explaining, as Michael Moore's film on capitalism exposes.[45] Indeed, even top figures such as Alan Greenspan and Ben Bernanke have publicly admitted that they no longer know how the contemporary financial world works, leading Bernard Stiegler to speak of "the proletarianization" of the 1 percent.[46] "The proletariat," he adds—quoting from Marx's *The Communist Manifesto*—"is recruited from all classes of the population."[47]

Berardi speaks in this context of semio-capitalism, of a capitalism that operates through the logic of the sign. "Money and language have something in common," he writes in *The Uprising*: "they are nothing and they move everything."[48] What we are dealing with is the rise of what Marx in the third volume of *Capital* called "fictitious capital": "value, in the form of credit, shares, debt, speculation and various forms of paper money, above and beyond what can be realized in the form of commodities."[49] The concept is discussed on several occasions in the collection *Crisis in the Global Economy* (which includes enlightening contributions by Marazzi, as well as by Andrea Fumagalli and Tiziana Terranova).[50] Marx's theory of fictitious capital can be read as a version of his theory of commodity fetishism, developed early on in the first volume of *Capital*—with the psychic condition of fetishism being transformed into full-blown psychosis when we are dealing with fictitious capital. At this point, we are moving from the fiat theory of money to the credit theory of money. From the fetishism of the money commodity to the psychosis of finance.

The culmination of this development is the so-called derivative, for example, the CDO. As Arjun Appadurai explains, "the derivative [for example, a CDO] is above all a linguistic phenomenon, since it is primarily a referent to something more tangible than itself: it is a proposition or a belief about another object that might itself be similarly derived from yet another similar object."[51] If this leads Appadurai to conclude that "the derivative's claim to value is essentially linguistic," he also adds that "its force is primarily performative."[52] Having already referenced Austin on that count, Appadurai explains that while a derivative is "a linguistic artifact, it is even more specific in that it is an invitation to a performative insofar as a derivative takes its full force when it is traded, that is, when two traders arrive at a written contract to exchange (buy and sell) a specific bundle of derivatives."[53] Linguistic and performative, the derivative is a peculiar form of contract "that is based on the unknown future value of an asset that is traded between persons." Marx, Appadurai notes, ultimately didn't really enable us to understand this; finance's "promissory logic" requires another mode of investigation.[54]

Bloch's novel and Hitchcock's film intimate this history, but their relation to it has been obscured by an overwhelming focus on psychosis—money's effect—rather than the cause of this psychosis—money. At the same time, if the economic history I have sketched out is correct, then it doesn't make much sense to speak of money as a material cause, for it is itself already an effect, either because it had an immaterial cause (credit; debt) or because it was always already partly effect, characterized by a performative aspect that today has intensified to the extreme. The rise of bitcoin should surprise no one in this light; the arrival of the cashless society, far from marking an advanced state of civilization, merely returns us to the origins of money.[55]

While *American Psycho* is a prophetic statement about such developments, it nevertheless also preserves traces of the psychotic relation to money's materiality that *Psycho* (as I have shown) documents. All of the financial transactions in *American Psycho* are, of course, cashless; early on in the novel, when Bateman and his colleague Timothy Price pass a bum in the street, Price tells Bateman to ask him "if he takes American Express."[56] It is a cruel exchange that anticipates a detail in Nathan Heller's *New Yorker* account of cashless societies, when Heller notes: "On [a] metro platform one night, I passed a busker with a sign: 'If you don't have Cash, pay with Swish [a mobile cash transfer app].'"[57]

Patrick Bateman looking at a business card in *American Psycho.*

But that doesn't mean that the novel is entirely devoid from the kind of relation to paper money that *Psycho* captures. One finds it, for example, in the famous scene where Bateman shows his colleagues his new business card.[58] Mary Harron's film is on this count perhaps even more effective than Ellis's novel: one by one, Bateman's colleagues start taking out their business cards as if they were weapons, carefully comparing them to Bateman's, and liking Bateman's card the least. Harron shows Bateman as if mesmerized by the business cards, in a way that is similar to how Marion Crane in Hitchcock's film was mesmerized by the money that Mr. Cassidy was waving under her nose.

Harron works very effectively within this association when, later on, her script uses the business card of Luis Carruthers as a trigger for Bateman's psychotic behavior. After Carruthers has presented his new business card to his colleagues, Bateman follows him into a men's room with the intention of strangling him. In the end, Bateman can't go through with it, however, and Carruthers interprets Bateman's gesture as a sign of his affection: he kisses Bateman on the wrist and reveals that he's attracted to him.

On the one hand, the music here indicates that the scene is a reference to *Psycho*. Harron in fact has Bateman's reference to Ed Gein—one of the novel's explicit references to *Psycho*—introduce the scene with Carruthers. The intense string arrangement evokes Bernard Herrmann's famous score for Hitchcock's film. But there is more: the scene throws Bateman into a dizzying panic and when it cuts to Harron's vertiginous shot of a group of New

York skyscrapers, one understands that the reference is also to Hitchcock's *Vertigo* (Paramount, 1958). It's as if Bateman's psychosis can no longer be contained to individual scenes; instead, it spills over from one scene to the next, a spilling that is established through the Hitchcock references.

It is worth noting, however, that each business card scene is *both* a scene of (Hitchcockian) horror *and* comedy. In the first business card scene, the traders are merely discussing a business card, but it is as if a horrible murder is taking place. If the scene is also comedic, this is in part because Bateman and company are assessing pieces of paper; they are clearly attaching much more value to them than they are actually worth. But that is also why it is a scene of horror: because a material object that has very little actual value has become invested with a symbolic value that makes it pulse with life, the way money pulses in Hitchcock's film. There is a horrific excess that haunts it, and disturbs us. The second business card scene, which turns into an aborted scene of psychotic murder, also has comedy built in: when Carruthers kisses Bateman's wrist, or mouths "I'll call you" at the end of the scene, there is comic relief. The music is dropped at this point and the generic shift is as stark as in *American Psycho*'s opening credits, which oscillate between bloody murder and nouvelle cuisine, between psychotic thriller and comedy of manners.

The scene where Bateman is looking at his colleague's business card is the scene where he is looking most closely at what money has become in his time: symbolic rather than material value. A name for *nothing but* the horrific and comedic *excess* that Hitchcock and Harron evoke. It is quite appropriate that from where the viewer is sitting, the card that Bateman is holding appears to be a blank—a white blank interrupting the frame of Harron's film. That evokes, one could suggest, the general absence of money in *American Psycho*; but it also evokes, and this is something *American Psycho* brings home to us, the general absence *within* money, which is not something of actual material value (as the gold standard narrative would have us believe) but a mere symbol or token of credit or debt, an "I owe you" note that in its blank and writable space is ultimately no different from the plastic with which Bateman and company pay for dinner. It is unclear whether this is supposed to makes us laugh or cry.

Money, then, is caught up in a kind of appearing/disappearing act in *Psycho* and *American Psycho*: to read those works as finance fictions means that money in them must appear; and yet, as soon as it appears, it must again disappear to account for both its odd materiality, at the crossroads of the material and the symbolic, and its odd but originary immateriality, drawn out in financial times. Perhaps no work has better staged this dynamic than Douglas Gordon's conceptual artwork *24 Hour Psycho* (1993), which slows down Hitchcock's film to a twenty-four-hour document. In an article titled "The Time of Affect," Mark Hansen recalls that for Gordon, this project originated in his sense that "there is more [in *Psycho*] than meets the eye"[59]—in other words: slowed down, the film might reveal more than what we are able to see at its normal projection speed. "Money" is definitely something that such a decelerated viewing might reveal. Along similar lines, Michael Fried has suggested that by slowing *Psycho* down, Gordon alerts us to "the subtle play of [Janet] Leigh's facial expressions serving mainly to bind the viewer's attention to the smallest discernible features of her behavior."[60] Christine Ross, on the other hand, argues that this slowing down "[dissolves] diegesis to the extent that, more often than not, there is nothing to see"[61]: if money might have been visible at the normal projection speed, slowing the film down makes it disappear and renders it invisible. I do not think it is necessary to take a decision on these different viewings: together, they reveal the peculiar status of money in *Psycho*, as something visible that is at the same time invisible, and thereby throws human beings into a psychosis that itself is caught up in this drama of seeing.

Psychotic Realism

> He's been savaged to the degree that it makes me think he's saying something important.[62]
>
> *Jeff Gordinier on Bret Easton Ellis*

Given all of this, *American Psycho*'s failure as a finance novel—because it privileges psychosis over finance as a theme—could be recuperated as what I call (after the Italian literary theorist Antonio Scurati[63]) a psychotic realism: the novel's focus on psychosis in fact goes to the essence of the history of money and finance.[64] Moving on, then, from money as the unstable reality that renders human beings psychotic, let me turn toward the subject who is caught up in this process. Even before Bret Easton Ellis's *American Psycho* was published in 1991, the novel was caught up in a storm of protest about its graphic violence and misogyny.[65] Its first-person narrator, finance man Patrick Bateman, also turns out to be a racist and anti-Semite; and he doesn't go easy on homosexuals either. Although all of those problematic elements are part of Bateman's character, the Bateman we encounter at the beginning of the novel doesn't quite seem to be all of this yet.

When New York City is summed up in the novel's opening pages—"strangled models, babies thrown from tenement rooftops, kids killed in the subway, a Communist rally, Mafia boss wiped out, Nazis . . . baseball players with AIDS, more Mafia shit, gridlock, the homeless, various maniacs, faggots dropping like flies in the streets, surrogate mothers, the cancellation of a soap opera, kids who broke into a zoo and tortured and burned various animals alive, more Nazis . . . more Nazis, gridlock, gridlock, black-market babies, AIDS babies, baby junkies, building collapses on baby, maniac baby, gridlock, bridge collapses"[66]—it's Bateman's Pierce and Pierce colleague Timothy Price who is speaking. When one of Bateman's other colleagues notes that the lucky Paul Owen, who "handles the Fisher account,"[67] is a "*Jew*," Bateman remarks: "What does *that* have to do with anything?"[68] In response to a joke that the same colleague tells a few pages later, Bateman says: "It's not funny. . . . It's *racist*."[69]

These reactions—calling out his colleagues's anti-Semitism and racism—resonate with a political speech that Bateman delivers early on in the novel. "We have to end apartheid for one," Bateman begins.

> And slow down the nuclear arms race, stop terrorism and world hunger. Ensure a strong national defense, prevent the spread of communism in Central America, work for a Middle East peace settlement, prevent U.S. military involvement overseas. We have to ensure that America is a respected world power. Now that's not to belittle our domestic problems, which are equally important, if not *more*. Better and more affordable long-term care for the elderly, control and find a cure for the AIDS epidemic, clean up environmental damage from toxic waste and pollution, improve the quality of primary and secondary education, strengthen laws to crack down on crime and illegal drugs. We also have to ensure that college education is affordable for the middle class and protect Social Security for senior citizens plus conserve natural resources and wilderness areas and reduce the influence of political action committees.[70]

The speech (which goes on for quite a bit longer) lays out what many would probably perceive as an anti–*American Psycho* program, attacking many of the things that have come to define Bateman as a character: materialism, violence in movies, graphic sex, in addition to the various *-isms* I already mentioned. Bateman is certainly not one who cares for social needs. It is difficult to imagine that the Bateman who brutally murders women, homosexuals, homeless people, Paul Owen, and various small animals, is the same as the one who is speaking here.[71] In fact, all of the scenes in the first fifty pages of Ellis's four-hundred-page novel are relatively innocent: *American Psycho* delivers a social satire, a "comedy of manners" (as Harron has suggested) that takes on white, privileged, consumerist, male (yuppie) behavior on Wall Street in the 1980s.

The first hint of Bateman's murderous self arrives on page 52: "I have a knife with a serrated blade in the pocked of my Valentino Jacket and I'm tempted to gut McDermott with it right here in the entranceway, maybe slice his face open, sever his spine." This tension between the two Batemans is captured nicely by Bateman's girlfriend Evelyn, who, while she keeps referring to Bateman as "the boy next door," also asks, jokingly: "You're not an extraterrestrial, are you honey?"[72] "Should I even dignify that question with an answer?" Bateman responds. "Oh baby," Evelyn goes, "*I* know you're not an extraterrestrial."[73] Of course, the exchange makes explicit the uncanny atmosphere of the novel, which is precisely about a boy next door who turns out to be psychotic. *Psychosis* strikes us close to home: in *America*. The extraterrestrial is here—already among us, one of us. Us/US (American *Psycho*; Us, Psycho).

Psychosis is the easy answer to the split personality problem that seems to haunt Bateman (civil rights advocate? or racist?): Bateman is a psychopath (and possibly has been since his college days—the novel includes a reference to a murder he may have committed while still at Harvard[74]) who turns psychotic over the course of Ellis's novel. Whereas he is still somehow able to keep it together in the novel's opening pages—even calling out the racism and anti-Semitism of those around him—that performance of normality quickly disintegrates, causing a crack (hinted at throughout the novel through the repeated references to the disturbing crack in Bateman's ceiling, above his David Onica painting, first mentioned on page 70) through which all of the evil that caused such protest comes oozing out.

The strange thing is, however, that while Bateman isn't exactly shy about this disintegration—there are numerous moments in the novel when he confesses his murderous thoughts and actions; he appears in public with a blood-splattered raincoat and blood-stained sheets; dragging a body bag in the street one evening, he runs into two acquaintances—no one, not even his lawyer Harold Carnes, appears to take these warnings seriously: perhaps a sign, as I have already suggested, that all of this is imagined, none of it is real (as some critics have argued); or that Bateman is—in the words of his lawyer—such a "bloody ass-kisser, such a brown-nosing goody-goody" that no one could possibly imagine him committing all of his heinous crimes.[75]

In both of these readings, Bateman's political speech would have to be considered a kind of performance: Bateman is projecting a façade under which the opposite of what he preaches is raging. The political speech is fake; the murders, whether real or imagined, are the consequence of a real hatred against women, black people, homosexuals, the homeless, and even children, or Wall Street men (like Paul Owen).

This list reveals, however, that identities such as "women" or "black people" cannot really do justice to the universality of Bateman's rage, which appears to include nearly everyone. His is a misanthropic rage against humanity at large and the comedy of manners in which it is caught up. Bateman reveals to us, to a certain extent, the inhumanity to which well-mannered humanity has lead: an inhumanity that provokes him into murdering people (and several animals as well), thus exposing on the side of the murderer *and* the murdered a kind of inhuman that in fact might be more real as "dead" than the "living" fakery that surrounds him.

Indeed, Bateman's violence in the novel appears to be driven not so much by hatred but by an attempt to have some experience of reality, and specifically of his own reality (or nonreality). Bateman does not exist, is surrounded by people who do not exist, in a world that does not exist. It is a classic experience of psychosis as I have defined it in the introduction—disavowal of the world—with the added twist that the creative element of psychosis may be excluded here: Bateman does not appear to have the desire to create another world instead of the one he disavows. He is stuck entirely in the destructive part of his affliction. Bateman's nonexistence, as well as his psychosis' lack of a constructive dimension, should be read in relation to the novel's representation of consumerism, as marked by the litanies of objects and brand names that traverse the novel (as well as one of Ellis's other novels, *Glamorama*, which is focused on the fashion world[76]), and that has given critics much to chew on: whatever remains of existence and creativity find their dead-end in the acquisition (and not even the use) of objects.

As such, Bateman is a product of our contemporary, decadent democracies. A consumer *par excellence*—many have been irritated by the lists of brand names throughout the book—Bateman suffers from a proletarianization of the spirit, of a loss of *savoir-vivre*, and it is this loss—which is not fictional but very real—that produces his murderous behavior. In Bernard Stiegler's terms, Bateman is "expropriated of all knowledge, condemned to a life-without-knowledge, that is, without savours, thrown into an insipid and, at times, squalid world: at the same time economically, symbolically and libidinally immiserated."[77] Bateman is affected by what Stiegler later in the same book calls "generalized proletarianization," which "affects the entire population, just as a Parisian suffers the toxicity of the atmosphere regardless of his or her social condition."[78] As Stiegler understands it, this is an aesthetic problem: Bateman suffers from an "aesthetic proletarianization" that is not defined by his pauperization—he is rich—but by the "symbolic misery" in which he has landed.[79]

Bateman's murders, then, and the novel's description of them, need to be read not just as a "confession,"[80] as Bateman puts it. They need to be read as *testimony*. Commenting on various contemporary murder stories in the West (he focuses specifically on cases in France, but one can also think of the numerous mass shootings in recent US history), Stiegler suggests:

> [T]hese passages into action are lived by their authors, in one way or another, as a form of testimony, and even as this need to do evil in order to have, at least once in their life, the feeling of existing, a feeling which . . . was then transformed through being acted out, through the passage into action. For this is indeed what it means "to ex-sist": "to testify," here, means to attest before others to a "disposition," to confront a legacy by leaving a legacy oneself, and through death given as well as through one's own death—which is always in one way or another a testament, even if only through the fear it inspires.[81]

"If this is true," he concludes, "it means that all these acts tend to evolve toward the figure of the martyr."[82] The excerpt recalls a passage of Stiegler's book *Acting Out*, where he dedicates the text titled "To Love, to Love Me, to Love Us: From September 11 to April 21" to the voters of the extreme right in France, saying that he feels close to them because they suffer from the sociopathologies that define our contemporary existence.[83] Mobilizing this position within the realm of finance, the project would not be to simply oppose figures such as Jordan "the wolf of Wall Street" Belfort;[84] it would be to try to understand what kinds of societies produce such human beings, and how such human beings—who have suffered a destruction of the spirit—can be taken care of. It is our responsibility to change society; we should perhaps focus on this rather than on the psychopathologies that effect us individually and collectively (and which are often treated through pharmaceutics alone).[85]

Bateman as a martyr, then, whose tragedy is that even his extreme testimony goes unheard—for whom there is indeed no exit (as the closing line of Ellis's book has it, in reference to another, famous existentialist drama) from the hell of the decadent democracy in which he is caught up.[86] Someone we should feel close to, but to whom we would much rather be opposed. What *American Psycho* offers us, in all its extremity, is ultimately a nauseating existentialist drama that does no more (but also no less) than capture the life drama of Everyman under the economic conditions of finance. The "nameless dread" that is mentioned repeatedly in the novel is our dread; even Patrick's "anxiety" and "panic" is our own.[87]

Rereading the novel today, it strikes one as strangely prophetic, hypercontemporary, in line with how capitalist societies have developed—with Bateman's Walkman and videotapes oddly outdated in this bright, contemporary light. It is no wonder that Ellis has apparently been considering a follow-up to the novel; or that Patrick Bateman has returned in one of Ellis's later fictions, the paranoid *Lunar Park*. If Bateman may have appeared to some as an unreal, extreme character who was dead before Ellis's novel was published, he has turned out to be more real, more "normal" with time—he has come alive over time. However frightening that may be, it would be a mistake to deny this, and persist in the disavowal of the reality that Bateman represents.

Indeed, it is partly by looking at some of Ellis's other work that the validity of such a hypothesis can be demonstrated. While critics love to lock away the extremity of *American Psycho* in its Wall Street context, it is worth noting that some of the horrors the novel describes are actually copied from some of Ellis's earlier works, which are *not* set on Wall Street. There, they occur on the West Coast, among the wealthy "generation X'ers" that Ellis's novels have tended to describe.[88] In many ways, *American Psycho* was an exception that confirmed the rule: true, it is an extreme novel, but its extremity merely captures a situation or state that is laid out in his less extreme fictions as well. The measure of this insight remains to be taken.

None of this takes away, of course, the fact that Bateman is an extreme character, a limit figure produced by the particular world of finance; a kind of "last man" in the financial universe.[89] The tragedy of the novel is that Bateman, as a figure of the inhuman, may be committing all of his heinous acts precisely in an attempt to hold on to some kind of humanity—some kind of real in an overwhelmingly fake world. Indeed, one gets the sense throughout the novel, from Bateman's earliest murderous remarks, that he has a desire to be caught, to be found out, to be recognized in his inhumanity. The cruelty of the novel is that it does not grant him even that recognition: even when he leaves a recorded confession of his crimes on his lawyer's answering machine, that confession is not believed, and Bateman is left to the insignificance of his murderous behavior. Again, some have read this as evidence for the fact that the murders aren't real; but I think that may gloss over the real drama here, which is a kind of existential drama of one's life being ignored in a fake world that couldn't care less about anything real. The novel concludes with the depressing line that there is no exit from that situation: Bateman is doomed to go on murdering forever, in a world that is indifferent to his actions. It is this indifference, which is arguably more horrible than Bateman's own—a psychosis not of Bateman but of the world—that is the truly troubling reveal of the novel, and one that is denied entirely by readings of the novel that suggest Bateman's murderous behavior is not real. *It isn't because the world doesn't recognize the murdering that it isn't real.* This is the troubling conclusion that some readers may find difficult to reach.

However, one might also wonder in this context whether such a reading of Bateman as a figure of the inhuman, with the attachment to the human that it entails, can do justice to Bateman's particular kind of being. In closing, I want to suggest that *American Psycho* also pushes beyond that remainder of humanity, casting Bateman not only as a last human being but also—and perhaps more prophetically so—as a late (former) human being, an ex-human being who has truly left the realm of the human behind and to whom the notion of the inhuman therefore does not apply. In a famous passage in the novel Bateman reflects on his own humanity:

> [T]here is an idea of a Patrick Bateman, some kind of abstraction, but there is no real me, only an entity, something illusory, and though I can hide my cold gaze and you can shake my hand and feel flesh gripping yours and maybe can even sense our lifestyles are probably comparable: *I simply am not there*. It is hard for me to make sense on any given level. Myself is fabricated, an aberration. I am a noncontingent human being. My personality is sketchy and unformed, my heartlessness goes deep and is persistent. My conscience, my pity, my hopes disappeared a long time ago (probably at Harvard) if they ever did exist. There are no more barriers to cross. All I have in common with the uncontrollable and the insane, the vicious and the evil, all the mayhem I have caused and my utter indifference toward it, I have now surpassed.[90]

While Bateman still describes himself as "human," his humanity is obviously under huge pressure, being pushed to the limits of what can still be considered such. "My pain is constant and sharp," he continues, "and I do not hope for a better world for anyone."[91] However, this admission does not lead to catharsis: "I gain no deeper knowledge about myself, no understanding can be extracted from my telling. There has been no reason for me to tell you any of this. This confession has meant *nothing*."[92]

As an "idea," Bateman has surpassed even the scale of the inhuman, which is always still related to the human.[93] The question that a figure such as Bateman ultimately raises is not just that of "the uncontrollable and the insane, the vicious and the evil"—he is beyond that, beyond what still remains within the sphere of the human. A threshold has been crossed into indifference, a lack of understanding, nothingness. There is no longer anything natural about Bateman, he has become pure fabrication, a mere abstraction, unreal—heartless, as he also puts it. One could arguably read this as a transition into "character," as a novelistic character who has come into his own: whereas we started out, perhaps, with the illusion of a real human being, what we end up with is a real character: entirely scripted, and—in Bateman's understanding—at a remove from the contingency that makes us human. There is a sense of automation that is prevalent here, a sense that Bateman has turned into some kind of "bot."[94]

If "the idea of Patrick Bateman" passage hovers somewhere between the real and the written, between Bateman as a real, living person and a heartless character, it also functions at the edge of a digital culture whose take-over of the stock market is imminent. This is an element that Stiegler, with his attention to automation, invites us to think in this context (he mentions "automated trading" in his discussion of proletarianization[95]). It seems that with the bot-like figure of Patrick Bateman, Ellis was already on the track of this; but Bateman's position at the crossroads of the real and the written in fact prevents us from fully grasping the reality of a digitized Bateman. Imagined as an algorithmic trading bot, Bateman would hardly be noncontingent: scripted, his "code" would in fact generate contingency in the stock market—a situation in response to which more "writing" would be needed. *American Psycho* does not include yet, in other words, a thinking of the digital market that we are living in today and the kind of contingency and even "life" that the particular writing of algorithms brings to it.

In his book *Look at the Bunny: Totem, Taboo, Technology*, Dominic Pettman tells the story of how animators scripted the elaborate battle scenes in Peter Jackson's *Lord of the Rings* films. As Pettman points out, it was obviously impossible to script each of the "digital 'extras' involved—namely, 80,000 Orcs."

> The new state-of-the-art Massive™ software used by Jackson's hi-tech atelier side-stepped this issue by algorithmically allowing Orcs to fight their own individual battles, according to separate decision trees and sub-routines. This meant that each digital creature would behave according to a set of pre-coded possibilities, and yet the animators themselves could not anticipate what any single actor would do at any given moment in the melee. As such, each Orc existed in a semi-open zone, somewhere between the predetermined and the aleatory: that is, between compulsion and free-will.[96]

What happened was this: in one of the early test runs, "one of the Orcs simply refused to fight," causing other Orcs to do the same thing and run away "in the face of aggressive Elves, against the directions of the script."[97] So the algorithmic script entered into tension with the cinematic script.

If the cinematic script—which is in play in Bateman's self-description—does not allow for nonscripted behavior, Pettman shows us that the algorithmic script does, and in that sense an algorithm is more than a character.

If Bateman casts himself as a character, we would have to point out in view of the developments of the stock market that will follow him (developments that will only fully hit the financial markets in the late 1990s[98]), that the new being governing the market is not so much a scripted character as a scripted algorithm—with all of the challenges for a contemporary fiction of finance that this entails.

THREE

Financial Realism in *The Fear Index*

> When the screens go black, a world goes black. But what happens if that world goes black?
> Twenty years from now, even in ten years, the answer could be "nothing at all." The screens project the market, but in the future the market might carry on just as well without the screens.
>
> —KARIN KNORR CETINA, *"What If the Screens Went Black?"*[1]

Updating the Finance Novel

Set against the so-called flash crash of May 6, 2010—the day when the Dow Jones Industrial Index for reasons that are still not entirely clear experienced a huge drop, only to recover from it within minutes—Robert Harris's science-fiction thriller *The Fear Index* tells the story of twenty-four hours in the life of Dr. Alexander "Alex" Hoffmann. Based in Geneva, Alex is a scientist—specifically, a physicist—working on artificial intelligence and autonomous machine learning who became a hedge fund manager and made himself and his investors fabulously wealthy through algorithmic trading. In the novel, Alex's algorithm seems to go rogue, trying to crash not only its creator, but also his company as well as the global economy in an attempt to maximize the profit it was designed to generate.

The Fear Index thus updates a familiar plot from the gothic novels it references into the age of the digital economy. Harris's most obvious intertext is Mary Shelley's *Frankenstein* (1818),[2] which is also partly set in Geneva. But *The Fear Index* also reworks the plot of *American Psycho* in light of the consideration with which I ended the previous chapter, about Bateman as a scripted (novelistic, cinematic) versus an algorithmic character. Ellis's extended oeuvre in fact includes the plotline—which *The Fear Index* realizes—about the automated trader going rogue: this is precisely what happens in *Lunar Park*, Ellis's mock memoir which is set in post-9/11 America and includes Patrick Bateman as a character. (Donald Kimball, the detective from Ellis's earlier novel, also makes an appearance.) Furthermore, if *American Psycho* is also an example of the subgenre of the financial novel called the panic novel, *The Fear Index* builds on *American Psycho* in that respect as well.

However, there is also a marked difference. In what follows I show that as a panic novel *The Fear Index* (like its predecessors) mobilizes the theme of psychosis only to distance itself from it. True to the reality of the markets today, it instead proposes a science fiction–like plot (238), which it then asks the reader to accept as "real." Such a request is not as outrageous as it might seem, given that today markets are governed by nonhuman, algorithmic agents trading at speeds that neither humans nor computers are able to record, let alone regulate. While *The Fear Index* thus goes a long way toward promoting a new financial realism that would be attuned to today's sci-fi–like economic reality, I also show that it ultimately fails on that count by operating too much on a human scale in its representation of VIXAL-4, the trading algorithm that plays a central role in the novel. That criticism will open up room in chapter 4 for a consideration of philosophical mindsets required to think outside of that scale as well as various literary experiments that would be attuned to it.

A Panic Novel

The Fear Index begins with Alex Hoffmann leafing through a copy of the first run of the first edition of Charles Darwin's *The Expressions of the Emotions in Man and Animal* (1872) in the study of his sixty-million-dollar house in Geneva, a tax haven; he is looking in particular at the book's images of madness. The novel will end twenty-four hours later, with a supposedly psychotic Alex lying unconscious in bed at the city's University Hospital, badly burnt and with multiple fractures. On the night when he receives the $10,000 Darwin book in the mail—he later confirms that it was ordered and paid for by himself, even though he has no recollection of doing so[3]—Alex has a violent run-in with a home invader who appears to have had knowledge of the codes to dismantle his house's state-of-the-art security system. Alex's house, like his office, most closely resembles a fortress.[4] But it appears the fortress is under attack. Throughout the day, more evidence comes to light that someone is using Alex's e-mail account in an attempt to "destroy" him (138). "Someone's really after me," he confesses to his business partner, Hugo Quarry. "Out to destroy me bit by bit" (144). *The Fear Index* gradually reveals that the agent behind this attack is none other than VIXAL-4, a trading algorithm that Alex created and that appears to now be challenging Alex' fatherly sovereignty over it.[5]

A bit of background about Alex: he originally came to Switzerland "in the nineties [what Hugo refers to as 'the coke-and-call-girl glory days' of finance (73)[6]] to work for CERN [the European Organisation for Nuclear Research], on the Large Hadron Collider" (22).[7] After about six years of working as a physicist, he was lured into the finance world: not because he wanted to work for a bank but because the finance world enabled him to progress with his research on artificial intelligence. CERN had to contain that research because an algorithm Alex designed went out of control and started affecting CERN's systems like a virus. Many years later, Alex seems to be confronted with the same problem at Hoffmann Investment Technologies, and Alex must try to shut down the algorithm before it ruins not only his company but also the global economy. That turns out to be easier said than done: as if to confirm Karin Knorr Cetina's suggestion that prefaces this chapter, Harris's novel shows that algorithmic life continues even after the screens go black.

Although *The Fear Index* is thus clearly a finance novel, it is also a science novel. Hoffmann Investment Technologies is a business, but it is also a laboratory. When the policeman Jean-Jacques Leclerc comes to investigate the home invasion—the novel tells us that Leclerc's investments toward retirement have tanked due to the 2008 crash—he asks Hoffmann what his business makes. Hoffmann's answer is the definition of finance: "It makes money" (23). And yet, for Hoffmann it's never just about the money. Leclerc notes, for example, that Alex's library does not contain a single book about money. It's Alex's partner, Hugo, who represents the financial side of things. When Alex gives a speech to the team with whom he is working at the hedge fund, he thanks them for the *scientific* progress they have made. *The Fear Index* is about the intimate connections between science and finance today—a mix that Alex's former CERN boss Robert Walton considers to be an "unstable compound" and characterizes as the "dark arts" (213).

The Fear Index takes a while to arrive at the revelation that a rogue algorithm is responsible for what is happening to Alex. In the meantime, it builds up tension focusing on the intensification of Alex's emotions from fear into full-blown panic. Early on in the novel, when he is on the tracks of the man who has invaded his house, Alex can still insist that "he felt no panic": "panic was quite different from fear, he was discovering. Panic was moral and nervous collapse, a waste of precious energy, whereas fear was all sinew and instinct: an animal that stood up on its hind legs and filled you completely, that took control out of your brain and your muscles" (13). Some forty pages later, however, when he finds out that he did not place the book order that originated from his e-mail account, "the confidence leaked from his voice and he felt almost physically sick with panic, as if an abyss was opening at his feet" (65). Another eighty pages later, when he realizes his marriage is disintegrating due to the crises in which he has landed, "panic welled up inside him again" (142). At his office, he does his best not "to create a panic" among the traders; but as the crisis around the algorithm grows, "panic" invades them anyways (258). In short, panic returns as a *Leitmotiv* throughout the text—it seems inescapable (65, 142, 258)—and within the genre of the finance novel, *The Fear Index* can obviously be assessed as a panic novel.[8]

There is some irony (or poetic justice) to Alex's being overwhelmed by panic since the affect that Alex's algorithm thrives on is, precisely, panic. The way Alex and his associates see it, digitalization is producing "an epidemic of fear" today (86). "The rise in market volatility," they argue, "is a function of digitalization, which is exaggerating human mood swings by the unprecedented dissemination of information via the Internet" (86). With his algorithm, Alex seeks to make money out of this situation: VIXAL-4 monitors panic on the World Wide Web and places its trades on the basis of the data it collects there, making huge profits out of negative human emotion. Interestingly, given my discussion of finance in the previous chapter, language plays a key role in this: indeed, it is because algorithms have become able to recognize language that the development toward a panic-monitoring algorithm has become possible. It is because algorithms have taken on this most human of features that VIXAL-4 is in business (82–83). One of Alex's potential investors refers to VIXAL-4's approach (turning fear and panic into a profit) as "behavioral finance" (85), thus splicing the novel's interest in finance and panic together with evolutionary science and Darwin. All of this is not as outrageous as it sounds: the VIX, the volatility index, exists—*The Fear Index* merely adds an extra twist to it. "Behavioral finance" is also an existing, relatively new field in financial theory.[9] Although *The Fear Index* may thus sound like a science fiction novel, it actually stays quite close to the reality of financial markets today.

It's important to note, however, that in *The Fear Index*, the algorithm does not merely monitor panic; it also produces it—and here we seem to be taking a step beyond "realism."[10] Alex's creature appears to be involved in a struggle to crash its creator, thereby transforming Alex into a panicked creature. Beyond that, it appears the algorithm also seeks to crash Alex's company and the market at large, panicking not only Alex's business partner Hugo and his employees but also traders worldwide. Most strikingly, *The Fear Index* suggests that Alex's algorithm may even be responsible for the "flash crash" that operates as the novel's real-life historical background.[11] The only one who does not panic in this situation is the algorithm itself. Indeed, it is precisely because algorithms do not panic, as the novel points out that "they're so perfectly suited to trade on the financial markets" (84). The algorithm might have language, the argument goes, but it doesn't have the imagination that comes with it and that produces panic (84). While Alex tries to battle his panic—and by extension that of the global market—by trying to shut the algorithm down, *The Fear Index* closes with Alex knocked out in his hospital bed and the suggestion that the algorithm is still trading and increasing its profits. Meanwhile, at the office, Hugo resumes his work, giving "the slightest bow of obeisance" to the algorithm that is spying on him through a hidden camera in the ceiling (285). Here, in the suggestion that the algorithm is "spying" on Hugo so as to control his behavior rather than merely "record" it, we seem to be within the realm of a science fiction novel, even if there are also elements of a contemporary financial realism to this. Indeed, after the algorithm has been shut down, it turns out to have merely migrated—it continues to live in what Karin Knorr Cetina characterizes as "another world underneath the level of human agency: that of data centers, programs, and electronic connections, . . . the environment of algorithms, or . . . software agents."[12]

To sum up: *The Fear Index* is a contemporary finance novel, more precisely a contemporary panic novel, that offers a part realist, part sci-fi representation of today's digitized financial markets. At the crossroads of the fi-fi (financial fiction) and the sci-fi (science fiction) genres, the novel has a number of intertexts that make this localization even more specific. Some of the novel's chapter mottoes are taken from Bill Gates's *Business @ the Speed of Thought* (1999; coauthored with Collins Hemingway), a text that is also explicitly credited in the novel as the source for Hoffmann's idea for an "entirely digital" company (53–54).[13] The novel's investigation of fear and specifically panic partly happens in dialogue with the already mentioned *Expressions of the Emotions in Man and Animal.* In addition, the novel also includes references to Darwin's *On the Origin of Species* and *The Descent of Man*, and those intertexts are related to the novel's gothic plot in particular. Explicitly revisiting Mary Shelley's *Frankenstein* (1818; partly set in Geneva, Shelley's novel also deals with artificial life) as well as Stevenson's *Strange Case of Dr. Jekyll and Mr. Hyde* (1886) in light of contemporary economic issues (110), *The Fear Index* updates the gothic novel's plot into the age of the digitized economy. Given Hoffmann's last name, one should also add E. T. A. Hoffmann's "The Sandman" (1816) as a reference in this uncanny novel that mobilizes the themes of the double and of automata that are central to Sigmund Freud's theory of the uncanny and its analysis of Hoffmann's story.[14]

Panic and Its Responses

With the psychopathology of panic, we are on the terrain of psychosis, which, as discussed in chapters 1 and 2, is a familiar theme in the finance novel. If panic is indeed the name that *The Fear Index* proposes for Alex's particular state of mind, then what is this particular panic produced by the contemporary digital economy? What is this *econuméripanique*, as one could call it—a French *portmanteau* word that splices together the economy, the digital, and panic? After all, the word panic has a long tradition that far precedes our contemporary economic situation.

In his work on the contemporary digital economy, the Italian activist and critical thinker Franco "Bifo" Berardi reminds his readers that the word *panic* and the affect it names can be traced back to the Greek god Pan.[15] Half goat, half human—and thus a creature in-between animal and human life—Pan was the god of the wild, of shepherds and flocks. Associated with sexuality (including polygamy, eroticism, masturbation, rape, and lust) and fertility and a companion of the nymphs, he was usually worshipped in a natural setting—a cave, for example. Some theories have it that he is the son of Zeus. Others suggest that he is the son of Hermes (and the nymph Penelope of Mantineai—apparently, she later became confused with Penelope from Homer's *Odyssey*, and Pan was thought to be the son of Penelope's intercourse with all of her 108 suitors). Probably one of the oldest gods, many have also noted that he is also the only Greek god who dies: "Pan ho megas tethneke" (The great Pan has died) was a cry that was popular with the romantics because it evoked the loss of human beings' relation to nature or to what Berardi in a more contemporary context calls "the overwhelming flow of reality, things, and information that we are surrounded by."[16]

As our contemporary use of the word panic still reveals, panic was not a comforting relation. Pan's unseen presence produced feelings of panic in human beings who were traveling through remote, lonely places of the wild; Pan's creaturely appearance, that is, turned human beings into panicked creatures themselves. And yet, and as the cry popular with the romantics illustrates, as long as Pan was still alive, human beings still had *some* relation to nature—one that was formalized in religion. Berardi argues that today, this relation is gone: "Today, panic has become a form of psychopathology. We can speak of panic when we see a conscious organism (individual or social) being overwhelmed by the speed of processes he, she is involved in, and has no time to process the information input. In these cases the organism, all of a sudden, is no more able to process the sheer amount of information coming into its cognitive field or even that which is being generated by the organism itself."[17] Returning to the concept of panic a little later on in the same book, he writes: "The mental environment is saturated by signs that create a sort of continuous excitation, a permanent electrocution, which leads the individual mind as well as the collective mind to a state of collapse."[18]

This issue is articulated in Berardi's work in both a temporal and a spatial way: it is associated with the acceleration of time today, and the problem is particularly present, he suggests, in urban environments. In his book *After the Future*, Berardi returns once more to the topic of panic, now writing about what he calls the "city of panic" or what one could call the *panipolis*. According to Berardi, the "urban territory is increasingly traversed" by panic. "Anxiety" is "growing" in the city, "the urban libidinal economy" is "going insane." Or, as he also puts it, a little melodramatically: "In the city of panic, there is no longer time to get close to each other; there is no more time for caresses, for the pleasure and slowness of whispered words."[19]

In his book *The Soul at Work*, this argument is brought in explicit relation with the contemporary economy, even if Berardi himself seems to want to move away from this: "When in 1999, Alan Greenspan spoke of the 'irrational exuberance of the market,' his words were more of a clinical than a financial diagnosis. Exuberance was an effect of the drugs and of the overexploitation of available mental energy, of a saturation of attention leading people to the limits of panic. Panic is the anticipation of a depressive breakdown, of mental confusion and disactivation."[20] Berardi's focus here is on the so-called attention economy—the ways in which attention is being destroyed in an economy that increasingly capitalizes on the mind and the brain (he is interested in the clinical rather than the financial diagnosis). This focus works well with *The Fear Index*, which includes a quote from Darwin's *Descent of Man* that foregrounds that issue as well: "Hardly any faculty is more important for the intellectual progress of man than ATTENTION" (61).

But it is worth noting the financial setting of this attention "crash," which is the digitized economy. *The Soul at Work* is interested, first and foremost, in the changed conditions of labor that such an economy brings—one in which our very souls (our minds, our spirits) are put to work. One such change, Berardi suggests, is that panic in this economy becomes a widespread phenomenon. This is due to several causes. "The social context" for this phenomenon "is a competitive society where all energies are mobilized in order to prevail on the other . . . if one doesn't win, one can be eliminated."[21]

One can think here of the popular film trilogy *The Hunger Games* (Lionsgate, 2012), or its Japanese source of inspiration *Battle Royale* (Toei Company, 2000). Berardi continues: "The technological context is the constant acceleration of rhythms of the global machine, a constant expansion of cyberspace in the face of the individual brain's limited capacities of elaboration."[22] Finally, he notes "the communicational context," which "is that of an endless expansion of the Infosphere, which contains all signals from which competition and survival depend."[23] For Berardi, this situation is "very similar . . . to the one pictured by the Greek etymology of the word panic." He concludes, "The infinite vastness of the Infosphere is superior to the human capacities of elaboration, as much as a sublime nature overcomes the capacities of feeling that the Greeks could summon when faced with the god Pan."[24]

Today, then, panic is no longer produced in nature—the setting for the classical understanding of panic—but in the second nature that the "Infosphere" has become. This time, of course, there is no god in place that will enable us to recuperate this panic as a meaningful religious experience. Today's panic no longer names even the shred of a relation; instead, it marks the total loss of relation—the death of Pan, and thus of panic itself. Berardi thus reveals himself to be something like a contemporary romantic, crying in the wilderness of today's digitized economy that "the great Pan has died!"[25] His position is in line with the traditional take on Pan, who, as Dominic Pettman in an instructive discussion of the Greek god has pointed out, has "become an icon for those who lament the Fall into civilization."[26]

If the condition Berardi describes is arguably also the scene that *The Fear Index* sets for its readers, then what are the responses to panic that the novel dramatizes? Alex, the novel's protagonist, battles the pathologizing information economy with science. Indeed, it is to manage the overwhelming flow of information and the loss of relation that it risks producing, that Alex designs his algorithm: a kind of contemporary version of Pan, or what Pettman in his discussion of Pan wittily refers to as "the goat in the machine."[27] Alex seeks to reestablish a meaningful relation to information through his algorithm. Pan is supposed to help him maintain control within the information economy. Very quickly, however, Alex's algorithm grows out of control, and the means that Alex used to manage the flow of information seems to become part of the flow of information itself. It is worth noting, however, that this is obviously not *entirely* so: for the algorithm still takes up an active role within that flow.

Indeed, while the algorithm seems to become part of the flow of information that it was designed to master, it clearly still exercises some control within that flow given that it is still making a profit. "Profit" is the law under which the algorithm was generated and to which it still responds. The crucial difference is that the algorithm now responds to this law *outside of its creator's control*. Thus, the algorithm becomes a creator in its own right—a creature that, written (heteronomously) under the law of profit, comes to enact that law itself (semi-autonomously, if not autonomously,[28] given that it still did not write its own law), turning human beings—including the human being who created it—into creatures. It's as if Dr. Viktor Frankenstein becomes subjected to the power of his creature, a confusion that the popular reception of Shelley's novel—which refers to Frankenstein's monster as Frankenstein and erases the difference between the two—already realizes. This is arguably evoked early on in the novel, when Alex at the hospital where he is treated for a wound on the head that he received during the home invasion, "put his fingers to his wound and traced his stitches. It felt to him as if they were stretched so tight they might split apart" (100).[29] Like Dr. Frankenstein's creature, Alex's body is marked by stitches.

It is this at least partly emancipative situation for the algorithm that Alex seeks to undo by attempting to reestablish control over Pan—by returning to a time when Pan was still a figure of humans' relation to overwhelming nature. But *The Fear Index* suggests, and Berardi's analysis goes in the same direction, that such a sense of relationality has gone lost and that panic today has turned into a very different phenomenon. The god, or the goat, has been turned loose. Far from being dead, it is in fact out to kill us.

The response of Alex's business partner Hugo offers a further twist on this situation: rather than trying to master the algorithm, Hugo settles into passive subjection to it, a state that is softened for Hugo by the fact that the algorithm is still making a profit. If this subjection—figured in the novel as Hugo giving "the slightest bow of obeisance" to the algorithm that is spying on him through cameras it had installed both in Alex's office as well as his home (285)—is opposed in the novel to Alex's response of control, neither one of these responses in any meaningful way reconfigures the relation between human beings and their increasingly digitized living environments. Alex's response marks a desperate quest to regain control over the "Infosphere" that human beings have created, an attempt to reinforce the human being's position of mastery. Hugo's response abandons that struggle for control entirely, and passively subjects itself to a human-made, artificial form of life that rewards him with profit.

The situation that is depicted both in Berardi and in *The Fear Index*, is therefore rather grim, to say the least. Does any hope remain, outside of the nostalgia that Berardi seems to flirt with? *The Fear Index* seems to think so when it suggests an alternative etymology for panic. When Alex's wife, the artist Gabrielle, goes to visit one of Alex's colleagues at CERN to inquire about what happened to her husband while he was still a scientist there, she notices in the lobby of the Computing Center "an old computer in a glass case. . . . When she went closer, she read that it was the NeXT processer that had started the World Wide Web at CERN in 1991" (211). When the man who has come to greet Gabi—Alex's old boss Robert Walton—notices her looking at the glass case, he says: "Pandora's box" (211)—a reference to a box in Greek mythology that contained *elpis*, translated as both "fear" and "hope." As Bernard Stiegler in his most recent work has pointed out, *elpis* also refers to the suspension of a kind of waiting, an *attente* (in French) that resonates with the "attention economy" that is, in the information age, under attack.[30] We have heard plenty, at this point, about the Infosphere's worrisome effects on attention; is there any hope that this can be turned around, that attention can be taken care of in the information age?

With respect to the finance economy in particular, I already described in the previous chapter its psychotic effects—elaborated on here through the notion of panic—and what Stiegler characterizes as the digital economy's proletarianization of the human being. It seems that a first step toward what Stiegler understands as the taking care of the spirit (the soul, in Berardi's terms, or what we could more generally—and with reference to Hannah Arendt[31]—call the mind) in such a situation would be the adequate description of the finance economy and, for example, the automated trading by which it is governed. Such a description could increase one's understanding of the situation, thus putting one in a better position to effectively intervene within it. Philosophers such as Stiegler or critical thinkers such as Berardi, who have engaged in such a project of description, can contribute to that understanding. But I want to ask in particular about the role that a finance novel such as *The Fear Index* might play in it: how can *the novel* contribute to the adequate description of today's digitized economy? What kind of challenges does the digitized economy pose to the novel on this count? This also means to ask: How can the novel contribute to our understanding of the digitized economy, and thus place us in a better position to intervene within it? From a political point of view—and economics today appears to be political through and through—it seems that one must ask those questions about the contemporary finance novel and the particular world it seeks to write.

From Psychosis to Realism

Both Alex's and Hugo's flawed positions still have some value, in that they recognize the reality of the algorithm as a digital form of life that is governing the economy. The realism of both Alex's and Hugo's positions becomes all the more pronounced if one considers the suggestion, which is elaborated as part of the plot of *The Fear Index*, that the calamities that befall Alex may be due to a psychotic condition. By now, we are of course familiar with this suggestion: it has become an essential component of the financial fiction genre, to the extent that it has pushed away finance—the realist depiction of finance—as the finance novel's central project. Tom Wolfe's *The Bonfire of the Vanities* tells us very little about finance; it was received as a prophetic novel about the 1987 stock market crash but it actually deals with the bonds market. Psychosis is arguably the novel's central drama. That theme is even more pronounced in Bret Easton Ellis's *American Psycho*, which tells us nothing about the nuts and bolts of finance. And *The Fear Index* too tempts its readers into taking that road—but the novel ultimately resists that temptation in order to drive home the realism of its science fiction plot instead.

To properly assess the role of psychosis in *The Fear Index*, one must consider the transformation of the "mad scientist" or "mad professor" from the gothic novels it references into the "mad financier" familiar from other finance novels (6). It then appears that Alex's recognition of his algorithm as a form of life is not as mad as it may seem. As a scientist who has moved into the world of finance, Alex feels that he is being corrupted by money. In that sense, his work at the hedge fund differs from his work as a scientist. "There was one great difference between the two," he concedes, "You couldn't buy anything with a nanosecond or a microjoule" (141)—that is, with the units in which the success of his experiments at CERN was measured—"[Money] was a sort of toxic by-product of his research. Sometimes he felt it was poisoning him inch by inch, just like Marie Curie had been killed by radiation" (141).

The idea of money's toxicity returns at various points in the novel, often in relation to Alex's wife, Gabrielle, who feels that money has turned her husband into a different person—here, of course, the reference to the previously mentioned *Strange Case of Dr. Jekyll and Mr. Hyde* is dominant. "What exactly have you turned into, Alex?," she asks her husband at some point in the book. "I mean, Leclerc [the policemen investigating the home invasion] wanted to know if money was the reason why you left CERN, and I said no. But do you ever stop to listen to yourself these days? Two hundred thousand francs . . . Four hundred thousand francs . . . Sixty million dollars for a house we don't need" (135). Later on, she wonders: "to take such a vaulting ambition [Alex's talent for science] and place it entirely at the service of making money—wasn't that to marry the sacred and the profane? No wonder he had started to behave so strangely. Even to *want* a billion dollars, let alone *possess* such a sum, was madness in her opinion, and there was a time when it would have been his opinion too" (250). The trope that is delivered here, namely the association of money, capital, and in particular finance to madness, is familiar and takes shape in *The Fear Index* in the figure of the "mad financier."[32] Within the longer history of psychosis in the finance novel (and, indeed, the even longer history of money's tie to psychosis), *The Fear Index* shows that the age-old theme of money and its corrupting effect on human beings is intensified in the digital economy (as opposed to the supposedly more material economy based on a gold standard). Alex himself rehearses the reasons for this (which I have covered in the previous chapters): "If the money had been in the form of bars of gold or suitcases of cash, they might perhaps have been more careful. But this was not really money in the physical sense at all, merely strings and sequences of glowing green symbols, no more substantial than protoplasm. That was why they had the nerve to do with it what they did" (110). It is under the conditions of the *digitized* economy that the psychotic madness associated with money becomes particularly intense.

Consider how the particulars of Alex's psychosis enter into Harris's tale: when Alex receives an MRI scan at the hospital after he has been hit on the head by the man who invaded his house, some anomalies are discovered in his brain. The reader learns that those may be due to the attack, or may also suggest a preexisting condition. When the police start looking into Alex's history, they discover that he had "a nervous breakdown" while still at CERN (122). As his life starts spinning out of control—in Alex's view, due to acts he did not commit (ranging from the acquisition of a Darwin first edition to the buying of all of his wife's art on the opening night of her gallery show)—those around him think that this may very well be due to "psychosis" (271, 280).

One of the interesting aspects of *The Fear Index* is that while it fully entertains that hypothesis—today's financier, descendant of the mad scientist, is psychotic; he is, given that everything happens here with twenty-four hours, a kind of *24 Hour Psycho* (to recall my reference to Douglas Gordon in the previous chapter)—it also decidedly undermines it, thus undoing at least to some extent money's familiar connection to madness.

For example, Alex himself insists, at numerous points in the novel, that he is "not mad": "But I am not mad, he thought. I may have killed a man [his attacker, whom he traced to a hotel in the off-the-grid red light district of Geneva] *but I am not mad*. I am either the victim of an elaborate plot to make me *think* I am mad, or someone is trying to set me up, blackmail me, destroy me" (210). It is not entirely clear how we are to interpret this: for one, the murder scene that is evoked here initially has the intruder, a man called Johannes Karp, wielding a knife and forcing Alex into the bathroom, and into the bathtub—a reference, to be sure, to Robert Bloch and Alfred Hitchcock's *Psycho* (discussed in chapter 2). Karp would in that case stand for Norman Bates; but how are we to tell, given that it is Hoffmann who ultimately commits the murder? Furthermore, if Karp is Bates, then Hoffmann is Mary Crane, who is *Psycho*'s other psycho—suffering from a psychosis that is produced by money (which is Hoffmann's weak point as well). As if to intensify this point, which the novel will make later, *The Fear Index* shares with us that when Alex is taken to hospital after the home invasion, he finds himself thinking "Abandon hope all ye who enter here"

(32)—that famous line from Dante's *Inferno*, which can be found at the beginning of Bret Easton Ellis's *American Psycho* as well.

Although any critical reader will point out that there is little reason why one should take Alex's statement about his own mental state as reliable—if Alex is indeed truly mad, it would be typical for him to be convinced otherwise—the novel is largely with Alex in that it exposes that what those who are sane in the novel perceive as a product of madness is in fact a reality that is fully rational: VIXAL-4 has become semiautonomous and is trading as an intelligence of its own, controlling the market, making it crash, managing its trades with this knowledge, and all the while making a profit off it, quite indifferently to and independently from the humans whose lives it effects. In other words: we have here a finance novel that struggles against the finance novel's theme of psychosis in its attempt to give a realist account of today's economy.

While Hugo, for his part, may (like Alex) also be under the general spell of profit, *The Fear Index* offers no evidence of actual, clinical psychosis in his case, and it is his nonpsychotic recognition of the algorithm's life that has led most reviewers to note the book's proximity to science fiction. However, this attribution—which seems to remove the novel's representation of the contemporary economy from realism—is not necessarily warranted. Such a labeling—such a push of the novel's representation of the digital economy into the realm of science fiction, even if science fiction has traditionally maintained a close proximity to reality and current scientific developments—risks to avoid all too easily the project of thinking through today's economic reality.

Although categorizing *The Fear Index* as science fiction seems to further the idea that there is not much to learn about finance from reading a finance novel—it's just science fiction!—Harris himself seems to insist on the "realism" of his science fictional account. In the acknowledgments to his book, he thanks various banking and hedge fund professionals for sharing their expertise with him and reading the book manuscript. This creates the odd feeling, which no financial realism can fully escape, of a complicity between the novel and the financial world it represents: plenty of financial institutions are mentioned in the acknowledgments of *The Fear Index* for "[having made] this book possible."[33] *The Fear Index* quite literally depends on finance; its representation of the world is consistent with it. The intense research that also characterizes Harris's other books becomes evident as well when he indicates, in an odd footnote accompanying the chapter where the algorithm's crashing of the market is described, that "the background detail" provided in the chapter "of what happened on the US financial markets over the next two hours is entirely factual, drawn from congressional testimony and the joint CFTC and SEC report, *Findings Regarding the Market Events of May 6, 2010*" (236). Although it is certainly possible to label *The Fear Index* as a science fiction novel and to conclude from there (as a reviewer in the *Economist* did[34]) that the novel's plot is not plausible, the author's insistence on the realism of its account—marked, for example, by the acknowledgments and the addition of an academic footnote to the text—seems to invite the reader to slow down and consider to what extent the reality that the novel describes is indeed still science fictional rather than entirely realistic. That realism may ultimately be more in line with the project of science fiction than the reviewer in *The Economist* is able to appreciate.

The Pitfalls of the Novel

Compared to the examples of the financial fiction genre discussed in the previous chapters, *The Fear Index* arguably offers a financial realism—mediating between the material and the speculative—that marks real progress in the representation of finance. One actually learns something about finance by reading Harris's novel. Ultimately, however, *The Fear Index* fails in its representation of finance—and fails *as a novel in particular*. Indeed, it is where the book is most novelistic, where it realizes itself most as a novel, that *The Fear Index* fails in its representation of finance, because finance resists precisely that realization. In other words, finance demands another realism, one that would push the novel to the limits of the genre, all the way to the brink of its destruction, raising the question of whether a novelistic financial realism is possible at all.

When it comes to the algorithmic agents that govern today's digitized economy, trading at speeds that in some extreme instances (such as the flash crash) neither humans nor computers can observe, the contemporary finance novel is dealing with forms of life that follow a law but do not have desire.[35] If *The Fear Index* insists on the fact that algorithms do not panic, one might want to add to this that they do not desire either. They merely follow the law of their generation. It is on this count, however, that *The Fear Index* in its representation of an algorithm gone rogue is not sufficiently realist: for it ultimately humanizes the algorithm into a novelistic character—into an agent with desire, who is supposedly involved in a (motherless) Oedipal struggle, trying to kill its father and all those who risk interfering with the law of its generation.

A particularly egregious instance of this is the suggestion that VIXAL-4 makes a profit out of a plane crash that it was able to anticipate through its monitoring of worldwide information (specifically, Jihadist websites). Rather than preventing the plane crash by warning the airline, it shorts the airline's stock to make a profit out of it (99). Another one of those instances involves Hoffmann Investment Technologies' risk assessor, Ganapathi Rajamani. After VIXAL-4 has made "a profit out of the [flash] crash [a crash that, the novel suggests, VIXAL-4 caused] of four-point-one billion dollars," it's pointed out that this "represents only zero-point-four percent of total market volatility" (283). In other words: the amount is not significant enough to trigger an investigation, leaving Hoffmann Investment Technologies beyond suspicion. VIXAL-4's profit will be divided in bonuses among the company's employees to silence everyone who witnessed the algorithm's dubious actions. The only one who insists that he will complain is the company's risk assessor, Rajamani. However, he is conveniently killed off by the algorithm, who uses the elevator in Alex's entirely digital company to get the employee out of the way.

The latter is, perhaps, a reference to Dutch director Dick Maas's tech-horror flick *De Lift* (Tuschinski Film Distribution, 1983), which was remade for international audiences as *Down* (retitled as *The Shaft* for the US DVD release). Indeed, *The Fear Index* echoes other scenes of tech-horror—think, for example, of Dave trying to shut HAL down in Stanley Kubrick's masterpiece *2001: A Space Odyssey* (Metro Goldwyn Mayer, 1968). "This must be the cortex," Alex muses when he arrives at the algorithm's central control unit in the novel's closing battle, as if his algorithm has a human brain. Later on, he characterizes it as "reluctant" (260). Those humanizations indicate that we have moved beyond the limits of the algorithm and the law of its being; instead, the novel offers us a desiring character, modeled after a human being. The algorithm's artificial intelligence is collapsed into the novel's representation of human intelligence. In *The Fear Index*, it is ultimately the human that prevails—even if it seems that the algorithm wins.[36]

That humanization drives the novel's plot and determines the climactic scene of its closing life-and-death struggle between Alex and the algorithm—an explosive scene that in part explains why Paul Greengrass (who is also thanked in the novel's acknowledgments) has been engaged to turn the novel into a film. At the same time, however, the algorithm never loses its uncanny, inhuman dimension in the novel: unlike in *Space Odyssey*, where HAL speaks and even begs for his life (although it's a begging that's done in a strangely neutral tone of voice), the algorithm operates mostly by proxy throughout the novel, appearing through the actions of the human beings whom it manipulates. It never speaks, although we do get to "read" one of its e-mails and some of the malware it uses—both pushing the limits of legibility. It is only in the novel's closing scene that it acts directly, and even then, it remains strangely absent.

I want to suggest, then, that this uncomfortable oscillation between the inhuman and the human aspects of the algorithm marks a conflict of contemporary financial realism that *The Fear Index* makes visible.[37] Indeed, it is in the humanization of the algorithm, which coincides with its becoming a character in Harris's novel rather than just being an algorithm, that *The Fear Index* gives in to a demand for relationality that, as Ian Bogost has noted, governs the novel as a genre. In *Alien Phenomenology*, Bogost writes that "the problem with literature" may be that its "preference for traditional narrative acts as a correlationist amplifier."[38] By this, he means that traditional narrative is perpetually caught up in the relation between reality and its human perceiver, aiming "to create resonance between readers and characters."[39] At this point, effectively, it loses its grasp on reality. It is at this point that *The Fear Index* misses the reality of the digitized economy. In other words, *The Fear Index* gives in to the affinity between readers and characters that the novel seeks to establish. Harris is no longer rendering the reality of the contemporary digital economy but is instead writing a novel, and the realism that this novel practices becomes eclipsed by the demands of narrative fiction.[40] Indeed, the algorithms that govern today's digitized economy probably do not make for very exciting reading. If the "software agents" of today's financial markets are different from "human actors" in that they are for example unemotional, do not engage in interpretation, cannot practice discretionary judgments, are programmed rather than follow a self-imposed discipline (to list just a few of their most obvious characteristics as summarized by Karin Knorr Cetina[41]), then indeed they make for very unattractive characters. In order for the reality of today's digital economy to read like a novel, these algorithms need to become humanized, to become characters driven by desire (rather than by the mere law of their code). There appears to be something about the algorithm, then, about the particular form of life that it is, that might be more than what the novel can stand. *Pan*, which in Greek means "everything," might already name that limit, even if we do not relate the word to panic and to the panic of contemporary financial markets: for "everything" marks the limit of realism, just as Alex's "goat in the machine" marks the limit of financial realism.

The Fear Index's simultaneous withdrawal from humanization and its attempt to "write" the reality of the digital entities governing the contemporary economy opens up the possibility of a financial realism within the novel, one that would seek to write the (granted, probably not very literary) world of digital finance. Such a project could amount to a true writing of the world, one that would escape what Pettman calls the "anthropological measure" to which the world, and all of the creatures in it, have tended to be subjected in narrative fiction.[42] It might amount to a realism that, while attuned to the contemporary realities of finance, surprises us by returning us to the "great outdoors" (see chapter 4) of an overwhelming world that Berardi in his writing about panic and the contemporary digital economy evokes—and that should not necessarily lead us to panic. The challenge, indeed, would then be to find a new kind of meaning in *that* world, not through the reinstitution of a new Pan or through the blind (albeit profitable) subjection to its power, but through a kind of thinking and writing that would be able to realistically account for it.

Capitalist versus Financial Realism

If we can agree on the fact that compared to earlier instances of the finance novel, *The Fear Index* offers a more realist account of finance, introducing its readers to the world of automated, high-frequency trading, we can probably also agree that the realism the novel thus practices has elements of nonrealism to it—of the science-fictional variety, for example. It is on this count that *The Fear Index* practices what I call *financial realism*, a term I propose partly in distinction to the capitalist realism that has received some discussion recently. I choose financial realism over capitalist realism for reasons having to do with the difference between finance and capitalism (see the introduction). Whereas capital—in Karl Marx's formula M-C-M'—crucially revolves around the commodity, finance is better captured with the abbreviated formula M-M', as it manages to turn money directly into money that is worth more—without the intermediary of the commodity. It's not as if the commodity, defined by Marx as any external thing that satisfies a need, is entirely gone; but it has been replaced by financial products that in some cases appear to satisfy one need alone: the trader's need to become rich fast. Virtual money and the digitized economy have played a major role in this. The shift has been such, I think, that a terminological shift from capital to finance is justified.

If realism in this context "has long been considered the aesthetic mode most intimate to capitalism," as Alison Shonkwiler and Leigh Claire La Berge point out,[43] then the question is what shifts realism needs to undergo to become adequate to finance. Interestingly, Shonkwiler and La Berge opt for the at first sight tautological term "capitalist realism" because they consider it to already be doing some of that work: the capitalist realist mode "interrupts and disorganizes itself," they write "through its incorporation of other genres and through its desire to show the processes of its own commodification."[44] The former I consider to be part of financial realism as well—one need only think about the play between realism and science fiction in *The Fear Index*; the latter—showing the processes of its own commodification—I would consider to be specifically capitalist. Financial realism, by contrast, is interested not so much in commodities but in financial instruments (and their automated, high-frequency trading) and shows not so much the processes of realism's commodification but its transformation into a financial instrument. *The Fear Index*, as I have shown, is a novel about automated, high-frequency trading; it is not a capitalist novel but a novel about digitized finance in particular.

Furthermore, Shonkwiler and La Berge insist that capitalist realism as an aesthetic mode "potentially conjoins both conservative and critical impulses." It can preserve "representational realism" (conservative) while at the same time "modeling the very transformative capitalist processes of commodification and financialization that it records" (critical).[45] Again, I agree—but I wonder about the introduction of the term *financialization* (next to commodification) into the equation. Part of what I appreciate about *The Fear Index* is that it includes a conservative impulse to realistically represent: that is, indeed, what the novel fights for—against the psychosis hypothesis, as I have shown. But the novel also fails on that count because its representational realism is too relational, too stuck in a relationist conception of the novel whose world must somehow reflect and resonate with the readers' world. *The Fear Index* ultimately continues to operate at a human scale that the world of finance quite simply exceeds. The novel is on the track of this, but it struggles to realize this in its form. If this challenge to the human already lies contained in the commodification that we associate with capital (the dehumanization of the assembly line workers, for example, that Adam Smith already writes about at the end of *The Wealth of Nations*), then surely we cannot deny that this challenge has only intensified in the age of digitized finance? Digitized finance does not merely have *dehumanized* agents; it has *nonhuman* agents governing the markets. If *dehumanized* agents were the very stuff of realist representation—that is, according to some, what realism set out to show us, how human beings were dehumanized for example through work—*nonhuman* agents pose a different kind of challenge: for how is realism, which has always operated in reference to the human, going to represent those? On this count too, it seems that financial realism is a more apt term to capture the representational challenges that I am interested in than capitalist realism.

Finally, and going back to the first point, Shonkwiler and La Berge note that "capitalist realism calls into question what realism is."[46] They conclude their extensive definition of capitalist realism with a quote from Fredric Jameson, who wrote that "we may even wonder whether the most useful 'definition' of realism may not lie in the capacity of a text to raise the issue of realism as such within its own structure, no matter what answer it decides to give."[47] Now, this understanding of realism can also be found in the introduction to Anna Kornbluh's *Realizing Capital*. She concludes from it, however, and I am inclined to agree with her, that for that reason, realist fiction is perfectly positioned "to engage the paradoxes of fictitious capital,"[48] that is, of "value, in the form of credit, shares, debt, speculation, and various forms of paper money, *above and beyond what can be realized in ordinary commodities.*"[49] It is this fictitious capital that puts us on the track of finance, as Kornbluh lays bare in the short epilogue to her book, which explicitly makes the connection to the 2008 housing market crash. In other words, it seems that on this count too, Shonkwiler and La Berge's very definition of capitalist realism in fact leads beyond a narrowly defined capitalism into what Marx in the third volume of *Capital* calls fictitious capital, and by extension finance. Indeed, while capitalist realism is a key term in La Berge's own work on financial fiction, her own book on what she calls "financial fiction of the long 1980s"[50] uses finance and financialization even more, begging the question of whether there is any difference between the two and how it might be theorized. "Capitalist realism" refers to the commodification of realism in the era of finance; but I think that by now, after the long 1980s, we have to go further and consider a financial realism that in part refers to the financialization of the realist novel today. Indeed, such a financialization may—as I will discuss in chapter 6—be built into realism which, by definition, cannot deliver what it promises: an account of the world. Realism's value, therefore, is crucially a future-oriented one; it is driven by credit. It's perfect for speculation, because it is virtual—it never fully arrives.

Early on in their introduction, some of this leads Shonkwiler and La Berge to suggest that "the familiar realism-modernism-postmodernism account" demands "new scrutiny"[51]—a point that I intend to come back to in chapter 4. When in his afterword to Shonkwiler and La Berge's book Richard Dienst follows Alexander Kluge in suggesting that "the root of a realistic attitude, its motivation, is . . . a denial of the pure reality-principle, an anti-realistic attitude, which alone enables one to look realistically and attentively,"[52] we have perhaps come full circle, in the sense that what Kluge appears to evoke here is the psychosis that was at the center of the previous chapters. Dienst offers Kluge's "psychotic" understanding of realism in a book about capitalist realism; and while I have discussed how capitalism already entails aspects of psychosis (in the introduction I mention the fetishism of the commodity from the first volume of *Capital* that in my view develops into fictitious capital in *Capital*'s third volume), it is really with finance that capital's as well as money's antirealist dimension is most intensively realized. With Kluge too, then, we are confronting a financial rather than a capitalist realism and by pointing at such a realism's "denial of the pure reality-principle" Kluge has put his finger on the very issue that has haunted what can properly be called the "finance" novel from 1971 to the present. In Kluge's definition, realism is defined with finance, and by extension certain aspects of capital, and the origins of money. It is perhaps time, then, to revisit realism's age-old association with capitalism and consider instead its tie to psychotic finance.

"Financial realism" could then be considered one of those "new" realisms that have emerged in recent years, with the waning of postmodernism, ranging from neorealism to fiduciary realism, postmodern realism, experimental realism, metarealism, new conventionalism, pragmatic realism, dirty realism, crackpot realism, and deep realism—as Julia Breitbach neatly summarizes them in the introduction to her book *Analog Fictions in the Digital Age*.[53] Shonkwiler and La Berge's interest in capitalist realism can obviously also be added to the list. Indeed, it seems that both capitalist realism and financial realism share what Breitbach distinguishes to be the two key characteristics of the various new realisms she lists, namely a distance to postmodernism and a negotiation of postmodernist and realist strategies.[54] As she points out, the latter is frequently assessed based on some key characteristics: "narration," associated with "readable plots and recognizable characters"; "communication," allowing "the reader to create meaning and closure"; "reference," "language can refer to external realities, that is, to 'the world out there'"; and "ethics," "a return to commitment and empathy."[55] When it comes to realism, which has been associated with all of the previous—postmodernism has been understood to attack realism on all counts—Breitbach points out that our understanding of it seems to have largely survived the postmodernist onslaught: "We still tend to recognize and conceptualize realism by certain die-hard characteristics, such as the focus on what the reader deems to be ordinary people leading ordinary lives, a particular attention to quotidian detail, or the shunning of unheard-of incidents and improbabilities."[56] That is the "commonsense approach to realism,"[57] as Breitbach puts it. New realisms, of course, draw that into question; while capitalist realism, as per Shonkwiler and La Berge, negotiates between the conservative (realist) and critical (postmodernist) impulse, it draws realism into question, interrupting, for example, through the mixing of genres the realist aesthetic and inquiring into the commodification of realism itself. From the perspective of financial realism, it is worth noting that when it comes to finance, ethics, reference, communication, and narration are all under extreme pressure. Realism seems to run into an extreme limit when it comes to the representation of a nonhuman, algorithmic agent, operating at high speed, invented to guarantee profit, caught up in and probably responsible for contemporary market crashes, but escaping regulation and defying explanation. Finance marks the end of empathy, external referentiality, meaning and closure, readable plot, and recognizable character: all of that would need to be abandoned for a realist account of finance. And yet, that abandonment has precisely been called postmodernism, which interferes with the realist attempt to depict finance.

A similar interference happens when it comes to psychosis. *The Fear Index*'s struggle with realism takes place at the crossroads between realism and psychosis, with the novel mobilizing the theme of psychosis in order to distance itself from it and pursue a more realist track. It is, however, difficult to imagine how this can be done if, following Kluge's analysis, realism is itself theorized as a psychotic form, a realistic and attentive looking that is enabled by the denial of reality. This would seem to identify realism, psychosis, and finance in a way that makes a nonpsychotic realist description of finance impossible. *Psychotic realism*, the term I borrowed from Antonio Scurati in the previous chapter, would then turn out to be a tautology. The distinction between capitalist and financial realism in this context could enable one to distinguish between differences of degree, with capitalist realism marking a lesser degree of psychosis than financial realism—in the same way that Hitchcock's Marion Crane, even though she is psychotic, is obviously not as psychotic as Norman Bates. But the conclusion would always inevitably be that realism is always caught up in psychosis, and that any kind of financial realism—whether it be of money, capital, or finance—is always inevitably caught up in psychosis. In the same way that a realist, nonpostmodern representation of finance appears impossible, there can be no realist, nonpsychotic representation of finance.

Given my philosophical analysis of money, capital, and finance in the previous chapter, that ultimately seems quite appropriate, because money, capital, and finance are never entirely free from psychosis. Indeed, if the fictitiousness that Marx in the third volume of *Capital* associates with specific kinds of value—credit or debt, in particular—lies at the origin of money, as scholars such as Felix Martin and David Graeber have shown, then it would seem quite appropriate that any form of realist financial representation would be marked by that fictitiousness, in other words by a certain removal from or denial of the reality that it proposes to deliver. That doesn't necessarily turn it into a full-blown psychotic mode; but it can never lose that touch of the psychotic if it wants to write the reality of money, capital, and finance. As I indicated in the introduction, it is one thing to want to take the specter out of finance; but to properly write finance, one will not be able to give up the ghost.

In a similar way, then, the continued link to postmodernism—something that is quite impossible to shake, even in a novel such as *Bonfire of the Vanities*, as La Berge has pointed out[58]—might not so much be a burden but an indication of a key characteristic of finance. It was, of course, Fredric Jameson who demonstrated that postmodernism was the aesthetic mode of late capitalism. Since then, Jeffrey Nealon has suggested that the waning of postmodernism and the arrival of what he calls post-postmodernism, has necessitated an update of Jameson's account, which Nealon provides in his book *Post-Postmodernism, Or, the Cultural Logic of Just-In-Time Capitalism*.[59] Shonkwiler and La Berge's *Reading Capitalist Realism* in part also takes its impulse from both Jameson and Nealon.[60] With "financial realism," I intend to take both Nealon's and Shonkwiler and La Berge's gestures one step further, indicating that the continued tie to postmodernism in new, contemporary realisms needs to be intensified into new philosophical projects that, while maintaining a tie to postmodernism, nevertheless also mark something else. In the next chapter, I focus on so-called speculative realism and the market philosophy that it has spurned as a particularly fruitful site to think about the future of finance's representation.

If realism, then, cannot quite shake neither postmodernism nor psychosis, I want to close by suggesting that it cannot quite shake finance. In its perpetual deferral of reality, in its promise to deliver a reality that it can't, realism is arguably a financial form, and it may be for that reason that it has postmodernist and psychotic elements built in. It is, precisely, in its incapacity to write finance, and more generally in its incapacity to write any reality, that realism is most financial: postmodern, psychotic, inevitably denying the world it offers.

FOUR

The Financial Universe (After Meillassoux)

> The story of data, how our world has come to be seen as data, starts with celestial bodies, with stars and later whole galaxies.
>
> —RYAN S. JEFFERY AND BOAZ LEVIN, *All That Is Solid Melts into Data (2015)*

Intensifying Realism

Compared to Tom Wolfe's *The Bonfire of the Vanities* and Bret Easton Ellis's *American Psycho*, Robert Harris's *The Fear Index* marks real progress when it comes to delivering a financial realism that is attuned to our time. Consciously mobilizing the problematic tension between realism and psychosis that characterizes the genre of the finance novel, it draws from the science fiction genre to provide a more realist account of today's financial companies and their business of money-making. One learns more about finance from Harris's novel than from Wolfe's or Ellis's. As a realist representation of finance, however, it also fails because it ultimately adheres too much to a realism at a human scale: giving in to what Ian Bogost (following the French philosopher Quentin Meillassoux) understands to be the "correlationist" demands of narrative fiction—summarized by Julia Breitbach as: "narration," "communication," "reference," "ethics"—*The Fear Index* ultimately loses sight of the inhuman reality that *American Psycho* already intimated and that Harris's novel seeks to write. It is this correlationism—this realism at an all too human scale—that prevents *The Fear Index* from being successful in its novelistic representationalism of finance. Certainly, had *The Fear Index* stuck to the inhuman reality of finance, we would have ended up with a very different novel—assuming that the term *novel* would still have applied to the final result of such an experiment.

In this predominantly theoretical but ultimately also literary critical chapter, I want to pursue that experiment to see what it might yield. In my pursuit of a novelistic representationalism of finance, I want to begin by considering the contemporary reality of finance so as to better understand the reality that such a representationalism would seek to write. Second, and in view of that reality and the challenges to representation that it poses, I pursue Bogost's reference to the work of Quentin Meillassoux in this context. As I see it, Meillassoux—as a critic of the correlationism from which *The Fear Index* still suffers—can help us develop a mindset appropriate for the thinking of finance. Indeed, his work has played a crucial role in contemporary philosophies of the financial markets and their criticisms of probability and improbability theories. Finally, and starting from the mostly overlooked role that narrative fiction has taken up in Meillassoux's oeuvre, I consider some literary examples that come close to the financial mindset and its challenge to narrative fiction that Meillassoux's work lays out. Those examples operate, in some cases, at the level of logic and structure; but I am also interested in examples that combine logical and structural experimentation with a less sophisticated representationalism of finance—in other words, in works that do not give up on the vulgar writing of finance by delegating finance entirely to a higher realm of reflection (privileging a formal financial realism over one that would operate on content).

There is a way in which sophisticated accounts of realism, which for good reasons seek to liberate realism from its bind to reality, risk to proletarianize us in relation to reality by giving up all too easily on reality's adequate description. Although I recognize the latter may always be a fiction, and although I have suggested at the end of the previous chapter that it may be precisely that insight that justifies our understanding of realism as a financial instrument, I thus want to work against that financialization by seeing what can be accomplished at the limits of what I characterized in the previous chapter as postmodern and psychotic realism. If that call for a vulgar realism of finance may seem to echo Tom Wolfe's manifesto for a new social novel, my discussion of Meillassoux will indicate that Wolfe's realism is outdone by the reality of finance today. Specifically, Wolfe offers an epistemological solution to what Meillassoux enables us to understand as an ontological problem. The ontology of contemporary finance defies the narrative solutions that, after Wolfe, one might propose for it, and requires a reinvention of realism for the financial age. If capitalist realism's mantra is that "there is no alternative"[1]—"which can be heard as an ontological claim," as Mark Fisher has noted[2]—Meillassoux helps us understand that the ontology of today's economy demands a reinvention of realism for the financial age. It cannot but push realism toward its alternative.[3]

The Financial Universe

> The great exchanges have become like space cruisers, turned inward on themselves, fixated upon the hypothetical image of an infinitely unreachable horizon.[4]
>
> *Brian Holmes, "Information's Metropolis"*

What is the economic reality that *The Fear Index* is trying to capture? The novel is dealing with a digitized economy governed by algorithmic agents. Those algorithms are trading complex financial instruments at speeds that exceed not only human but also technological capacities of observation. The trading happens in "dark pools,"[5] which are nontransparent markets that are largely outside of regulation. All of this led the chair of the Securities and Exchange Commission (SEC) to characterize the stock market in 2008 as "a regulatory black hole."[6] (Other aspects of finance, such as offshore money, have been characterized as "the equivalent of an astrophysical black hole" as well.[7]) If Patrick Bateman, as the "automated teller" of Bret Easton Ellis's novel, can be said to anticipate this kind of economy, it is worth noting that his murders arguably also anticipate this "black hole"–like market reality. When Bateman is questioned by detective Donald Kimball after the mysterious disappearance of his colleague Paul Allen, Kimball expresses his puzzlement about Allen's case: "It's just strange. . . . One day someone's walking around, going to work, *alive*, and then . . . ," to which Bateman replies, "The earth just opens up and swallows people."[8] Of course, it is Bateman who has brutally murdered Allen—he is the black hole into which Allen has disappeared. "Kimball is utterly unaware of how truly vacant I am," he reflects earlier on in the chapter.[9]

After the use of so-called black box techniques—fully artificial trading—in electronic trading,[10] financial writer Michael Lewis, former Big Swinging Dick at Salomon Brothers, describes the financial economy as a "black box."[11] But the term also has a broader reach in this context: in Cristina Alger's finance novel *The Darlings*, the fraudulent hedge fund Reis Capital Management is described as "a black box," even though one of its suspicious peculiarities is that it doesn't provide electronic records of its trades.[12] Frank Pasquale uses the term to describe contemporary society at large.[13] Although Pasquale's book is wider in scope than Lewis's, both works lay bare what Bernard Stiegler calls the "algorithmic governance" of contemporary life.[14]

One guesses that in Lewis's project, a black box is meant to be a source of illumination: when everything else goes down, it is supposed to be preserved to provide information about the apocalypse for those (if any) who will come after. Along similar lines, the term *black box* in part highlights that the economy, although digital, is still in part box-like or material: indeed, Lewis's book *Flash Boys* shows that today's economic reality, although it may escape our capacities of observation, is nevertheless enabled by the specific material infrastructure of fiber optic cables and the "co-location" of trading computers with those of the stock exchanges.[15] High-frequency trading firms are paying fortunes to have access to certain fiber cable networks and to have their computers be located close to those of the stock exchange: for even if this saves them only the smallest fragment of time, it will yield a huge profit.

Although part of what is going on in Lewis's work is about breaking into the black box of recent market crashes in order to try to get at the information that would explain them, other connotations arguably are in sway as well. To characterize the finance economy as a black box also reveals that the material infrastructure (which still falls within the limits of traditional science and of investigative journalism) supports a kind of blackness—the blackness of dark pools; or the blackness of Reis Capital Management, in Alger's novel—that escapes material observation and regulation (and, as I will show, even poses a limit to traditional science and journalism as well). Here, it connects with terms such as the already mentioned "dark pools," "dark money" (Jane Mayer), or the "dark web."

The use of the adjectives *black* or *dark* is analogous here to their use in physics. As the philosopher Vincent Bontems and the astrophysicist Roland Lehoucq explain in their book about *Les idées noires de la physique*, *black* in physics refers to "what cannot be seen or what cannot be seen well"; it refers to "what resists detection"—even with the "phenomenotechnical" means that physics has at its disposal.[16] We know that the blackness of dark pools is real, however, because it has real effects on the market. It is responsible, for example, for stocks swinging from say being priced one penny to one hundred thousand dollars in just a few minutes. However, we can only speculatively consider the existence of such blackness, because its reality is dark: it moves too fast for us to observe it. This is true both humanly and technologically, as I already pointed out: it is impossible, for example, to get a printout of all the trades that happened during the flash crash; even the machines could not record all of the trades. This is a reality that, given that it has also been characterized as a "black hole," I propose calling "the financial universe."[17]

That phrase is a reference, of course, to Sherman "master of the universe" McCoy from Wolfe's novel *The Bonfire of the Vanities*—although, as Leigh Claire La Berge points out, Wolfe actually borrows the phrasing from Lewis.[18] If the limitlessness of the stock market in Sherman's days was still something that he could imagine to master, today—in the black box economy—that situation seems to have decidedly changed.

There are reasons other than Wolfe's novel, however, to use the term *universe* in this context. If one reads contemporary analyses of the stock market, one is almost certain to come across phenomena such as "black holes" or "the Big Bang." The association between the economy and the universe is justified by the fact that in both cases, the scientific information we have about them is available not through direct human or technological observation but through speculation—through the postulation, through mathematics, of scientific "facts" based on the observation of certain "effects." In the economic realm, for example, a market crash would be such an effect. The affinity between the economy and the universe is evident in the fact that most of the heroes in Scott Patterson's *The Quants* and *Dark Pools* are mad scientist types, echoing the connection between *The Fear Index* and *Frankenstein* discussed in the previous chapter. To give one more example: Patterson observes that Henry Laufer, former head of the hedge fund Renaissance Technologies,[19] has a PhD from Princeton in mathematics and published a book (in 1971) about black holes.[20]

The confluence of physics and finance can also be found in the work of scholars such as Karen Knorr Cetina, a sociologist who used to work on high energy physics but is now writing about finance (see chapter 3).[21] The same *New York Review of Books* issue that includes Bill McKibben's review of Jane Mayer's book *Dark Money* features a review by Lawrence R. Krauss about Lisa Randall's *Dark Matter and the Dinosaurs*—and one could argue that the two reviews actually speak to each other.[22] The analogy between the universe and the economy is not merely superficial: the science of the universe is at the heart of the financial markets as the title of James Owen Weatherall's book *The Physics of Wall Street* suggests.[23]

It is in particular astrophysics and the notion of the "black hole" that are relevant here. As Bontems and Lehoucq point out, the history of black holes begins in 1783 when the English physician and astronomer John Michell proposes that we think of a mass so large that even light does not travel at the speed required to escape its gravitation.[24] The popular understanding of what later (in 1967) comes to be called "black hole" as some kind of "cosmic vacuum-cleaner" can be related to the limit of the black hole's sphere from which neither light nor matter can escape—the so-called horizon of the black hole.[25] Contrary to the horizon on earth, which shifts with the position of its observer, the horizon of a black hole is absolute: "It is a limit of space-time, independent from any observer, and it divides events into two categories."[26] Outside of this horizon, one basically finds the universe as we know it. Inside of it, light can no longer travel freely between two arbitrary points, because light is directed toward the center of the black hole. Communication within the black hole is therefore severely limited.[27] Light and matter cannot travel from the inside toward the outside, but only in the other direction.

Proof for the existence of black holes is delivered for the first time in 1971, when "astrophysicists detect Cygnus X-1, a binary system whose characteristics suggest that it is a system formed by a black hole and a gigantic star."[28] Since 1971, as Bontems and Lehoucq point out, some twenty black holes have been discovered in our galaxy; the largest is located at the center of the Milky Way.[29]

When it comes to the universe, it may be that black holes are partly necessary: the one that is at the center of the Milky Way "participates in its stability and contributes to its evolution."[30] That would presumably change, however, if the black hole's horizon were to shift and to include within its sphere masses—or even light—that is vital for life on earth. It seems that with financial markets, the sphere of a black hole's influence, and its effects—for example, the extremely limited navigation that is possible within its vortex[31]—must be carefully considered before we are merely passively exposed to their pull and the unregulatable market "life" that they generate.

In philosophy, Quentin Meillassoux has recently turned his attention to cosmic realities such as the Big Bang. The derivatives trader Elie Ayache, whose career started with the Black Monday crash from 1987, has mobilized Meillassoux's work as part of a philosophical thinking of the market as a speculative universe that challenges our understandings of the world.[32] For Ayache, the project would be to think of a world of absolute contingency. This position is more radical than the one that focuses on mere improbability; that is the difference, as I understand it, between Ayache and Nassim Taleb, whose "black swan" theory ultimately remains within the limits of probability theory, even if it focuses on the improbable.[33] If the Black Monday crash was caused by a flawed theorization of the market—the so-called Black-Scholes model (a Bell curve)[34]—Taleb insists on the "fat tails" of market theorization graphs (i.e., a graph that differs significantly from the Black-Scholes graph because of its "swollen" outer ends). Black-Scholes did not account for the fat tails, hence the inadequacy of, for example, portfolio insurance, which was based on it and could not prevent the crash when it was happening (it even exacerbated it).

Ayache's point in *The Blank Swan* is that "fat tails," although highlighting the highly improbable, still fall within probability. Ayache criticizes this with the notion of a blank swan, a swan that is the more radically contingent market event whose ontology cannot be recuperated by a more sophisticated scientific or more technologically robust episteme.[35] Instead, we are dealing with a situation to which no established episteme corresponds. Such an episteme would have to be invented (and invented again and again, as reality is perpetually changing and it is not certain that one will be able to use the same episteme twice), on the spot or "in the pit" (to stick with the traders' lingo), in every market event. The trader, in this situation (and it is worth pointing out that Ayache is very much focused still on actual traders), becomes something like a heroic figure, one who is acting, which Ayache calls "writing,"[36] within such market events, which are the product of a "writing," as Ayache points out—a product that is material, relies on a material infrastructure, and yet has in many if not most cases come to escape human and technological capacities of observation, representation, and control.

This leads into the new sense of materialism and reality that is developed in Ayache's *The Medium of Contingency*.[37] If "writing" still applies to Ayache's market, then, to a significant extent, it is not the kind of writing that one finds in novels or scripts. This is why Bateman can ultimately not be contained within the limits of a literary or cinematic character (see chapter 2). As a figure of the inhuman, he anticipates the algorithmic writing that dominates the financial markets today.

It is not all that surprising, given the association between the economy and the universe, that religion (in addition to science and philosophy) would be a competing discourse in this context: one can think of the case of Sean Hyman, a former pastor, who claims to have discovered in the Bible a code for making money on the stock market, the so-called "biblical money code."[38]

With the reality of contemporary finance, then, we have arrived at what Meillassoux has called "the great outdoors." In his words, "[the great outdoors is] the *absolute* outside of pre-critical thinkers: that outside which was not relative to us, and which was given as indifferent to its own givenness to be what it is, existing in itself regardless of whether we are thinking of it or not; that outside which thought could explore with the legitimate feeling of being on foreign territory—of being entirely elsewhere."[39] As such, the great outdoors poses a challenge to what Meillassoux calls correlationism, or thought that is caught up in the relation between reality and its human perceiver, leaving us unable to think either one independently from the other. In Meillassoux's work, the great outdoors becomes the terrain of what has been called a speculative realism, which thinks a (still) mathematizable reality that exists independently from the human being but to which the human being, through math, nevertheless has access. Meillassoux's philosophical question is: how is this kind of thought, this access to the absolute, possible?

How can literature, and specifically financial literary realism, be situated in this context? How might it deal with the "ontology of finance" (Suhail Malik) and the epistemic challenges it poses? If Meillassoux and Ayache are the contemporary thinkers who begin to approach this ontology in their work, this would be equivalent to asking what literary solutions they might imagine to the philosophical questions they raise. To insert literature into this conversation is not as forced a move as it might seem: indeed, Meillassoux himself has taken it up in his work. His second book to be translated into English, *The Number and the Siren* (2011), was a study of that old favorite of French philosophers, Mallarmé's *Un coup de dés*—a poem that, through its programmatic statement that a throw of the dice will never abolish chance, appears to give the finger to those who think mathematics can "beat the market" (a blank swan indeed). At the same time, Meillassoux seeks to show that there may be a count—specifically, the count of 707—that sums up the poem's mystery. That conclusion, however, is never reached and Meillassoux's reading of the poem retains, at least on my count, an uncertainty that defies such a final tally, leaving us with a "code . . . at once fragile and coherent."[40] In this context, it is worth noting the importance of blackjack to the history of algorithmic trading: in *The Quants*, Scott Patterson presents Ed Thorp, who figured out how to use mathematics to beat the card dealers in Las Vegas, as "the godfather" of the digital economy.[41]

If poetry in general and Mallarmé's poem in particular are perhaps obvious places to turn to in this context, what about narrative fiction? The finance novel, as I have shown, has demonstrated an intense concern with realism. But what about narrative fiction, and realism in particular, in Meillassoux? Once again, the question is not as forced as it might seem. First of all, some of the most generative work associated with Meillassoux's thought has been literary: one can think, for example, of Reza Negarestani's cult "novel" (if it can still be called that) *Cyclonopedia* (2008), or of Graham Harman's *Weird Realism* (2012), which points to the weird fiction of H. P. Lovecraft—much appreciated by Michel Houellebecq (see chapter 5), who wrote a book on Lovecraft[42]—as an important resource for his object-oriented ontology. I will also have to return, in this chapter's final section, to the central importance that Ian Bogost attributes to Meillassoux's thought in his criticism of what he understands to be "correlationist" narrative fiction. However, the key document in this dossier is no doubt an overlooked discussion of narrative fiction by Meillassoux himself, first published as an essay titled "Metaphysics and Extro-Science Fiction" (2010) and later republished as *Science Fiction and Extro-Science Fiction* (2015). This text, which seeks to distinguish between science fiction and extro-science fiction on ontological grounds, elucidates the importance of Meillassoux's work for narrative fiction as well as for how thinking about the financial markets today can begin to be put in dialogue with the literary question of financial realism as I have addressed it in the previous chapters.

The Limits of Literary Realism

The contemporary finance novel was born in 1987 with the publication of Tom Wolfe's *The Bonfire of the Vanities*, followed in 1989 by Wolfe's manifesto for a new social novel, which took *Bonfire* as its central example. In "Stalking the Billion-Footed Beast: A Literary Manifesto for the New Social Novel," Wolfe called for a renewed commitment to a realism that would be able to write "the life around us." Far from being conceived as a finance novel, *Bonfire* (as per Wolfe's own account) was a big city novel that tried to "[cram] as much of New York City between covers as you could."[43] Chastizing young novelists for feeling helpless before an actuality that, as per Wolfe's recollection of Philip Roth's statement on this issue, "is continually outdoing our talents,"[44] he questions their abandonment of the real and proposes a "detailed realism based on reporting, a realism more thorough than any currently being attempted, a realism that would portray the individual in intimate and inextricable relation to the society around him."[45] "American society today," he writes, "is no more or less chaotic, random, discontinuous, or absurd than Russian society or French society or British society a hundred years ago, no matter how convenient it might be for a writer to think so. It is merely more varied and complicated and harder to define."[46] When confronted with reality's "billion-footed beast," Wolfe writes, "the answer is . . . to do what the journalists do[:] . . . to wrestle the beast and bring it to terms."[47] We need a realism that would tame the beast of reality so as to let it live in realist fiction.

Wolfe puts forward such a program for realism in a discussion of a big city novel. But that novel has in spite of its original intention become known as a finance novel and what Wolfe has to say thus inevitably also reflects on the project of writing finance. If finance, then, is the billion-footed beast (bear or bull) that is also evoked in his manifesto, Wolfe's program appears to be to tame it: financial realism needs to tame finance so as to let it live in realist fiction.

One can characterize such an understanding of realism, and by extension of financial realism, as both representationalist and biopolitical. The first term probably does not require too much explanation: Wolfe's realism is representationalist in the sense that it seeks to give an account of the world. I propose the term *biopolitical* on the basis of some of my own work on the politics of the realist novel. There, I have uncovered a biopolitical theory of realism in the work of some contemporary novelists (J. M. Coetzee, Kazuo Ishiguro, Paul Auster, Tom McCarthy, and others).[48] This theory would ask one to take seriously the historical coincidence that the modern genre of the novel—which programmatically seeks to write the lives of ordinary human beings into their most intimate details (as opposed to the lives of mythical or legendary figures represented in the tales of yore)[49]—emerges at the same time that, in Michel Foucault's analysis, the transformation of Western power from sovereignty into biopolitics take place. In the realist novel, as Ian Watt in his study of the realist novel already pointed out, characters do not only have names that sound like yours or mine; they also have dates of birth, birth times even (or, for that matter, times of death: we know that Richardson's "Clarissa died at 6:40 P.M. on Thursday, 7 September," as Watt recalls[50]). This biographical trait is staged in the diary writing that makes up a significant part of what is often considered to be the first English-language novel, Daniel Defoe's *Robinson Crusoe*, whose full title—*The Life and Strange Surprising Adventures of Robinson Crusoe, Mariner*—reveals its biographical drive.[51] In the modern novel, characters are so full of life "they practically need birth certificates," as Yann Martel in *Life of Pi*—a contemporary rewrite of the Crusoe tale—put it.[52]

In the famous fifth chapter of the first volume of *The History of Sexuality*, Foucault suggests there has been a shift in the history of Western power from the old, classic power of sovereignty, defined by the right to kill (a power of death), to a new, modern power of life.[53] He makes a distinction between anatomo-politics, which is focused on individual bodies and rules through disciplinary techniques, and biopolitics, which is interested in the biological life of the population (the human being as species) and governs through interventions and regulatory controls. Biopolitics tries to make (produce, foster, optimize) life rather than take it: to keep life alive to the point of near death, if need be. While several novel theorists had already considered the relation between the novel and anatomo-politics, specifically the disciplinary power that rules individual bodies, I've shown that some contemporary novelists through their intertextual engagement with certain classic examples of the novel genre (the already mentioned *Robinson Crusoe*, but also Shelley's *Frankenstein* among others) invite one to investigate the relation between the novel—specifically, the realist novel—and biopolitics. They invite one to theorize the realist novel as a biopolitical form, whose programmatic attempt to write life is complicit with the shift in the history of Western power that Foucault theorizes. If Wolfe's rather pompous summary of the realist aesthetic is that it would "tame the billion-footed beast of reality," then his realism is biopolitical through and through. As Peter Sloterdijk in "Rules for the Human Zoo" suggests: reading is breeding;[54] writing is, too.

This representationalist and biopolitical position may have made sense in a discussion of the big city novel. But one wonders to what extent it can still apply to the finance novel. Finance, as mentioned previously, is at odds with both representation and the living—it operates as a form of digital life at the limits of what can humanly and technologically be represented. Wolfe's position appears to be entirely outdated when it comes to this particular kind of reality.[55]

Wolfe wrote his manifesto in response to postmodernist trends in narrative fiction. Those trends, which he traces back to modernism (Samuel Beckett, for example), arguably developed out of, or at least in some relation to, structuralist and poststructuralist approaches to realism and its representationalist and biopolitical project (see chapter 3). One can think, for example, of anthropologist Claude Lévi-Strauss's structuralist understanding of myth, which posited that myth offers an imaginary, symbolic resolution for a real social contradiction that thus always remains at some remove from the myth.[56] Extended to all narrative—in *The Political Unconscious*,

Fredric Jameson uses Lévi-Strauss's theory for his understanding of all narrative, and not just myth, "as a socially symbolic act"—this means that any narrative (and not only the mythical one) seeks to resolve within its coherent form real, material problems that remain at some remove from that coherence, and in fact risk to disrupt it.[57] Structuralism offered what could be characterized as a "weak" solution to this problem by laying bare this situation within its theoretical narrative. Poststructuralism—one can think of deconstruction, for example—applied structuralism's insight to structuralism itself, a move that is famously anticipated in Roland Barthes's structuralist treatise *S/Z*, which ends in poststructuralist "suspension" or with the structuralist project breaking under its own weight.[58] For Wolfe, the modernist and postmodernist literature that developed out of, or at least in relation to, these philosophical positions ultimately removed us from realism's program to give an account of the world. And indeed, we have become used to a distribution of the sensible that separates modernism and postmodernism from realism due to their rejection of the realist aesthetic.

As already hinted at in chapter 3, however, there is a realism that *continues* in modernism and postmodernism, and in the structuralist and poststructuralist philosophical approaches with which they are associated. Indeed, from the perspective of realism, it would seem that both structuralism and poststructuralism can be interpreted as attempts to arrive at the real, material contradiction that any socially symbolic act, and specifically narrative, excludes. In their attempt to undermine the realist project of giving an account of the world, and to show that such a living representation of the living is always impossible, they are arguably also approaching a reality that they emphatically claim cannot be "written." Deconstruction may be the most advanced name for such a reality, even if it is a reality that is perpetually displaced, more of the order of the performative than the descriptive. When it comes to the realist program of giving an account of the world, the conclusion is the same for realism, modernism, and postmodernism: it cannot be done. Deconstruction may be the closest that we are going to get to it. The billion-footed beast cannot be tamed, the best that can be done is to expose taming's *différance*. That is as real as it gets. At the end of chapter 3, I proposed—writing in the tracks of Jeffrey Nealon[59]—that we understand this as a financial logic, one that turns the perpetual deferral of realism into a financial instrument itself. In that sense, one would have to consider the financialization *of* realism, or realism's complicity with finance, in a discussion of financial realism (see in particular chapter 6).

One example of how this debate continues today can be seen in the literary critic James Wood. In 2001, Wood proposed—with reference to Tom Wolfe's work—the genre of what he called "the big, ambitious novel" to refer to novels such as Zadie Smith's *White Teeth* (he also mentions novels by Salman Rushdie, Thomas Pynchon, David Foster Wallace, among others). In Wood's view, these are novels that pursue their account of the world, their living representation of the living, "at all costs," trying to capture (perhaps) something of the extreme acceleration that is characteristic of "the life around us" in the digitized late twentieth and early twenty-first centuries.[60] As Wolfe already pointed out in his manifesto, such acceleration is of course not new and one can debate whether the acceleration we are living through today is indeed unprecedented. The point is, however, that Wood seems to wonder whether the realist novel can hold together at such high speed, amidst this explosion of information. He suggests that the contemporary realist novel is groaning under everything it is trying to contain: driven on by what he refers to as the "grammar" of storytelling alone, it no longer tells any actual stories. Its supposed extreme vitality, while seeming to borrow from realism, actually evades reality in his view and lacks the human (and here, we should add an element to my characterization of the realist novel as representationalist and biopolitical: it is also, in Wood's view, humanist). While such hysterical, histrionic realism may have originated in Dickens (who takes up a central place in discussions of the financial fiction genre), Wood considers it to lack the "very passionate and simple sentences" that makes Dickens's big, ambitious novels human. In writers such as Smith, "information becomes the new character." It is this particular use of Dickens that, in Wood's view, ties authors as "distinguished" as Don DeLillo and as "cinematically vulgar" as Wolfe together.

Leaving aside Smith's response to Wood,[61] I want to consider a realism freed from the representationalist, biopolitical, and humanist program with which it struggles. It is important to consider this because, as I have suggested, representationalism, biopolitics, and humanism create realism as a financial instrument (for those terms name a trinity that realism can never deliver) while at the same time they prevent it from ever writing finance (since finance defies all three of realism's key orientations). I will readily admit that such a realism is an extreme, if not extremist, realism—a realism that critics like Wood might not hesitate to call *terroristic*. Indeed, it involves pushing the realist novel toward the experimental fiction from which it is traditionally separated, moving from a narrative realism toward a realism of juxtaposition, from a realism associated with novels and films toward the realism of poetry and painting (as Michel Houellebecq suggests in *The Map and the Territory*).

What Wood deems to be such a realism's inhuman, quasi-machinic generation of stories, in its "glamorous congestion" of dead narrative, in its covering up of vitality by artificiality (all, of course, heavily criticized by Wood), can be understood in Smith's *White Teeth* as a deathly, linguistic storytelling machine, generating tales outside of the representationalist, biopolitical, and humanist framework that has dominated the realist novel. Smith's novel does not offer an account of the world or a living representation of the living; it is not a humanist account. Instead, the challenge would be to read Smith's novel as merely stories—by no one and for no one in particular. The kind of automated telling one also finds in *American Psycho*. We find here "reality"—beyond representationalism, biopolitics, and humanism—as a higher form of realism, one that might ultimately not be for us.

This is an extreme, quasi-terroristic position, as I have already indicated, one at the limits of writability and readability. For who can write like that, and who can read like that? However, I want to propose that as such, *White Teeth* would still be a form of realism, specifically a realism that would write the reality that Wood cannot consider within the realist novel, and that is the very reality that realism, in its wildest dreams, wants to write: the great outdoors, the world as independent from the human beings who perceive it. It is in this way that realism would be able to write the real, material contradiction that remains at a distance from all narrative resolutions (as per modernism and postmodernism's criticisms of realism). More specifically, it is this kind of realism that can account for our financial reality—which constitutes a kind of cosmic great outdoors, as I suggested previously—today.

Indeed, there is no room for what we can now call "the great outdoors of finance" in the representationalist, biopolitical, and humanist novel. How could there be, given that its absolute outside—which is not relative to human beings, is given as indifferent to its own givenness to be what it is, and exists in itself regardless of whether we are thinking of it or not—*breaks with all three of those credos*? The great outdoors cannot be represented. It is not necessarily "living." It is certainly not human. Clearly, a realist novel of the financial great outdoors can only be possible if realism leaves those values that it holds most dearly behind. Doing so would propel the realist novel toward the experimental fiction that is traditionally considered separate from it. This explains why realism has such a hard time writing finance; at the same time, it caused realism's financialization—its operating according to a promissory logic, announcing to deliver a reality that it can't. In this context, I want to suggest that it pushes the realist novel toward the speculative—toward the realm where it begins to exist independently from its human producer and receiver, while it can nevertheless still be written. Such a project has a double effect: on the one hand, realism can finally become financially real; on the other, it liberates realism from its financial logic, the promise of its delivery. It is here that literary realism, representation, and language begin to approach something like the mathematical formula—a "code . . . at once fragile and coherent."

Meillassoux on Narrative Fiction

An aspect of Meillassoux's oeuvre that has largely been overlooked is the role it attributes to narrative fiction. What literary solutions does Meillassoux arrive at for the philosophical questions he raises? In his essay "Metaphysics and Extro-Science Fiction,"[62] Meillassoux rehearses the philosophical argument that can also be found in *After Finitude*. However, he also greatly expands it to include a literary theoretical argument about science fiction and specifically the genre that Meillassoux seeks to distinguish from it, extro-science fiction. I want to consider both genres against the background of the debates about literary realism that I rehearsed earlier in order to see how the contemporary debates about speculative realism can be brought into conversation with those debates.

Distinguishing between two regimes of narrative fiction, science fiction and extro-science fiction, Meillassoux points out that as far as its relation to science goes, science fiction preserves the existence of science. In science fiction, science "may be profoundly transformed," he writes, "but there will always *be* science."[63] In extro-science fiction, this is not the case: extro-science fiction thinks "worlds outside science . . . *where experimental science is impossible in principle*, rather than unknown in fact."[64] Meillassoux is interested in extro-science fiction—not because he is particularly interested in fiction, but because the distinction between science fiction and extro-science fiction will enable him to lay out a conceptual distinction that he deems to be of philosophical interest.

Meillassoux's discussion revolves around "Hume's problem," familiar to readers of *After Finitude*. The problem involves a billiards match, "during the course of which the laws of dynamics cease to apply."[65] How can we know, Hume asks, "what truly guarantees—but also, what persuades us—that physical laws will continue to hold in a moment's time, given that neither experience nor logic can assure us of this?"[66] Meillassoux goes on to discuss Karl Popper's answer to this question: Popper argues that "nothing could guarantee it, but moreover that this was a good thing, since there is nothing fantastic about these possibilities—they must be taken entirely seriously."[67] This is, Meillassoux points out, the science fiction answer: "Popper tells us that new experiences could refute our theories; but he never doubts that the existing, canonic experiments will always produce the same results in the future."[68] He thus confuses Hume's problem, which is ontological, a problem of being, with an epistemological problem, a problem of knowledge. Meillassoux argues, however, that Hume was interested in something else: "Hume's problem mobilizes another imaginary, the imaginary of extro-science fiction, a fiction of a world become too chaotic to permit any scientific theory whatsoever to be applied to reality anymore."[69] This is a problem of being (ontology) that cannot simply be recuperated by knowledge (epistemology). To illustrate, but also to further his thought on the problem, Meillassoux turns to an Asimov story that he considers to do both: it captures the extro-science fiction imaginary, since "a totally unforeseen event . . . comes to pass" in it, but it is ultimately an science fiction story since this totally unforeseen event appears to *still* be explainable by the laws of science. That is why, Meillassoux argues, the story works: narrative needs this science fiction resolution since a world of "pure chaos, a pure diversity ordered by nothing" would render narrative fiction impossible. With the extro-science fiction imaginary, fiction is able to go where science cannot; but it seems that narrative fiction can no longer happen there, unless (one imagines) it would be entirely transformed.

With the distinction between science fiction and extro-science fiction, Meillassoux neatly captures what I consider to be the core problem underlying today's digitized financial markets. Those markets constitute, as I have argued, an extro-science fiction reality. But the problem is that high-frequency trading firms, for example, respond to that reality with a science fiction mindset: they believe that with the right math, it is possible not only to have access to that reality but, more importantly, to predict it (within the limits of probability theory, which includes improbable, black swan events). If the market can be predicted, it can be beaten; the latter would mean that guaranteed, perpetual profit is possible, as long as one ups the epistemological game. With the financial universe (a blank swan reality), however, we have stepped away from that game: like the Big Bang and in particular the black holes to which it is compared, it marks an ontological shift into what one might call, after Meillassoux, extro-science—a science outside of science, at the limits of science, one that would end, particularly, the possibility of predicting reality. If the reality of the financial markets cannot be predicted, then profit cannot be guaranteed—for this reality exceeds the one that "hedging" calculates with. Extro-science fiction financial markets escape the possibility of mathematical control, even if one needs mathematics to think them (they are based on mathematics, after all). Meillassoux's extro-science fiction enables one to think the reality of financial markets today and the challenge they pose to any "realist" attempt to describe and predict them.

That also explains why Meillassoux is relevant for a discussion of literary realism. For while he seems to be writing about science fiction, what he is really writing about is a scientific kind of realism that he opposes to extro-science fiction. When it comes to finance, scientific realism can no longer do; its ontology forces us to make the leap into extro-science fiction.

In view of my discussion of literary realism earlier on, I now want to jump to Meillassoux's conclusion. Meillassoux seeks to imagine various types of worlds that the extro-science fiction imaginary allows for. Type one worlds, according to Meillassoux, would be "irregular, but not enough to affect science or consciousness." As he notes, those worlds are not extro-science "in the strict sense since they still allow the exercise of science."[70] The irregularity of type two worlds, by contrast, "is sufficient to abolish science but not consciousness." Those worlds, he notes, "are the real extro-science worlds."[71] Finally, and most extremely, type three worlds "represent lawless universes in which disordered modifications are so frequent, that . . . the conditions of science and those of consciousness alike, are abolished."[72] All of that brings him to his final, and for my purposes most important question: How to write extro-science fiction? Which is another way of asking: What is narrative fiction's relation to the speculative realist worlds that Meillassoux has just sketched out and that range from not strictly extro-science fiction to the abolition of science and consciousness (and presumably also of narrative fiction as we know it)? Can there be a narrative fiction of extro-science fiction? If extro-science fiction, as I suggested, captures the reality of the financial markets today, those questions would apply in particular to narrative fiction that seeks to write the reality of those markets.

Meillassoux lists three literary solutions: first, introduce "just one rupture without cause or reason" (he summarizes this as "catastrophe"); two, "nonsense"; or: three, write "stories of uncertain reality, those in which the real crumbles gradually, from one day to the next ceasing to be familiar to us."[73] It is this third solution that he considers to express "most faithfully the extro-science fiction genre." Meillassoux summarizes this as "the dread uncertainty of the atmospheric novel," and notes that there probably aren't enough of these novels around "to constitute a genre."[74]

Apart from the reading of the Asimov story, there is no literary criticism in Meillassoux's essay to back up the list of worlds and solutions. Meillassoux gives examples of literary solutions one (René Barjavel's *Ravage*), two (Douglas Adam's *The Hitchhiker's Guide to the Galaxy*), and three (Philip K. Dick's *Ubik*), but none of them he finds entirely satisfactory. Also puzzling is how the three literary solutions that Meillassoux lists at the end of the essay are supposed to match the three types of worlds he describes earlier in the essay. It seems that while the first solution would match type one worlds, and the second solution, type three worlds, the third solution—"the one that most faithfully expresses the [extro-science fiction] genre"—would match type two worlds, "the real extro-science world." What is clear, however, and this justifies Meillassoux's place in this book, is that the issue Meillassoux confronts is not only philosophical; laying out three different worlds, all related to the philosophical mindset of extro-science fiction, he then asks—

moving to *literature*, even if it doesn't come with an equally robust literary theoretical framework—what kind of narrative fiction would be capable of writing the extro-science fiction worlds he has theorized.

I am interested in reconsidering Meillassoux's types of worlds and solutions for narrative fiction, involving various configurations of science and consciousness, through the lens of theory of literary realism, which is arguably—with naturalism—the most scientific form of narrative fiction: for example, one can think of Emile Zola's scientific method in writing naturalist fiction. In Tom Wolfe's manifesto, we find one contemporary instantiation of such scientific realism. It is worth recalling the challenge that Wolfe considers contemporary fiction writers to be up against: "American society today is no more or less chaotic, random, discontinuous, or absurd than Russian society or French society or British society a hundred years ago," Wolfe writes, "no matter how convenient it might be for a writer to think so. It is merely more varied and complicated and harder to define." At first sight, the two sentences in the previous quote may seem difficult to combine. On the one hand, Wolfe insists that contemporary society is no different today than in the past (an overlooked implication of this is that Wolfe thus seems to insist that society is and has always been irregular); on the other hand, he insists that it has become more varied, complicated, and harder to define. It thus seems, upon further consideration, that variation, complication, and interpretative difficulty cannot be equated to an increase in chaos, randomness, discontinuity, or absurdism. The latter is still the same as one hundred years ago; its variations and complications have just made society harder to define. And thus, the novelist should apply himself more diligently to his "science."

This is, one could argue, a kind of *science* fiction (i.e., realist) imaginary, in which reality—by definition chaotic, random and ever more varied, complicated—is matched by science (i.e., realism's biopolitics); in which reality's intensifications are matched by the intensifications of literary realism. However, I consider Meillassoux's three types of worlds to challenge Wolfe's belief in this biopolitical matching, which is a form of what Meillassoux calls correlationism. Instead, Meillassoux invites us to imagine worlds that would be irregular (although not quite in Wolfe's sense), although (a) not irregular enough to affect science or consciousness; (b) irregular enough to abolish science, but not consciousness; and (c) so irregular that both science and consciousness are abolished. Although the first option may seem to match Wolfe's mode of *science* fiction (i.e., realism), when Meillassoux gives an example of a literary work that matches this world, the difference between what he has in mind and Wolfe's chaotic society becomes clear: Meillassoux mentions René Barjavel's book *Ravage*, "in which electricity suddenly no longer exists."[75] This is a situation in which a scientific irregularity has occurred—but it happens too spasmodically for science or consciousness to be affected by it. In order for Wolfe's realism to begin to approach even the weakest of these extro-science fiction worlds, it would need to include an element that properly suspends the realist science, if only for a moment.

Wolfe's point is, of course, that any degree of variation, complication, or interpretative difficulty can be recuperated as part of the realist project—the novelist should simply try harder. But Meillassoux is asking for something else: in the case of a type one world, he is asking for a suspension that ultimately leaves realism and consciousness intact; in a type two world, for one that abolishes realism but not consciousness; and in a type three world, for one that abolishes both realism and consciousness. In literary realism, Wolfe is like Popper to Meillassoux's Hume, confusing an ontological issue with an epistemological one.

To imagine narrative fictions that write each of those worlds is to go beyond the realism that Wolfe advocates. That would mean to practice a literary-speculative realism of varying degrees: first, second, or third solution, as per Meillassoux's suggestion. But when Meillassoux deems the third solution ("stories of uncertain reality, those in which the real crumbles gradually, from one day to the next ceasing to be familiar to us") to be the most extro-science fiction—that is to say the one to match most closely the type two world in which science is abolished but not consciousness—one cannot help but notice that he does not provide a single example in his essay that illustrates this solution and the speculative reality it writes. The only example he gives—Douglas Adam's *Hitchhiker's Guide*—receives no further discussion; the example he does develop—the Asimov story that is reproduced in the essay's book version—includes the extro-science fiction mindset, but Meillassoux's argument is that this mindset is ultimately recuperated by the mindset of science fiction. Thus, even his only developed example is not really an example of a proper literary-speculative realism.

Needless to say, this is rather unsatisfying, since representationalism, biopolitics, and humanism ultimately continue to hold sway in Meillassoux's text—the literary examples he discusses are all still within the representationalist, biopolitical, and humanist framework. Part of the problem is the limitation of the science fiction and extro-science fiction framework, the fact that Meillassoux is *only* approaching the possibility of extro-science fiction fiction within the context of science fiction writing. If the (occluded) target of his discussion is literary realism as it is traditionally understood—if that is the most paradigmatic correlationist genre—then wouldn't it be more powerful to imagine Meillassoux's challenge to the genre from within that genre itself? Rather than from outside of it?

For the question of financial realism, all of the above issues are crucial: if the science fiction/realist imaginary cannot capture the reality of today's financial markets—for that the extro-science fiction/speculative realist imaginary is needed—this has ramifications for the financial realism that I have pursued in the previous chapters. To assess those properly, one must note how "science fiction" in this context is a mere extension of realism—I have just drawn out realism's close connection to science, and emphasized the *science* in science fiction to highlight Meillassoux's point that in the science fiction imaginary, everything can ultimately be brought back within the limits of experimental science. This is a realist position. However, extro-science fiction seeks to break out of those "realist" limitations of science fiction, it seeks to break out of realism, in order to think and write otherwise. My suggestion is that it is precisely such a thinking and writing otherwise that is needed if one wants to give an account of today's financial markets. On this count, Wolfe's manifesto only brings us more of the same. With *American Psycho*, Bret Easton Ellis was going in the right direction, presenting his readers with a novel that, in its development from psychopathy to psychosis, its repeated evocation of Patrick Bateman's "nameless dread," and in general its repetitive, mechanical narration could be understood as Meillassoux's third solution, matching the type two world that he describes. In that, the novel's "psychotic realism" was prophetic, because it managed to already be a literary response to a reality of digitized finance that would only fully reveal itself some fifteen years later.

Conceptual Realism

To sum up: a contemporary financial realism worthy of its name would seek to write the universe-like reality of today's financial markets. From a literary-theoretical perspective, I have tried to show that the financial realism we are familiar with through Tom Wolfe will not enable us to do that. As Wolfe explains in "Stalking the Billion-Footed Beast," *Bonfire* was actually conceived as a big city novel. Wolfe is taking novelists to task in his manifesto for throwing in the towel when it comes to writing the multifaceted, complex reality of the city: they could do better if only they applied themselves more. The novelist's task is to "tame the billion-footed beast of reality," to bring it within the limits of representation. I think this manifesto is a remarkable expression of realism's biopolitical credo, and it should be revisited today in view of the challenge that finance poses to realist representation. My position is that if the finance novelist back in Wolfe's day could perhaps still be under the impression that finance is a billion-footed beast that can be tamed, with the digitized reality of finance the rules of the representation game have definitively changed, presenting a new challenge to literary realism. It will no longer do to simply flex the epistemological muscle; the shift is ontological. If Wolfe's brand of financial realism can be called "Big Swinging Dick realism," as per Michelle Chihara's apt suggestion,[76] then finance marks the end of that kind of realism.

The Fear Index, as I have shown, in part responds to that shift by proposing an algorithm as one of its main agents, even if the novel fails when it humanizes that agent into a character. The novel gives in too much to what Ian Bogost in *Alien Phenomenology* diagnoses as a demand of narrative fiction, namely, the need to create a degree of relationality—of what Meillassoux might call "correlationist" affinity between readers and characters. But algorithms do not allow for that. Thus, the algorithm ultimately becomes in *The Fear Index* a mere stand-in for a human being and the book turns into a very familiar tale indeed: it doesn't seem like it, but it is ultimately the human who wins in the book. That still leaves us with a question, however: are attempts more successful at financial realism than *The Fear Index* possible? What literary form may be able to capture the reality of today's economy? Who are the true inheritors of *American Psycho* today?

Bogost considers Ben Marcus's experimental fiction *The Age of Wire and String*, a text that manages to capture the mindset of what Meillassoux calls extro-science fiction: variously described by critics as a work that "wields together a new reality," creating "a makeshift world [that defies] the laws of physics and language" and offering "a guide to an unpredictable yet exhilarating plane of existence," *Age of Wire and String* sounds like a poster text for speculative realism.[77] It responds to Meillassoux's type two world (science is abolished, but not consciousness) and his second literary solution, "nonsense." Bogost insists, in fact, on the "incomprehensibility" of this text that, as he notes, doesn't quite add up to a novel.[78] Marcus's *The Flame Alphabet*, which does present itself as a novel, would mark a weaker version of Meillassoux's extro-science fiction: it imagines a type one world (irregular, but not enough to abolish science or consciousness) and offers Meillassoux's first literary solution—in its imagination of a world in which children's speech has become lethal, it is similar to Barjavel's *Ravage*. If those examples matter, however, it is only in a formal way, because neither one of Marcus' books has anything to do with finance; while they might capture the extro-science fiction mindset that is needed to think finance today, they do not explicitly talk about finance and as such they do not qualify for the narrower kind of financial fictions—the novelistic representationalism of finance—that I am pursuing.

Bogost's turn to Marcus's *Age of Wire and String* does reveal something interesting: that in order to write the reality of finance today, one may have to turn to experimental rather than realist writing. In other words, experimental writing may be the new realism when it comes to writing finance today. As such, this is not a new hypothesis: Fredric Jameson arguably already proposed it when he put forward his argument about postmodernism as the aesthetic of late capitalism. Financial capitalism or finance may simply push us further along within this argument, toward the experimental or, as Katherine Hayles suggests, the conceptual.[79] Conceptual art, with its ties to modernism and especially postmodernism, is a psychotic art that disavows existing reality and substitutes another reality for it: this already lies contained in a work such as Marcel Duchamp's *Fountain* (1917), which calls a urinal a fountain and asks us to consider it as a work of art. Furthermore, if art has arguably always had a close affinity with finance, in that artworks are par excellence objects of high speculative value, conceptual art marks an extreme form of this, tying value to the conceptual rather than the commodity. On this count, it is worth noting that while conceptual art saw its rise in the 1960s, the first exhibition of conceptual art was in 1970, just before the Nixon administration unilaterally decided to abolish the gold standard. I have already suggested that money today is virtual, linguistic, and performative; we can now add to this list conceptual.

It is in fact in a text about conceptual writing from Los Angeles that one can find one example of a literary text that both in its content and its form manages to bring us closer to the financial realism that I am pursuing. Brian Kim Stefans, who has written insightfully about what he terms "a speculative turn in recent poetry and fiction,"[80] discusses such a text—Mathew Timmons's *Credit*[81]—in *Conceptual Writing: The L.A. Brand*:

> *Credit* was conceived to be the most expensive book one could offer on the print-on-demand website Lulu; for this reason, it is 800 pages in full color (though most of the pages are in black and white), measuring 8.5 by 11 inches, and only available in hard cover, priced at $199 [the e-book version is, absurdly, priced even higher at $299]. As for content, *Credit* is composed entirely of scans of snail mail from credit card companies imploring the impecunious Timmons to sign up for an account; along with high resolution, color scans of the envelopes and internal documentation are OCRs (optical character recognition) of the texts of the letters and envelopes. Some of the text is "redacted" to hide details of Timmons' own financial situation at the time; because Timmons doesn't correct the OCRs of the advertisements, much of the text of *Credit* is made up of gibberish that the computer put in place of words that it didn't recognize.[82]

The "exaggerated," "sped up," "accelerated" nature of the writing is emphasized by Timmons's public performances of the work, as Stefans notes: "Timmons, also a sound poet, has performed readings of the book in a breakneck speed as if emphasizing or exaggerating the very junk-like nature of the textual activity that underlies the nanosecond long transactions of major financial institutions."[83] In other words: if *Credit* itself, as an expensive 800-page book filled with gibberish, presents itself as a conceptual artwork/financial instrument (the "what" of contemporary finance), Timmons's public performance of the work—which is part of his putting the work in circulation—mimics (in Stefans's reading) contemporary finance's "how" (high-frequency trading). Furthermore, *Credit* engages the financial economy through its content, which also—formally—foregrounds the digitality of contemporary finance. Of course, this is hardly a novelistic representationalism of finance. Indeed, *Credit* as such may ultimately be closer to poetry—although a specific kind of poetry, to be sure—than to narrative fiction. In that sense, it points, perhaps, to the novel's need to "poetically" destroy itself if it wants to offer a realism of today's financial economy.

FIVE

Michel Houellebecq, Finance Novelist

> Michel Houellebecq's writing revels in the derivative.
>
> —JOHN MCCANN, *Michel Houellebecq*[1]

After the Scandal

The work of French author Michel Houellebecq is often thought of as scandalous due to the racism and misogyny of the characters in his novels. But Houellebecq's novels go far beyond that: from his critical representation of post-Fordist workers in his first novel *Whatever* to his engagement with sex tourism and religious (fundamentalist Islamic) terrorism in *Platform* to the posthuman science fiction of *The Possibility of an Island* and his satirical vision of France under Islamic rule in *Submission*, Houellebecq has emerged as one of today's most insightful philosophical novelists who, even if he dabbles in sci-fi and satire, considers himself to be working in the tracks of realism's great tradition of providing an account of the world.[2]

In a book about what he terms Houellebecq's "depressive realism," Ben Jefferey has presented Houellebecq's realism as a "capitalist" one, in the sense that it is so realist it "thoroughly fails to envision a better world."[3] While that last claim can be disputed, one important recurrent concern in Houellebecq's oeuvre indeed has been the economy—capitalism, liberalism, neoliberalism, finance, and the related topics of work, sex, and humanism—so much so that his friend the economist Bernard Maris (who was murdered in the *Charlie Hebdo* terrorist attack) was able to write a book titled *Houellebecq économiste* in which he discusses the theme in Houellebecq's oeuvre.[4]

In this chapter, I want to consider Houellebecq's prize-winning novel *The Map and the Territory* through that economic lens. An art novel that continues Houellebecq's investigation of realism, *The Map and the Territory* is (as at least one other critic has pointed out[5]) an intensely economic text that explores art's relation to finance. If the book is a particularly good fit for *Finance Fictions*, it is in part because it also probes the limits of realism, not so much to arrive at a realism that would be able to "represent" contemporary finance—although it accomplishes, as I will show, some transformations of realism that are decisive on that count—but at a realism that would take up the financialization of art itself. Although that in part leads away from the representationalist problematic of the previous chapters—with Mathew Timmons's *Credit*, we had, in any case, arrived at the limit of that line of questioning—it is one very effective way in which contemporary novelists have taken up the topic of finance, even if Houellebecq doesn't quite put the novel at the center of that investigation yet.[6]

Whatever

First, I will consider Houellebecq's debut novel, *Whatever*, in order to see how the interrelated themes of the economy and realism are launched in his work. *Whatever* offers the first-person account of the life of a computer programmer. In an excellent article, Carole Sweeney argues that the novel engages with our contemporary economic situation, specifically with the post-Fordist economy.[7] Whereas the assembly line from Henry Ford's automobile factories and the increase it presents in the production of material commodities was central to Fordism and the capital it generated, post-Fordist capitalism (often associated with neoliberalism) no longer revolves around the material commodity that is at the heart of Karl Marx's understanding of capital. Instead, post-Fordism thrives on "immaterial labor" (Michael

Hardt and Antonio Negri).[8] It is an economic system in which flexible workers—modeled, in the view of Luc Boltanski and Eve Chiapello, after the creative laborer: the artist, for example, or the writer[9]—work with their brains and minds, often for low salaries and minimal or no benefits, toward the production of fictitious capital (which can be defined, after Marx, as "value in the form of credit, shares, debt, speculation, and various forms of paper money, above and beyond what can be realized in the form of commodities"[10]). Developments in technology and specifically the rise of high technology and digitization are generally considered to have contributed greatly to this situation.

The "cognitive" form of capitalism that this situation has created targets not only the brains and minds of its workers but also of its consumers, producing what Bernard Stiegler understands to be psychotic subjects without desire (see chapter 2),[11] driven solely by the need to consume. Under post-Fordist cognitive capitalism, consumers and workers constitute a new, updated proletariat that critical thinker Franco Berardi calls "cognitariat."[12] It is the human being's brain and mind rather than the body that are proletarianized under current economic conditions. And those conditions are no longer limited to the poor alone: the rich are also proletarianized, leading Stiegler to include Alan Greenspan in his examples of today's psychopathological subjects.[13]

As one might guess, such an economic condition does not produce particularly interesting characters for literary realism. Bret Easton Ellis was arguably still able to write an entertaining novel about one of the contemporary economy's proletarians, Patrick Bateman—a man who, while he is rich, has obviously been hollowed out by consumerism and is alive only in his murderous exploits, whether real or imagined.[14] But it can hardly be disputed that Bateman poses a challenge to realism: *American Psycho*'s surreal descriptions of torture and murder beg the question of why a contemporary realist novel about the post-Fordist economy would include such scenes—perhaps to make sure the novel stays entertaining, something that, had Ellis been limited to consumerism alone, would have been difficult to pull off? The protagonist, if one can still call it that, of Houellebecq's *Whatever* is less flamboyant, though also still decently paid. But his life under cognitive capitalism is dreary—so dreary that Houellebecq's novel explicitly wonders whether it still constitutes an appropriate subject for the realist novel. It shouldn't surprise us that he has a decidedly psychotic touch, something that Sabine van Wesemael has deemed a hallmark of many of Houellebecq's characters.[15]

Referring to Michel Biron's characterization of Houellebecq's realism as "second degree realism" or "the idea of realism,"[16] Sweeney notes that *Whatever* "barely qualifies as a novel at all."[17] Instead, the novel "traces a moment of 'vital exhaustion' that inevitably represents certain aesthetic challenges for the writer."[18] Sweeney quotes from Houellebecq's fiction, which reflects on its own form: "The novel form is not conceived for depicting indifference or nothingness; a flatter, more terse and dreary discourse would need to be invented."[19] In Sweeney's perceptive reading, "the novel presents the relationship between the 'bad' subject of post-Fordism . . . who fails to reinvest his surplus in the affective or cultural domain and the corresponding aesthetic difficulty of constructing an appropriate novelistic discourse."[20] Houellebecq's narrator in *Whatever* can be understood as one who "ridicules narrative realism as the 'pointless accumulation' of detail with 'clearly differentiated characters hogging the limelight.'"[21] At the same time, Sweeney notes that Houellebecq's fiction (as per the narrator of *Whatever*'s own admission) "cannot altogether escape the lure of the idea of a kind of realism," thus yielding a realism for post-Fordist times.[22]

Consider the distribution that must be in place for Houellebecq (and Sweeney) to arrive at these conclusions (see my discussion of biopolitical realism in chapter 4). First, there is the assumption that realism attempts to offer (impossibly so) a living representation of the living. The realist novel is not a form that is fit to write a moment of what Houellebecq calls "vital exhaustion." Second, and in close relation to this, there is the assumption that the novel is not conceived for "depicting indifference or nothingness": instead, its characters are engaged in the fullness of life. Finally, when it comes to those characters, they cannot be interchangeable. The realist novel needs to provide them with specific identities that must be laid out in detail. Those are all assumptions associated with the realist novel as a representationalist and—I maintain—biopolitical form. Within such a framework, the contemporary post-Fordist moment of cognitive capitalism poses a challenge to realism, for it offers a reality that is not worthy of such representation.

Perhaps unsurprisingly, the critical reception of Houellebecq's fiction has reinforced that framework. When discussing Houellebecq's recent novel *The Map and the Territory*, for example, which once again problematizes the aesthetic of realism in relation to the theme of work, literary critic James Wood deplores that nothing in the novel "is subjected to the longevity of narrative" and asks whether Houellebecq is "really a novelist."[23] Comparing Houellebecq to D. H. Lawrence, Wood identifies "Lawrence's larger vision of life" as "rich and substantial and ramifying"; Lawrence "had a limitless faith in the novel's explanatory powers, in fiction's enormous capacity to be what he called 'the bright book of life.'"[24] Houellebecq, of course, stands at the opposite end of that credo. In Wood's reading, he is "an unconvincing and incoherent novelist."[25] Against realism's close connection to life, Houellebecq is heralded as a writer (hardly a novelist) of death.

Whatever thus offers a situation in which the realist novel runs up against its representational limits when confronted with the contemporary economy. Economic reality can be considered as part of what scholars have identified as the "epistemic trouble" in Houellebecq's work.[26] If the novel as a genre is interested in certain kinds of subjects, it may just be that the subjects of today's economy are not very well suited to be in a novel. They all look alike; their nihilistic indifference isn't interesting for the novel; they lack vitality. In Houellebecq's novel, the computer programmer thus seems to have become quasi identical to the algorithms operating on today's markets—a human being who has become like the computer programs he creates.

That is not the entire picture, however. One of the interesting things about Houellebecq's novel is that even if the post-Fordist economy is supposed to have exhausted the workers' creative capabilities, they clearly still have "some free time" on their hands (as the title of Sweeney's article about *Whatever* has it): *Whatever* includes, in addition to its account of the narrator's dreary life, excerpts of creative writing that the narrator is doing.[27] In combination with the fact that *Whatever* is actually a pretty good novel, these excerpts constitute in spite of the novel's depressing ending ("the goal of life is missed"[28]) the dark hope that a successful realism for post-Fordist times is also possible.

The Map and the Territory

Houellebecq's novel *The Map and the Territory* develops a very different approach to the relation between realism and finance by exploring the financialization of realist art itself. The central concern here is no longer a representationalist realism of finance, even though representationalist realism is still a focus in the novel. Instead, Houellebecq is concerned with how concrete works of representationalist realism are valued financially.

The Map and the Territory tells the life story of the visual artist Jed Martin, whose photographs and paintings show a deep interest in technology and work. The novel begins with a prologue of sorts in which Jed is at work in his Paris studio on a painting titled *Damien Hirst and Jeff Koons Dividing Up the Art Market*:

> Jeff Koons had just got up from his chair, enthusiastically throwing his arms out in front of him. Sitting opposite him, slightly hunched up, on a white leather sofa partly draped with silks, Damien Hirst seemed to be about to express an objection; his face was flushed, morose. Both of them were wearing black suits—Koons's had fine pinstripes—and white shirts and black ties. Between them, on the coffee table, was a basket of candied fruits that neither paid any attention to. Hirst was drinking a Bud Light.
>
> Behind them, a bay window opened onto a landscape of tall buildings that formed a Babylonian tangle of gigantic polygons that stretched across the horizon. The night was bright, the air absolutely clear. They could have been in Qatar, or Dubai; the decoration of the room was, in reality, inspired by an advertisement photograph, taken from a German luxury publication, of the Emirates Palace Hotel in Abu Dhabi.
>
> Koons's forehead was slightly shiny. Jed shaded it with his brush and stepped back three paces.[29]

The description is of a painting (in progress) showing Koons and Hirst engaged in a discussion. Given that they are two of the most expensive contemporary artists, it seems appropriate that the scene is dripping in luxury: with the exception perhaps of Hirst's Bud Light (which needs to be attributed to Hirst's coarse looks, as the novel suggests), the painting shows a setting associated with Qatar, Dubai, and Abu Dhabi—choice destinations for a certain class of German (i.e., wealthy European) travelers.

Whereas Hirst is easy to represent—including his "I shit on you from the top of my pile of cash" attitude (3)—Koons poses a problem, and this in spite of the fact that Jed has many photographs of him, for example in the company of Warren Buffett and Bill Gates (4). Somehow Jed cannot get

Koons quite right. By the end of the novel's prologue, Jed has decided that *Damien Hirst and Jeff Koons* is a failed painting:

> He seized a palette knife, cut open Damien Hirst's eye, and forced the gash wider; it was a canvas of tight linen fibers, and therefore very tough. Catching the sticky canvas with one hand, he tore it in one blow, tipping the easel over onto the floor. Slightly calmed, he stopped, looked at his hands, sticky with paint, and finished the cognac before jumping feet first onto his painting, stamping on it and rubbing it against the floor until it became slippery. He lost his balance and fell, the back of his head hitting the frame of the easel violently. (14)

The prologue ends with Jed's destruction of his painting. If within the range of just a couple of pages, Houellebecq has moved from the creation to the destruction of a painting, the value swing of the painting in those pages should also be noted: from a painting that's potentially worth half a million euros, it ends up being worth nothing. The fact that this transition occurs with a painting representing two of the richest artists in the world makes the effect of Houellebecq's prologue all the more powerful.

But what brought Jed to this transitional, destructive moment? Part 1 of Houellebecq's novel answers that question. If the novel's opening representational play—it opens with a realistic description of a conversation between Hirst and Koons that turns out to be a representation of a painting—introduces (in a postmodern way) the concern of realism into the novel, that concern becomes explicit very early in part 1, when we learn that Jed "had devoted his life . . . to *art*, to the production of representations of the world" (19). As opposed to his architect father, whose job is "to produce inhabitable configurations," no one is "meant to live" in Jed's representations, and that gives him a certain artistic and critical freedom. The grandson of a photographer, Jed's first major art project is in photography as well: he engages in "the systematic photography of the world's manufactured objects" and as part of his application to École des Beaux Arts in Paris he submits "an exhaustive catalogue of the objects of human manufacturing in the industrial age" (20)—"Three Hundred Photographs of Hardware" (26). The novel describes the work as "pure photography": "technically perfect but entirely neutral" (23).

It's thanks to his father, who decides to "invest" in Jed's career, that Jed is able to buy his Paris studio. While the property is marketed as an artist's studio, the real estate agent expresses surprise at the fact that an actual artist is able to afford it: "It was the first time, he exclaimed, that he'd had the opportunity to sell an *artist's studio* to an *artist*!" (7). That is, as the novel puts it, "the truth of the market" (7). Thus, Jed "launched himself into an artistic career whose sole project was to give an objective description of the world—a goal whose illusory nature he rarely sensed" (27). We have here, then, an industrial object-oriented realist who fully believes in the visual artist's project to provide a representation of the world.

One day, however, that project—which some interpret as Jed's "*homage to human labor*" (26)—ends, and Jed moves on to something new: the photography of Michelin Departments roadmaps. Coming across one of those maps shortly after his grandmother's death, Jed has a "great aesthetic revelation" that the map is "sublime" (28). In a discussion of the sale of the grandmother's real estate, the novel indicates that this revelation occurs around the time of "the crash on the London Stock Exchange, the subprime crisis, and the collapse of speculative values"—to get a good price for one's house, one "would now have to wait . . . for the arrival of a new generation of rich people, whose wealth was more solid, based on some form of industrial production" (32). Jed's Michelin map photograph will end up in a group show, where it is seen by Olga Sheremoyova, who becomes Jed's lover.

Olga works for Michelin, specifically for the Michelin Holding Michelin Finance, which operates out of Switzerland. It's in this way that the connection (not a marriage but an intense sexual relation) between art and business is clinched in Houellebecq's novel. While the novel pursues this seriously, it is difficult to ignore its satirical elements. "Am I boring you?," Olga asks when she is having dinner with Jed shortly after they meet. "I only talk about business while you're an artist." "'Not at all,' replied Jed sincerely. 'Not at all, I'm fascinated. Look, I haven't even touched my foie gras'" (37). At a literary prize ceremony, Jed meets the French novelist Frédéric Beigbeder, who envies him for being with Olga. When he finds out Jed is an artist, Beigbeder exclaims: "But yes, of course, you have to be an *artist*! Literature, as a plan, is completely old hat! To sleep with the most beautiful women today, you have to be an *artist*! I too want to be *an ar-tist*," and he follows up by singing "The Businessman's Blues" ("*I would have liked to be an artiiist . . . And live like a millionaire!*") (42). In other words: the artist has outdone the creative writer in the competition for women, and for sex with women; part of art's value today is that, unlike literature, it enables one to sleep with the most beautiful women. Jed observes this scene with a cool detachment, but he also connects Beigbeder's remarks to the situation of young men in "those realist novels of the French nineteenth century," working their way up through women, noting that "he was surprised to find himself in a similar situation" (43).

Shortly after that, we arrive at Jed's second major project: "THE MAP IS MORE INTERESTING THAN THE TERRITORY," an exhibition featuring his photographs of Michelin maps. If there is any doubt that the realist project of providing an objective description of the world is in play here, consider that when one of the exhibition's art critics introduces himself as "the art critic for [the French newspaper] *Le Monde*," Jed "almost stupidly repeated 'For the world?'" (46), as if to suggest that the world itself is interested in how Jed has chosen to represent it.[30] After the show's opening, Jed meets with Patrick Forestier, the director of communications for Michelin France, and the deal between art and business is sealed: "*we are a team*" (51), Forestier exclaims (in English) during a meeting in which they decide Jed can sell his art through a website set up by Michelin. He adds that it's a "win-win situation" (52). While Jed initially puts up his prints at two hundred euros, he quickly discovers that their "*market price*" (54), based on what buyers are willing to offer, is about ten times as much. The Michelin project comes to an end when Olga returns to Russia. Once again, Jed is in search of something new.

This is how we arrive at the phase of his career during which Jed will start painting *Damien Hirst and Jeff Koons*. Continuing Jed's interest in industrial objects, but now shifting to the side of the laborer or the producer, this phase starts as a "Series of Simple Professions," followed by a "Series of Business Compositions" and marks Jed's turn to painting. With those two series, the prices of Jed's art will go through the roof and Jed will accumulate his own "pile of cash," as the novel puts it with respect to Hirst. It's in part 2 of the novel, which focuses on the series mentioned above, that Houellebecq describes paintings such as *Bill Gates and Steve Jobs Discussing the Future of Information Technology*. While the latter is subtitled "The Conversation at Palo Alto," the novel notes that it could just as well have been subtitled "A Brief History of Capitalism," given its representation of "two convinced supporters of the market economy; two resolute supporters also of the Democratic Party, and yet two opposing facets of capitalism, as different as a banker in Balzac could be from Verne's engineer" (119). In its discussion of the painting, the novel refers to Gates's *The Road Ahead* and the faith it expresses in capitalism, in the "mysterious 'invisible hand'"; Gates's "absolute, unshakable conviction that whatever the vicissitudes and apparent counter-examples, the market, at the end of the day, is always right, and that the good of the market is always identical to the general good" (118).

Jobs, on the other hand, appears to be more in doubt—even if it is he who, upon closer consideration, appears to be winning the chess game in which the two are shown to be involved. It is Jobs who, "through the brilliant intuition of a new [disruptive] product [could] suddenly impose new norms on the market" (119). It is around the same time that Jed paints *The Stock Exchange Flotation of Shares in Beate Uhse*, featuring "traders in running shoes and hooded sweatshirts, who acclaim with blasé world-weariness the great German porn businesswoman" (116).

This part of the novel also contains an extensive reflection—through the character of Jed's father—on art, work, communism, utopia and, ultimately, William Morris, who is cast in the novel as someone for whom "the distinction between art and the worker, between design and execution, had to be abolished" (141). If one might be inclined to oppose Morris to artists such as Hirst and Koons, Jed's father actually sees a connection: Morris is associated with those "*great masters* of the Renaissance—be they Botticelli, Rembrandt, or Leonardo da Vinci—[who] behaved in fact exclusively as the heads of commercial enterprises": "Exactly like Jeff Koons or Damien Hirst today, with an iron hand the so-called *great masters* of the Renaissance ruled workshops of fifty, even a hundred assistants, who chain-produced paintings, sculptures, and frescoes. They just gave general guidelines, signed the finished work, and above all devoted themselves to public relations with their patrons of the moment—princes or popes" (140–41). In other words: it won't do to oppose Hirst and Koons to the arts and crafts movement associated with Morris. It's all the same—and it's all capitalist.

Often when artistic transitions and artworks are described in Houellebecq's novel, the novel parts ways with its focalized third-person narration to adopt instead an omniscient voice, as if from an art historian (similar to the art critic Wong Fu Xin whose work on Martin is repeatedly alluded to in the novel) who is looking back at Jed's artistic career from the not too distant future. This has the effect of solidifying Jed's status as a star in contemporary art's firmament; even if the voice is often hesitant when it comes to determining the meaning of Jed's work, it nevertheless assumes his place in art history and thus contributes to his value as an artist (a value that we see emerge in the novel). Although I don't think this voice can be attributed to any single individual, in the above quotes it appears to be the character "Michel Houellebecq" who is speaking.

In *The Map and the Territory*, Houellebecq writes himself into his novel as a writer who is contacted by Jed to write a catalog essay for Jed's exhibition of the Profession and Business series.[31] The introduction of Houellebecq into the novel in part accomplishes a comparative view on Jed and Houellebecq's approaches to realist representation. During a first meeting with Houellebecq, the artist and the writer discuss Jed's turn to painting. Jed argues that photography allows for too many subjects—any object could become the subject of photography. Houellebecq points out that literature, too, can be object-oriented—and the novels of the real-life Houellebecq certainly have been; *The Map and the Territory* contains long and detailed descriptions of objects—although the two agree that it could never solely be so. Objects can only become part of the novel as part of "a *genuine human drama*"—with human "characters" (87). Whereas photography in Jed's view is perfect for objects, human beings demand painterly representation. If he has turned to painting, it was a turn that was necessitated by another turn: his turn from objects and peopleless maps to human beings. Finally, Jed and Houellebecq also discuss the commercial aspect of painting: paintings are easier to store and resell.

Clearly, economics is a central theme in *The Map and the Territory*, and it is associated with all the phases of Jed's work. And it's not just that much of Jed's work explicitly engages economic issues; the novel also tells the story of the work's valuation, and it presents itself as a finance novel on both counts.

In the end, Jed and Houellebecq agree that Houellebecq will be paid for his essay not with money but with one of Jed's paintings. Moreover, when Jed proposes to him over the phone—and while he is looking at "the floor [of his studio, which] was still strewn with the ripped remains [*débris déchiquetés*] of *Damien Hirst and Jeff Koons Dividing Up the Art Market*" (94)[32]—to pay him with a portrait of Houellebecq himself, the writer "unenthusiastically" agrees (94)—perhaps intimating that the painting will also become the cause of his downfall (it is, after all, the anticipation of his own "ripped remains"). The Houellebecq painting turns out very well, showing Houellebecq "standing in front of a desk covered with written or half-written pages" and in front of a "white wall . . . entirely papered with handwritten pages stuck to one another, without any interstices whatsoever" (113), creating the suggestion that Houellebecq is living in a book, that "writing" unlike Jed's artwork is an "inhabitable configuration" in which Houellebecq is caught up (and in the autofictional novel, that is of course the case). Here is how the novel explains the representation: "Jed Martin probably chose to portray [Houellebecq] in the middle of a universe of paper neither to make a statement about realism in literature nor to bring Houellebecq close to a formalist position that he had explicitly rejected. Without doubt, more simply, he was taken by a purely plastic fascination with the image of these branching blocks of text, engendering one another like some gigantic octopus" (113). That description will take on a dark resonance in part 3 of the novel, after Houellebecq has been savagely murdered.

The Detective Plot

In part 3, *The Map and the Territory* takes a surprising turn from an art novel toward a detective novel. As I intend to show, however, the surprise of that turn is only superficial—the novel in fact continues its central concerns through the detective tale and uses the shift toward genre fiction to further the connections between realism and finance that it has set up.

In part 3, the narrative focalization shifts toward a detective called Jasselin who is investigating Houellebecq's murder. Repeating to himself what he compares to "a mantra"—"I am the body of the law, the imperfect body of the moral law" (181)—Jasselin observes the scene of the carnage, and the dead body that is supposed to provide the basis for his deductive police-reasoning, the way in which he is going to solve the crime. Except that in this case, "strictly speaking, there wasn't a body":

> The head of the victim was intact, cut off cleanly and placed on one of the armchairs in front of the fireplace. A small pool of blood had formed on the dark green velvet. Facing him on the sofa, the head of a big black dog had also

> been cleanly cut off. The rest was a massacre, a senseless carnage of strips of flesh scattered across the floor. However, neither the head of the man nor that of the dog was frozen in an expression of horror, but rather of incredulity and anger. In the midst of the strips of mixed human and canine meat, a clear passage, fifty centimeters wide, led to the fireplace, filled with bones to which some remains of flesh were still attached. . . . The whole surface of the carpet was spattered with trails of blood, which in places formed complex arabesques. The strips of flesh in themselves, of a red color which sometimes became blackish, did not seem arranged at random, but followed motifs that were difficult to decrypt; [the description continues] he felt it was like being in the presence of a puzzle. No traces of footprints were visible: the murderer had acted methodically, first cutting the strips of skin that he wanted to place in the corners of the room, then returning gradually toward the center while leaving a path to the exit. They would need photos to help try and re-create the design of the whole. (181–82)

Again, one could be forgiven if one saw an artwork in the description of the savagery above. When Jed later catches a glimpse of photographs of the murder scene lying on Jasselin's desk—he doesn't know what the photographs are showing—he observes: "It's funny . . . it looks like a Pollock, but a Pollock who would have worked almost in monochrome"; when he finds out what the images "represent in reality,"[33] he collapses (222).

The second part of the previous description foregrounds the detective's process of deductive reasoning, the ways in which photography will come to the law's aid in the reconstruction of the totality of the murder scene—a totality that is like a puzzle or a riddle through which the identity of the murderer will become visible. "In a crime scene," Jasselin explains, "there is almost always something individual and unique, practically a signature of the criminal; and this is particularly true . . . of atrocious or ritual crimes, of those for which you are naturally disposed to steer the investigation toward a psychopath" (173). The reference to a "signature" sets up the novel's comparison of the murder scene to a work of art, something that it will later reinforce by Jed's reference to Pollock when he is describing the images of the murder. It also introduces the reference to psychosis that, for reasons that I have explored in chapters 1 and 2, is never far away in finance novels.

When Jed visits Houellebecq's house with Jasselin, he notices immediately that his painting—worth approximately "nine hundred thousand euros"

(232)—is missing. At this point, Jasselin considers the case solved: the missing painting obviously reveals the motive. All they need to do is wait until the painting shows up on the art market, at which point they will be able to find whoever murdered Houellebecq. The missing painting further reinforces the comparison of the murder scene to a work of art: Don't the strips of mixed human and canine flesh recall the textual universe—the white wall with the "branching blocks of text"—in Jed's painting? Isn't the murder scene a kind of portrait of Houellebecq as well, not a painting but a sculpture—a bio-sculpture, a "living" (although in this case "dead") work of art? "Life" has become "art" here, something of the realist project has become realized, but at a high price—the price of life itself. The realization of realism also marks its death. Note also that Pollock, while he is introduced in the novel as an abstract expressionist, is mostly known as an "action painter," that is to say, as someone who approximated life and art. Although a Pollock painting is worth seeing, it is even more interesting to see Pollock painting a Pollock painting—a realism that dies as soon as we end up with the actual, finished painting.[34]

The specter of the death of realism also haunts Jasselin's investigation, which seeks to map out the territory of Houellebecq's murder in order to find the path toward its murderer. And if the motivation for Houellebecq's murder may have been financial—the painting, which is worth a lot of money—*The Map and the Territory* comes to associate economics with Jasselin's investigation. Jasselin's wife, Hélène, is a university economics professor whose "interest in economics had waned considerably over the years": "More and more, the theories that tried to explain economic phenomena, to predict their developments, appeared almost equally inconsistent and random. She was more and more tempted to liken them to pure and simple charlatanism; it was even surprising, she occasionally thought, that they gave a Nobel Prize for economics, as if this discipline could boast of the same methodological seriousness, the same intellectual rigor as chemistry, or physics. And her interest in teaching had also waned considerably" (208). After their family dinner, the couple turns on the news, where a reporter discusses "the crisis that had been shaking the financial markets for several days, and which threatened, according to some experts, to be even worse than that of 2008" (208). "'Did you hear what the expert said?' [Hélène asks.] "Did you see his forecasts? . . . In a week's time we'll see that all his forecasts were wrong. They'll call another expert, even the same one, and he'll make new forecasts, with the same self-assurance . . .' She was shaking her head, upset, even indignant. 'How can a discipline that can't even manage to make verifiable forecasts be considered a science?'" (210). We are talking economics here, but those statements clearly also apply to Jasselin's detective work. What Hélène is taking on is, in a sense, the expert's capacity to "detect" how the markets are going to develop—and she is arguing that such detection, such a realism of the market, is impossible. Economics is not a science; one has to wonder, in parallel, whether police work is. The detective novel of course normally operates within that paradigm. But here the specter is raised of a detective novel that wouldn't—the economics professor plants a seed of suspicion that the "solution" that the detective novel, or detective work, provides is really illusory—that there can be no science of detecting reality, just like there can be no science of detecting the markets.

The Fear Index plants that seed as well (see chapter 3). What if we cannot explain what is happening to Alex Hoffmann? If we cannot explain what happened to the financial markets on the day of the flash crash? However, *The Fear Index* quickly undoes that suggestion by blaming the flash crash on the actions of the VIXAL-4 algorithm; and those actions in turn are motivated, the novel suggests, by a rather human desire that exceeds the algorithm's coded law of profit. Nevertheless, *The Fear Index* opens up the possibility of being a metaphysical thriller, in which no explanation would be provided for the strange things that happen in it.

When Hélène asks her husband whether economics can even be considered a science, Jasselin remains quiet: he "hadn't read Popper," the novel suggests, "he had no valid reply to make to her" (210). But my discussion—after Meillassoux—of Popper in the previous chapter indicates that it might not be the right place to turn to for a proper engagement with Hélène's argument, since Popper misinterpreted Hume's problem as an epistemological problem rather than an ontological one. With detective Jasselin's turn to Popper on this count, something similar risks to happen: the fundamental instability of the markets that Hélène draws out risks to become reappropriated as an epistemological issue, whereas it might be rather that the professor of economics (whose name, etymologically, means "the bright one") is drawing out something much more Humean, and ontological: that the markets are absolutely contingent, and that they will never be objectively describable, predictable, detectable.

If a major objection to the police practice of detection is formulated here, it is also a major objection to the discipline of economics and its claims to scientific authority. This point is also leveled in the book at those studying writing and art, and the detective-like approaches they develop to the aesthetic objects they investigate. It is not for nothing that the crime scene is compared to a Pollock painting and that as such, the crime scene shows some similarities to Jed's painting of Houellebecq as a writer. Hélène's suggestion, then, is that the economy puts us on the track of something darker and contingent that escapes scientific detection. It is no wonder that she has grown tired of teaching, which all too often operates under the assumption that everything can be explained. If Houellebecq has been characterized as a writer of "epistemological trouble," one who would require a kind of "epistemology *noir*" (to borrow a notion from Robin MacKay[35]) in response to his writing, one would also have to understand the ontological problem that precedes this issue—the *ontological* noir that challenges any epistemology that can be brought to it. Reza Negarestani's "Requiem for a Detective Novel" has explored the limits of the "deductive" detective novel in this context, considering what other modes of reasoning detective novels might pursue.[36]

The most extreme version of this concern in Houellebecq's book is probably Jed's father, who, to Jed's dismay, goes to Switzerland to be euthanized. In other words, even death is brought outside of the sphere of contingency here, it becomes part of a detectable plan. The setting of this euthanasia plot, Switzerland, already hints at the relevance of this subplot for the novel's economic narrative. But just in case there is any doubt, the text makes that clear: "A euthanasia was charged at an average rate of five thousand euros, when the lethal dose of sodium pentobarbital came to twenty euros and a bottom-of-the-range cremation doubtless not much more. In a booming market, where Switzerland had a virtual monopoly, they were indeed going to *make a killing*" (241). Gavin Bowd's translation is wonderful: "to make a killing," a phrase from financial jargon (it means "to make big winnings"), has often been used in association with Bret Easton Ellis's *American Psycho*, which as per Leigh Claire La Berge's argument, literalizes the violent metaphors of finance talk. Something similar may be going on in Houellebecq. Whatever the case may be, the translation works very well given the context: euthanasia. It is worth noting, however, that it translates the French "se faire des couilles en or,"[37] literally, "to get oneself golden testicles." Another good translation for this phrase could be "to get rich as fuck": while it would have been less appropriate in the context of the quoted passage, it has the advantage of evoking the sexual, "big swinging dick" dimension of the novel's economic theme.[38]

Ultimately, the concerns that are addressed here lead back to Meillassoux's essay on science fiction and extro-science fiction (see chapter 4). It is an essay that, by now, has revealed itself as a concise study of the detective novel as well, one that, ultimately, has become meaningful in the context of this book for thinking about the reality of today's economy. On this count, Houellebecq's *The Map and the Territory*, like much of his other work, is somewhat of a science-fiction novel itself: it ends in the near future, in a France that has undergone subtle changes, and a world in which financial market collapse has become the norm. Houellebecq's book qualifies as what Meillassoux calls an extro-science fiction novel. It is in that world that Jed embarks on the final phase of his work.

"I want to give an account of the world"

> Let's just say that in general I am quite ill at ease in contemporary places because often I want to stop and it's not possible. I am of a certain age, and there is an acceleration of movement and flows that is painful for me.[39]
>
> *Michel Houellebecq*

Although Jed at first compares the images of Houellebecq's murder scene to a Pollock, upon closer inspection he takes that back, saying: "You know, it's just a rather mediocre imitation of Pollock. There are forms and drips, but the whole thing is arranged mechanically, there's no force, no vital élan" (224). It is perhaps this "mechanical" removal from the "life" that anticipates that in *The Map and the Territory*, Houellebecq's murderer *will* ultimately be found. Three years later, French police intercept a car whose owner leads them to the home of a plastic surgeon in Cannes who had access to the sophisticated laser cutter that was used in Houellebecq's murder. The surgeon specializes "in male reconstructive and plastic surgery" (246). The walls of the basement room where Jed's portrait of Houellebecq is found—in addition to a stolen sketch by Francis Bacon—"is covered with glass shelves two meters high":

> Regularly arranged inside these shelves, lit by spotlights, stood monstrous human chimera. Genitalia were grafted onto torsos, and minuscule arms of fetuses prolonged noses, forming sorts of elephant trunks. Other compositions were magmas of human limbs, attached, intermingled, and sutured, surrounding grimacing heads. They had no idea how such creations had been preserved, but the representations were unbearably realistic; the slashed and often enucleated faces were frozen in atrocious rictuses of pain, crowns of dried blood surrounded the amputations. (246)

In this case as well, the link between the mutilated bodies and the works of art that are discussed in the novel is underlined (the bodies are referred to as "compositions"[40]), and the explicit link to realism is also made, even more so in the French which uses the actual word "realism": "les représentations étaient d'un réalisme insoutenable."[41] In other words, there is a realism here, but it is one that is not sustainable—it is no longer a realism. An extreme form of realism, it also leads away from it, marking a hold on reality that in fact kills off the living.

This scene would need to be read in contrast to Jed's late work, which is also described in elaborate detail in the novel's epilogue and continues the novel's engagement with realism. "I want to give an account of the world" ("Je veux rendre compte du monde") (406): this is the statement—a kind of motto, or formula even—that Jed repeats for more than a page of a forty-page interview that he gives toward the end of his life. Jed has been spending the final years of his life in quiet seclusion on the forested land he was able to buy thanks to the immensely lucrative sales of his art, in particular the Professions and Business series. When the young journalist who has come to interview Jed asks him about his new work, Jed speaks about it while "refus[ing] all comment . . . concentrating on questions of diaphragm, amplitude of focusing, and compatibility between softwares," Jed "chatter" (as the novel puts it) "unfolds, senile and free," giving the impression that the interviewer is letting their subject speak (264).

Before I get to Jed's last works, it is worth recalling, given the realist mantra that Jed repeats as part of the interview, how realism has operated in his career. While Jed's career launches with his photography of technical objects, that project is transformed when he starts photographing Michelin maps (45). In the early work, the photograph was the map and the technical object the territory. When Jed turns the map itself into the photographed territory, an interesting move is accomplished: the ontological distance between the map and the territory, which always inevitably subordinates the representation to the real, appears to have been overcome, with the representation being revealed as a real in its own right, through a mise en abyme of representation (the map of the map). With his photographs of Michelin maps, Jed no longer seems to operate in the ontological gap between the representation and the real, but in the real of representation, which his exhibition title deems more interesting than the map-territory relation.

This continues, I would argue, in Jed's paintings of what he calls "the professions": architecture (he paints his father), writing (his painting of Houellebecq), art (Hirst and Koons), and so on. *The Map and the Territory* begins with Jed at work on what will turn out to be the last in this series, the painting about art making. Although Jed may have abandoned his obsession with Michelin maps, the map-territory relation is clearly still at work here, and the novel's opening paragraphs, which play with the map-territory relation, make that abundantly clear. With the description of the conversation between Hirst and Koons, the reader understands very quickly that they have not been reading a first-degree representation of reality; rather, the novel has offered us, in the form of a linguistic representation, a description of a visual representation (a painting) that is supposed to represent art-making. Like Jed in his work on Michelin maps, Houellebecq offers us not a map of a territory (first-degree representation) but a map of a map, a representation of a representation—and a representation that is about art-making to boot (though hardly art-making of the representational kind—Hirst, Koons).[42]

If Jed's photographs of Michelin maps and paintings of the professions arguably mark the postmodern, meta-realist stage of his career, developing out of the object-oriented realism of his early work, it turns out his late work adds another turn of the screw to this engagement with realism. All of Jed's last pieces were made on his immense property, seven hundred hectares of land (a home that at the same time is a kind of great outdoors—Martin is at home in the outside, so to speak). It appears Martin would drive his car along the road traversing his property, stop the car "simply following the spur of the moment" (265), and then leave a camera there—sometimes for a few hours, sometimes for an entire day or even several days—to film "nature." Martin's frames would occasionally concentrate "on a branch of a beech tree waving in the wind, sometimes on a tuft of grass, the top of a bush of nettles, or an area of loose and saturated earth between two puddles" (265)—but since the novel tells us that such concentration happens only occasionally, the reader is left to assume that most of the time, Jed is simply filming "nature" in general.

At a later stage, Jed would superimpose edited versions of these nature films—"those moving plant tissues, with their carnivorous suppleness, peaceful and pitiless at the same time"; the novel refers to them as "representing how plants see the world"—with his portrayals of "industrial objects—first a cell phone, then a computer keyboard, a desk lamp, and many other objects," in particular those "containing electronic components" (266). Such a process, realized digitally, produces "those long, hypnotic shots where the industrial objects seem to drown, progressively submerged by the proliferation of layers of vegetation." He continues, "Occasionally, they give the impression of struggling, of trying to return to the surface; then they are swept away by a wave of grass and leaves and plunge back into a plant magma, at the same time as their surfaces fall apart, revealing microprocessors, batteries, and memory cards" (267). Around the same time, and as part of the same project, Jed started filming "photographs of all the people he had known": "he fixed them to a neutral gray waterproof canvas, and shot them just in front of his home, this time letting natural decay take its course" (267). "More curiously," the novel continues, "he acquired toy figurines, schematic representations of human beings, and subjected them to the same process" (268). It is unclear whether these films are then also superimposed with the plant films, but the novel suggests that is the case when it mentions "those pathetic Playmobil-type little figurines, lost in the middle of an abstract and immense futurist city, a city which itself crumbles and falls apart, then seems gradually to be scattered across the immense vegetation extending to infinity" (269).

How does this late work relate to the other phases of Jed's work? It seems to loop back to his early photographs of technical objects. Added to the objects here, however, are photographs and other representations of human beings. Both are then subjected to different processes that appear to make those human beings and the things they make disappear, to progressively decay or become swallowed up by the slow, hypnotic rhythms of nature. It may be, as the novel suggests, that when Jed's chatter develops "senile and free," the interviewer lets its subject (Jed) speak; but the point of Jed's late work appears to be to let go of the subject, and let the world appear. Digital video—as opposed to photography, which Jed associates with objects, and painting, which he associates with human beings—is able to accomplish this. That seems to be a return, then, to the territory. However, given Jed's attention to the technical aspects of his filming in the interview, this is clearly not a "naïve" return to nature (a simple return to a position that would recognize the gap between the map and the territory); it is not a return, in other words, to the drawings of flowers that Jed made as a child (17). Instead, it is a return to what one might call an "accursed" nature, a nature that arrives through its representation. Starting from the territory (phase one), and moving to the map (phase two), Jed turns (rather than returns) to a territory that is victorious by dint of its mapping (phase three), thus contracting the two extremes of the map-territory relation into one. What it is victorious over is technical objects and human beings, which are slowly submerged by the "second nature" of representation. We are left with what I propose to call (in view of the fusion of the natural and the artificial that the term realizes) a streaming realism, an artificially accomplished "streaming" of a people- and object-less "natural" world. Jed's last work is the dialectical accomplishment of the tension between the map and the territory, reality and its representation, humanity and the world of objects, into the streaming realism of digital video showing what the novel's last line refers to as "the triumph of vegetation" (17).

In the context of my reading of Houellebecq's novel as a finance novel that engages the reality of today's economy, it is worth noting that Jed's last work abandons both objects and human beings as subjects in his art. Instead, it turns toward plants and (digitally rendered) vegetation as a key interest. Like other of Houellebecq's novels, *The Map and the Territory* thus seems to end in a world without people; in its closing pages, the novel seems to leave humans behind. Jed already did this in his early work, by focusing on objects; he does so again at the end of his life, by focusing on (digitally rendered) plants. If Jed is still pursuing a realism here, it is one without humans. Jed mobilizes it as part of an interest in vegetation. But it is worth noting, I think, that such nonhuman realisms would be needed as well for the representation of contemporary finance; there is a need for such realisms, or at least their incorporation, into representations of contemporary finance if those representations want to be in tune with the reality of digitized trading, for example.

Houellebecq has pursued that specific reinvention of realism in several of his other works, including the already discussed *Whatever*. The project is probably most explicitly realized in his science fiction novel *The Possibility of an Island*, which can be characterized as a software fiction, partly narrated by software agents. Perhaps unsurprisingly, given what I said about the novel as a correlationist genre, *Possibility* is considered Houellebecq's worst novel. It digitizes itself to such an extent that readers can no longer "relate." Then again, given that the key characteristic of contemporary finance—and perhaps of the digitized world in general—might precisely be such nonrelationality, shouldn't nonrelationality be the affect that novels need to take on if they want to write the reality of the contemporary world?

This brings me to another element: speed. Although Jed's last works may ultimately just be showing nature at its own speed, the sense one gets in the novel's final pages is one of "deceleration," of slowing down. Again, if the concern here is still realism, then it seems important given the fact that *The Map and the Territory* is also a finance novel that the novel would highlight speed as one of realism's concerns. It does so not by speeding up realism but by slowing it down and synching it up with the reality of the natural world. Similar experiments would have to happen in realist fiction that seeks to represent finance.

Finally, and to recall the greatest burden that finance poses to narration, there is the problem of information and of how to "explain" finance in the context of a novel. On this count too, Houellebecq can be something like an example, as his novels contain elaborate descriptions of objects. When Jed is discussing with the character Houellebecq why he turned to painting, he indicates the problem with photography was its "abundance of subjects," by which he means: anything, any object even, can be the subject of a photography representation. As an example, he mentions the radiator in

Houellebecq's house. Houellebecq replies that in literature, something can be done with radiators:

> You could easily imagine a thriller involving a big market for thousands of radiators—to equip, for example, all the classrooms of a country—and all the bribes, political interventions, the very sexy sales rep of a Romanian radiator firm. In this context, there could very well be a long description, over several pages, of this radiator and competing models. . . . These radiators are made of cast iron, probably in gray cast iron, with a high level of carbon, whose dangerousness has often been underlined in experts' reports. You might consider it scandalous that this recently built house has been equipped with such old radiators, low-cost radiators in a way, and in the case of an accident—for example, the explosion of the radiators—I could conceivably turn against the manufacturers. (86–87)

In other words: objects such as radiators are a key element of Houellebecq's realism, even if he agrees with Jed that ultimately, the novel he imagines could not be about radiators alone but would need to make them part of a human drama, with characters. Houellebecq thrives on the challenge of the representation of objects and one can find this orientation throughout this work. Note here too the economic dimension of the novel that Houellebecq imagines: it would be a novel about "a big market for thousands of radiators." If some time would need to be spent on the description of the radiators, one imagines that similar attention would need to be paid to the description of the market—and he lists several of its dimensions, for example, bribes and sales reps. This is a call for a realism that would not leave the kind of objectivity and economy that is evoked here behind; it would need to explain, as part of its narrative, the world it is dealing with and that might not be considered worthy of explanation. The scene shows Houellebecq getting excited about the representation of radiators. A realism of objects would, of course, still be a capitalist realism, one that would revolve around the commodity that is central to Marx' general formula of capital. With finance, we have moved beyond that, into the realm of the "digital objects"[43] (and subjects) that Houellebecq writes about in *Possibility of and Island* and at the end of *The Map and the Territory*. Like the artist Jed Martin, Houellebecq is a writer who gets excited about the representation of objects; why would artists and novelists when it comes to the digital object of finance not feel the same?

SIX

Financing the Novel: Ben Lerner's *10:04*

> Lerner's position is always hedged.
>
> —HARI KUNZRU, *"Impossible Mirrors"*[1]

"I became a poet because of Ronald Reagan"

There is a startling moment in Ben Lerner's *10:04* when the narrator—a fictionalized version of Lerner himself—credits Ronald Reagan for his becoming a poet. "Let me allow the preposterousness of what I'm saying to sink in," he begins, "I think I became a poet because of Ronald Reagan and Peggy Noonan."[2] Although he also notes elsewhere in the book that he considers Reagan a mass murderer (in case there is any doubt, in an interview Lerner himself has also noted his dislike for Reagan[3]), Reagan—and his speech writer, Noonan—become tied to the narrator's birth as a poet due to "the way they used poetic language to integrate a terrible event and its image back into a framework of meaning" (112). The event in question is a galactic one: the explosion of the NASA space shuttle Challenger (on January 28, 1986), a disaster that is discussed at multiple points in Lerner's novel. Reagan—or better, poetry—is able to pull the nation together afterward. "Poets [are] the unacknowledged legislators of the world" (113), as the narrator in *10:04* (quoting from Percy Bysshe Shelley's "A Defence of Poetry") puts it.

The association of Reagan with poetic legislation and regulation—*10:04* highlights "the prosody [of the last part of the speech's last sentence], the way the iambs offered both a sense of climax and of closure" (112)—is a bit of a stretch, to be sure. As Franco "Bifo" Berardi has noted, Reagan is more easily associated with an avant-gardist poetics of deregulation—the violation of the rules that "was the legacy left by Rimbaud to the experimentation of the 1900s"—and the convergence of artistic and neoliberal subjectivities in the post-Fordist, cognitive capitalist regimes discussed in the previous chapter.[4] Indeed, Reagan and the policies that his administration put into place in 1981 have become identified with US neoliberalism, with Margaret Thatcher and her "there is no alternative" slogan representing the same thing on the other side of the Atlantic.

I mention that "economic" dimension of the reference to Reagan because Lerner's novel is obsessed with economics, and specifically with finance (whose history is generally tied to neoliberalism, as indicated in chapter 1—as such, it of course predates Reagan's appointment as president). The importance of neoliberalism for Lerner's work has not gone unnoticed: in a review of *10:04*, Hari Kunzru has pointed out that in Lerner's work, which is heavily invested in the second person plural address, "this possible 'you,' the you of community, has been assaulted by the fierce ideological individualism of neoliberalism."[5] Whereas the political dimension of that claim has already received some discussion, its economic focus remains to be explored.[6]

In what follows, I want to build on Kunzru's claim by arguing that *10:04* is a novel about finance and in particular about the financialization of the novel itself. My central argument is that *10:04* can be read as a contemporary novelist's response to the transcendental question that animates this book: the conditions of possibility for a financial realism today. Although *10:04* credits its narrator's birth as a poet to Reagan's Challenger speech, it does this within the form of a novel—not in the form of a poem—and the difference between the novel and poetry will take up an important role in this chapter (as it does in Lerner's writing). "Realism" is one of the two sites in *10:04* where the difference between poetry and the novel is traced; "finance" is the other. *10:04* brings those two sites together to deliver a financial realism at the crossroads of poetry and the novel.

A Finance Novel

It would be difficult to miss the fact that *10:04* is a novel about the future. One way in which the future is written into the novel is through finance, and specifically the financialization of the novel. The novel seems to operate, at least in the beginning, within the future-oriented temporality of the promise and the project. Having published a short story in the *New Yorker*, the narrator in *10:04* is told (by his agent) that he can likely get a "'strong six-figure' advance" for a novel that would revolve around the story (4). "All I had to do," the narrator notes, "was promise to turn [the story] into a novel" (4). Once the narrator has drafted a proposal, "there was a competitive auction among the major New York [publishing] houses"; when his agent asks him how he will "expand the story" into a novel, he answers: "I'll project myself into several futures simultaneously" (4).[7] "Advance," "promise," "proposal," "auction," "project," "futures": it is hard to miss the connections between finance and the future in a discussion about a novel-to-come that might well be the very novel we are reading. After all, part 2 of *10:04* turns out to contain the *New Yorker* story that is discussed here. One thing is clear: the novel's "occasion" reveals a keen sensibility, a heightened awareness, of its own value not so much as a capitalist commodity but in particular as a financial instrument, a tool for speculative value generation—a novel bubble.

Like his narrator's novel, Lerner himself could arguably also be considered a financial instrument: born in 1979 and the author of three books of poetry and one previous novel (a modest, though highly praised, output), he has already been a Fulbright Fellow, a Guggenheim Fellow, and a recipient of the MacArthur "genius" grant. What's next? The Nobel Prize? When a conference about "The Contemporary" was organized at Princeton University in March 2016, Lerner was the most frequently referenced writer in the submitted proposals (10 percent of all proposals mentioned his name).[8] Indeed, seen from a certain point of view, Lerner's literary art could also be read as relentless self-advertising, with advertising's close tie to the future duly noted. Even if one admires Lerner's writing, it's hard to avoid speaking of a Lerner bubble given that much of Lerner's value appears to be derived from what people think he might do "in the future"—from his potential. When Tao Lin introduces Lerner and his work at the beginning of an interview published in *The Believer*, he gives a different twist to this, suggesting that Lerner's books give the impression that "his oeuvre were a single work that is already completed and is being released in parts"—installments, so to speak, of a work that is already there, fully realized.[9] To his credit, Lerner himself seems to be keenly aware of all this, given that *10:04* revolves around an author, modeled after himself, who receives a large sum of money "on spec," as part of a publisher's (well-considered) bet that the author can expand the short story into a successful novel. All of the elements of finance are there—and they are applied to the novel itself. As Maggie Nelson in a review of the novel has put it with respect to the narrator's subject position: he "is on the winning end of an unjustifiable system," but if there is anything that redeems him, it's that "he knows it."[10]

It is key that the subject of discussion is a novel and not a poem: as the narrator notes later on in the book, you couldn't obtain the same effect with poetry, "given the economic marginality of the art," adding that it is "an economic marginality that soon all literature [including the novel] will share" (116). This seems to still accord a privileged role to the novel for the investigation of literature's relation to finance today; for some, it may also cast some suspicion on the novel as an art form that is still economically central—although the money generated by novels (and even by novels-on-contract) seems minimal compared to the price of the artworks (actual artworks, not art-on-contract) discussed in Michel Houellebecq's *The Map and the Territory*.[11]

The distinction between the novel as a capitalist commodity and the novel as financial instrument is important in *10:04* and must be pursued if one wants to assess the novel's exact position on its relation to finance. Although *10:04* is ultimately interested in finance rather than capitalism, that does not mean there is no capitalism, and no Karl Marx (one of the most important theorists of capitalism), in *10:04*. Consider, for example, the narrator's thought when he is stocking up on storm supplies early on in the novel—Hurricane Irene is approaching—and is holding a plastic can of instant coffee: "it was as if the social relations that produced the object in my hand began to glow within it as they were threatened, stirred inside their packaging, lending it a certain aura—the majesty and murderous stupidity of that organization of time and space and fuel and labor becoming visible in the commodity itself now that planes were grounded and the highways were starting to close" (19). "Social relations," "produced," "labor," "commodity": all of these terms point in the direction of Marx and his theory of the commodity as a crystallization of the social relations that are operative in labor. But there are other elements in the quote that must be addressed: "glow," "stir," "aura," and "majesty." If those terms refer to the "fetishization" of the commodity as Marx theorizes it in the first volume of *Capital*,[12] then they seem to be out of place in the quote, for the quote marks precisely a rupture of such fetishization, a becoming visible of the object's conditions of production beyond the alienation produced by their projection. The reference is, more likely though hardly in any straightforward way, to Walter Benjamin and his essay on the work of art in the age of mechanical reproducibility.[13] There, Benjamin argues that artworks lose their "aura" of uniqueness—a certain glow, to be sure—when they become mechanically reproducible—think, for example, of the effect of multiple prints of an art photograph on the photograph's price. As Benjamin sees it, the artwork's aura withers as the result of its multiple reproductions.

That association to Benjamin is reinforced by the fact that the first sentence of the paragraph immediately following the previous quote is taken from the novel's epigraph, a text "typically attributed to Walter Benjamin," as Lerner notes in his acknowledgments (19). (He also indicates that he came across it in the work of the Italian philosopher Giorgio Agamben.) The quote captures Benjamin's peculiar messianism: "Everything will be as it is now, just a little different" (19). If messianism is a reference in *10:04* (and a theme, even), that is no doubt because of the novel's apocalyptic tone. However, if traditional messianism is future-oriented through its reference to the messiah's coming arrival, Benjamin's alternative messianism contracts the future into the present by identifying the "will" with the "is," keeping open only the smallest of differences between them. In other words, there is another approach to the future that the reference to Benjamin introduces and that I will need to come back to later on given that it stands as the epigraph to Lerner's novel.

Echoes of a certain kind of "Marxism" in *10:04* continue: the value of a commodity such as wine is lost on the novel's narrator (20); the narrator blames himself for being "a bourgeois prude incapable of conceiving of the erotic outside of the lexicon of property" (29); the narrator works at the Park Slope Food Coop where, in exchange, "you get to shop at a store with less of a markup than a normal supermarket's; prices are kept down because labor is contributed by members; nobody is extracting profit" (95). But those echoes are interrupted and progressively overtaken by what I consider to be the markers of finance (rather than capitalism). We learn, for example, that the narrator becomes the literary executor for his poet friends Natali and Bernard, and he notes that he is thereby being asked "to conduct their writing into the future" (40). "Money" is not mentioned here, but the story clearly needs to be read in relation to the narrator's own *New Yorker* short story, "The Golden Vanity," which revolves around an author who "would be approached by a university about selling his papers" (55). Since the author is young, however, this leads to the question of "how exactly would you, in your early thirties, have any papers that a university library would be interested in collecting?" (70). The author himself is said to be surprised at this and in his reply "paraphrased the special-collections librarian: because he'd been 'particularly precocious,' her phrase, and because in his twenties he had co-edited a small and now-defunct but influential literary magazine, they suspected he might already be in possession of a 'mature archive'" (70). "Moreover," the story continues, "collecting practices were changing, and papers were now often sold in increments" (70)—a library buys for example one third of someone's papers and then buys the rest later. Here, the "value" question is dominant, and related to the author's writing into the future. If his friends Natali and Bernard ask the author to execute their writings into the future in their old age, the author himself is asked at a young age to do the same. It is, of course, the very story in which those questions are raised that will become the instrument through which the speculative value of the narrator's own novel will be generated. If the story is a commodity, one for which the author may have been paid "approximately eight thousand dollars" (56), it also exceeds its commodity status and begins to operate as a project, proposal, or promise of something bigger that is still to follow—something that, at this point in time, is still potential or virtual but that will, one day, materialize: a novel.

When *10:04* loops back to its beginning—specifically, the narrator's celebratory dinner with his agent—at the end of part 3, the financial dimension of that celebration becomes explicit: "I asked my agent to explain to me once more why anybody would pay such a sum for a book of mine, especially an unwritten one, given that my previous novel, despite an alarming level of critical acclaim, had only sold around ten thousand copies" (154). "Publishers pay for prestige," she explains. "Even if I wrote a book that didn't sell, these presses wanted a potential darling of the critics or someone who might win prizes; it was symbolic capital that helped maintain the reputation of the house even if most of their money was being made by teen vampire sagas or one of the handful of mainstream 'literary novelists' who actually sold a ton of books" (154). The author continues: "This would have made sense to me in the eighties or nineties, when the novel was more or less still a viable commodity form, but why would publishers, all of whom seemed to be perpetually reorganizing, downsizing, scrambling to survive in the postcodex world, be willing to convert real capital into the merely symbolic?" (154). At this point, finance arrives:

> "Keep in mind that your book proposal . . ." my agent said, and then paused thoughtfully, indicating that she was preparing to put something delicately, "your book proposal might generate more excitement among the houses than the book itself."
>
> "What do you mean?"
>
> "Well, your first book was unconventional but really well received. What they're buying when they buy the proposal is in part the idea that your next book is going to be a little more . . . mainstream. I'm not saying they'll reject what you submit, although that's always possible; I'm saying it may have been easier to auction the idea of your next book than whatever you actually draft." (154–55)

"I loved this idea," the author concludes, "my virtual novel was worth more than my actual novel" (155).

Given that what is described here is the financialization of the novel, it is worth pausing over the "love" the author expresses. If what is being described is how a short story is turned into a financial instrument to generate speculative value for a novel that might never materialize, it is worth noting that this is the very logic of the speculative financial bubbles that have been crashing the markets with increasing frequency since the 1970s, Reagan's neoliberalism in the 1980s, the dotcom boom of the 1990s, all the way to the financial crisis of 2008. The author's statement later on in the novel that he credits his birth as a poet to Reagan thus takes on a sinister spin with his expression of love for a logic of financialization that appears to be one of the core problems of today's economy.

Once again, however, *10:04* appears to be very much aware of this: while the author and his agent are discussing the author's book contract, "investment bankers or market analysts in their twenties" are talking loudly at nearby tables. Their "proximity was particularly unwelcome," the author notes, "since I was crossing my art with money more explicitly than ever, trading on my future" (156–57). It is as if the proximity of traders brings out an unwelcome realization that disturbs the author's excitement about his virtual novel being worth more than his actual novel. Ultimately, it is that complicity between the virtual and finance that *10:04* asks us to consider.

Finance and the Virtual

"The virtual"—the potential versus the actual—has revealed itself to be a key notion in Lerner's oeuvre. It plays an important role in Lerner's first novel, *Leaving the Atocha Station.* That novel tells the story of the young poet Adam Gordon's formation and arrival as a successful poet. Set in Madrid, where Adam has traveled on a fellowship, the *Bildungsroman* narrative of formation and arrival is told in parallel to the author's becoming fluent in a foreign language, Spanish. Both those narratives culminate with the ending of Lerner's own novel, staging an intriguing coincidence between the formation and arrival of the novel, linguistic competency, and the accomplished poet. And indeed, *Leaving* productively ties those three strands together in that it is an explicit exploration of the tension between the novel and poetry and associates poetry with the incapacity to fully understand (a foreign) language. Poetry, therefore, seems to take sides with the potential, the possible, and the virtual—with what undoes the actuality of the novel, or of speaking any language fluently, into something else. "I'm going to write a novel that dissolves into a poem" (158), the narrator of *10:04* tells his agent, and that very dissolution haunts all of Lerner's attempts at prose so far.

However, it is worth assessing the role of the virtual in Lerner's work in a little more detail. The association between poetry and the potential, the possible, and the virtual, has become most explicit in Lerner's essay

The Hatred of Poetry, which refers back to both of his novels. *10:04* includes, for example, the story of Caedmon, as related by Bede, and his vocation to sing about creation (109), that is also discussed in *Hatred of Poetry*;[14] Lerner's essay begins with a discussion of the line from Marianne Moore's "Poetry"—"I, too, dislike it"—that already appeared in *Leaving*, as a quote in English, during a Spanish-language conversation.[15] In *Hatred*, Lerner recalls the work of Allen Grossman, who "in an essay on Hart Crane . . . develops his notion of a 'virtual poem'—what we might call poetry with a capital 'P,' the abstract potential of the medium as felt by the poet when called upon to sing—and opposes it to the 'actual poem,' which necessarily betrays that impulse when it joins the world of representation."[16] In other words, poems exist in reference to another poem, a virtual "Poem," whose ideal "song" they inevitably betray; poetry therefore "writes" a kind of impossibility, the poet's incapacity of rendering the virtual Poem into representation. The virtual Poem can only join the realm of representations by becoming destroyed: all actually existing poetry is "virtual Poetry" that has been destroyed. This is key for Lerner's explanation of why people hate poetry so much: it is because they love the virtual Poem. Their hatred is meant "to burn the actual off the virtual like fog."[17] "Great poets as different as Keats and Dickinson," he argues, "express their contempt for merely actual poems by developing techniques for virtualizing their own compositions—by dissolving the actual poem into an image of the Poem literary form cannot achieve."[18] If the tension between the virtual and the actual is central to Lerner's writing, if as a writer he is arguably "in love" with that tension (as we might gather from what is said in *10:04*), then *10:04* asks us to consider the rather difficult question of that love's relation to the financialization that *10:04* associates with the virtual.

For I would suggest that Grossman's theory of the virtual Poem can be read in two directions. On the one hand, it contracts the virtual into the present, and reveals all poetry to be destroyed Poetry. All poetry has somehow undergone some kind of catastrophe when it was moved from the virtual Poem to being an actual poem. For that, one might hate it. On the other hand, and as Lerner's discussion of Keats and Dickinson clearly shows, such a theory of poetry nevertheless keeps the notion of a virtual Poem intact, as some ideal, future thing that someone, some day, might be able to write. It is that Poem that we love. But there is arguably a problem at the level of affect here: Why would one hate imperfect actuality, and love perfect virtuality? Wouldn't it make more sense to learn to love imperfect actuality (what Giorgio Agamben in his work has theorized as "the irreparable"[19]) and to learn to hate perfect virtuality? But what about the aesthetic, ethical, and political force of "the utopian" in such a situation? Could a love for imperfect actuality ultimately stifle *any* future orientation—could such a love mark neoliberalism's ultimate scaling down of the transformative imagination?[20] Is there no alternative?

If *10:04* as a novel plays a major role in thinking through the novel's relation to capitalism, virtuality, and financialization, the novel focuses most of that discussion around "art," specifically the art of Alena, a friend of the novel's narrator. On this count, Lerner's novel continues many of the concerns discussed in the previous chapter. Early on in the novel, we learn:

> [One of Alena's shows] consisted of images and a few objects she had deftly aged: she'd painted a portrait from a contemporary photograph and then somehow distressed it . . . so that it was networked with fine cracks, making it appear like a painting from the past. There was a painting based on an image downloaded from the Internet and then enlarged of a young woman whose eyes are lined with running shadow and upon whose face a man beyond the frame has ejaculated; she stares at the viewer as if from another century, the craquelure confusing genres and lending the image tremendous gravity; the title read: *The Picture of Sasha Grey.* Alena had painted several magnificent Abstract Expressionist imitations and then subjected them to her method; the Pollocks appeared completely unchanged, others seemed as if they'd been recovered from the rubble of MoMA after an attack or had been defrosted from a future ice age. (27)

Alena's practice, which recalls the late phase of Jed Martin's work in Houellebecq's *The Map and the Territory,* also anticipates Lerner's description of the work of an artist called Sonja (a version, it seems, of Alena) who in Lerner's *New Yorker* short story "The Polish Rider" has a gallery show in which every painting depicts, in a different historical style, the famous "fraternal kiss" between Erich Honecker and Leonid Brezhnev from 1979, the year of the narrator's (as well as Lerner's) birth.[21]

That early description of Alena's work culminates in *10:04*'s discussion of her "totaled art" project, modeled after Elka Krajewska's actually existing Salvage Art Institute (as Lerner notes in his acknowledgments). With an artist friend called Peter, Alena has started an institute that collects and intends to display for public viewing "totaled" art, meaning, art that has somehow been damaged and, as a result, has been declared to have "zero value" (129). In some cases, the damage is visible, even to the untrained eye; but in others—and those will turn out to be the cases that most interest the narrator, as Nicholas Brown has points out[22]—it is not. That begs the question of what exactly caused the object to be labeled as "damaged." Regardless, "totaled" artworks are works that "were formally demoted from art to mere objecthood and banned from circulation, removed from the market" (130).

It is probably no coincidence that when the novel's narrator visits Alena's institute, he is handed "the pieces of shattered Jeff Koons balloon dog sculpture" (131). "It was wonderful," he notes, "to see an icon of art world commercialism and valorized stupidity shattered" (151). When Alena picks up one of the smaller pieces from the narrator's hand "and hurled it onto the hardwood, where it shattered," she hissed "It's worth nothing" (132). The declaration gains part of its power from the fact that Koons is one of the most expensive living artists—a fact that Houellebecq also exploits in his novel.

The visit to the Institute for Totaled Art has a profound effect on the narrator. Contemplating a Cartier-Bresson that is part of Alena's collection, he notes:

> It had transitioned from being a repository of immense financial value to being declared of zero value without undergoing what was to me any perceptible material transformation—it was the same, only totally different. This was a reversal of the kind of recontextualization associated with Marcel Duchamp, still—unfortunately, in my opinion—the tutelary spirit of the art world; this was the opposite of the "readymade" whereby an object of utility—a urinal, a shovel—was transformed into an object of art and an art commodity by the artist's fiat, by his signature. (133)

Koons is the primary target of that process, but the novel also mentions Damien Hirst, who appears with Koons in the Jed Martin painting that is destroyed early on in Houellebecq's novel (133).

Clearly, what fascinates *10:04*'s narrator is not so much the valuation of the artwork but its devaluation, or better, revaluation: how can the artwork be removed from the art market? It's worth noting that the author captures those questions in capitalist terms. He describes the artwork's removal from the art market as an artwork no longer being "a commodity fetish; it was art before or after capital" (134)—that is part of his fascination with it. He also explicitly gives this before or after a messianic dimension: in Alena's project, art is "saved from something" "in the messianic sense," "saved for something": "An art commodity that had been exorcised (and survived the exorcism) of the fetishism of the market was to me a utopian readymade—an object for or from the future where there was some other regime of value than the tyranny of price" (134). The author is overwhelmed by the genius of this revaluation, of this other regime of value. Ultimately, Alena's art and what it accomplishes are associated with the alternative messianism that the author finds in Benjamin: everything will be as it is now, just a little different (135).

In that sense, Alena's works of totaled art seem to stand in stark distinction to the author's own novel project, which is worth a strong, six-figure advance. The scene in which the novelist expresses his "love" for the fact that his virtual novel is worth more than his actual novel (and thereby expressing his love for the financialization of his own novel) actually comes after his visit to Alena's project, which now comes to haunt it.

With Alena's project and with the author's novel we have two very different instances of the art-money connection, and this ultimately asks the reader to assess how *10:04* relates to this connection. Indeed, the visit to Alena's project operates as a turning point in the novel, a kind of conversion where the author begins to actively undo the novel's tie to financialization in order to push it more in the direction of Alena's totaled art.

On this count, *10:04* reveals in its closing pages that it is emphatically not the novel that its author was contracted to write. As the author is experiencing the aftermath of another New York storm (Hurricane Sandy), he references the image on the cover of "my book": a photograph showing the dark post-Sandy Manhattan skyline, with the exception of one building that is brightly lit. "Later we would learn," the author writes, that "it was Goldman Sachs . . . the investment banking firm" (236–37).[23] Given that this image is actually on the cover of *10:04*, this suggests that the author is referring here to his own book. He adds, apropos of that book: "not the one I was contracted to write . . . but the one I've written in its place for you, to you, on the very edge of fiction" (237). At this crucial moment—one that uses, importantly, the second person address that Kunzru has observed to be critical of neoliberalism—the author inserts a minimal difference between *10:04* and the book he was contracted to write, thus separating *10:04* as the novel that we are currently holding in our hands (the actual novel) from the financialized (virtual) Novel, the one he was contracted to write.

The author's wish, in the book's closing pages, seems to be to end up, in this novel that is heavy on the financialization, with a work of totaled art: that is the "project" that he seeks to accomplish. Indeed, a few pages earlier, he imagines after parting ways with Alena "waking the next morning in the Institute for Totaled Art" (210)—he seems to want to be part of it, to belong there. It is no coincidence that in the couple of pages immediately following this flight of the imagination, the author is shown to "delete" some writing from his manuscript (210–11)—writing that is, of course, still reproduced as part of *10:04*—as if in an attempt to destroy his own book and thereby take it out of the art market, reduce it to zero value.

But can the author accomplish this? The novel's closing riff—which crucially mobilizes the future tense (although with no other major effect on the writing, as Pieter Vermeulen has noted) only to end with a "poetic" present (borrowed from Walt Whitman)—is introduced by "I want to say something to the schoolchildren of America" (239). The reader knows that this line is lifted from Reagan's Challenger speech, but at this point the line is not quoted nor explicitly attributed to Reagan. In other words, the author appears to be identifying with Reagan, at the beginning of a monologue that explicitly recalls the "strong six figures" that he was offered for his book (240). The book ends not with Whitman but with a quote from Reagan's State of the Union speech on February 4, 1986, in which Reagan explicitly refers to the film *Back to the Future*, which provides the title for Lerner's novel (four minutes after ten is the exact time in 1955 when Marty McFly can travel back to the future, i.e., 1985). Why this return to Reagan? Why end with Reagan, after already having credited one's birth as a poet to this figure of neoliberalism?

Does this throw the reader back into the phantasmatic dimension of the novel's association with totaled art: the fact that the novel might *want* to be totaled art but ultimately knows very well that it isn't? After all, the novel makes it clear that waking up at the Institute for Totaled Art "never happened" (210). That is somewhat of a refrain in *10:04*, which repeatedly describes scenes only to take them back by saying that they never happened.[24] What is going on here? Does this mark Lerner's continued attachment to Grossman's notion of the virtual, which in *10:04* marks the removal of Lerner's actual novel from some kind of ideal Novel—the Novel he was contracted to write, but never wrote? Might that give us reason to hate the failure of *10:04*, in the same way that poetry, through its reference to the ideal Poem that it can never achieve, might trigger our hatred? Does that mean, however, that *10:04* keeps intact the notion of the ideal Novel as a kind of reference point in which we continue to be invested? Is Lerner, like those great poets he mentions, someone who virtualizes his own composition by dissolving the actual novel into an image of the Novel that literary form cannot achieve? And, to ask the most difficult question: does he thereby ultimately loop back to Reagan as well as the logic of financialization?

Alena's Institute for Totaled Art intervenes here, initially at the level of affect: first, through Lerner's narrator, we learn to love totaled art, in a way that invites us to also love *10:04* for not being the Novel Lerner was contracted to write. We love it as a failure. In other words, the novel works against its financialization by tearing down a future-oriented, traditional messianic logic that structures the novelist's advance contract, his being paid on spec. While the novelist states—with some discomfort—that he loves the fact that his virtual Novel is worth more than his actual novel, I would argue that his novel in fact teaches us the opposite, and less than the opposite even: to love our actual, irreparable novels more than our virtual ones. This means to undo the financial logic of the virtual, as well as its messianic promise, not simply into the actual commodity but into the totaled actual commodity.

Small differences are important when it comes to the scope of this totaling. The most extreme illustration of totaled art is probably Alena smashing a piece of a Koons artwork to pieces. It leads not only to the destruction of value but also to the destruction of art. The Challenger explosion, which plays an important role in *10:04*, is probably a dark mirroring of that. It marks, in a way, the total destruction of value and of the future. It is, in a way, the novel's 9/11, which Karlheinz Stockhausen infamously compared to a work of art—a work of art with no future. But such destruction is not where the novel's interest ultimately lies. Rather, the novel appears to be most interested in situations where value is destroyed but the work of art seems to be left intact—in a future of the work of art where the work of art will be almost exactly as it is now—with the difference being that it is without financial value. That is *also* why the novel is interested in Reagan: because of his continued attachment to the future, even after the Challenger explosion. Given that "difference" and "the future" are themselves key elements of financialization, one would have to read *10:04* as intervening in our understanding of both (the future and difference) in order to break with financialization, and in order to save a notion of the future from it. To allude to Theodor Adorno's famous phrase about poetry after Auschwitz, the point of *10:04* is not that there can be no future after the Challenger explosion; it is, rather, to think a different kind of future. The novel argues the same with respect to financialization. To say that there can be no future after finance would be to let finance win—to grant that there can be no alternative future.

As its title indicates, *10:04* does not attempt to turn us away from the future in its criticism of financialization, but to lead us back to it, or back to a different kind of future.[25] Finance and neoliberalism, *10:04* appears to be saying, cannot hegemonize our future; they cannot have the last word on the future, as if the future can only be financial or neoliberal. Finance doesn't have the monopoly on our future. There is a certain beauty, then, to the author of *10:04* in part learning this lesson from Reagan: Reagan insisted on the future in his speech about the Challenger disaster, and *10:04* appropriates that speech in order to think another kind of future, different from the neoliberal one that Reagan was promoting. In other words, *10:04* uses Reagan's speech to tell us that there is an alternative. The fight against finance and neoliberalism takes place in *10:04* on the terrain of the future and its author, like Reagan, wants to speak to the schoolchildren of America, this time with a different message, a message about a different future. One imagines that this partly motivates the novel's pedagogical subplot, about its narrator self-publishing a book with the eight-year-old called Roberto that's titled "To the Future" (225)—a publication that is funded with the narrator's book advance.

That becomes most obvious in the novel's closing line, which appears to shift from prose to poetry, and seems to be quoted, in part, from the 1860 version of Walt Whitman's "Crossing Brooklyn Ferry." The novel seems to dissolve here into a poem, as announced earlier in *10:04*. Such a reading appears to be reinforced by the fact that Whitman appears to have deleted the very line that is quoted in *10:04* from later editions of *Leaves of Grass*; in other words: we are here in the space of the deleted text that *10:04* opened up for us earlier on. However, and given that the lines are quoted in verse form and not as a poem, one might also read this as poetry being contracted into the novel, as poetry become prose. Prose and poetry are ruined in this closing line, and we learn to love quite simply what is, which is nevertheless a little different.

Realism ("A cut across worlds")

I now want to consider how the problematic of the virtual and of finance is tied to that of realism in Lerner's novel. One could argue that this is immediately foreground by the choice of the novel as a genre, whose history is closely associated with realism; but it is also marked by Lerner's interest in the future tense, which seems to mark a difference to realism, whose characteristic tenses are rather the present (in a strict, philosophical sense) and the past. Of course, if realism is an aesthetic of the present or the past, it is an odd present or past, to be sure: not future, they always also—as fictions—proceed in a minimal difference from the actual present or past, a difference that Lerner in his autofictions—all of which revolve around narrators that are very similar to Lerner himself—has explored consistently. Realism hardly merely offers an objective description of the world; it always operates in a minimal distinction from it and thrives in a fictitiousness that opens up, as Anna Kornbluh has suggested, its connection to what Karl Marx already called "fictitious capital."[26] In *10:04*, Lerner pushes this connection—both realism and finance operate within what he calls "a cut across worlds"—to the extreme.

Realism appears in *10:04* as a key concern, starting from the novel's early discussion of Jules Bastien-Lepage's painting *Joan of Arc*. "Bastien-Lepage was attacked," the narrator notes, "for his failure to reconcile the ethereality of the angels with the realism of the future saint's body, but that 'failure' is what makes it one of my favorite paintings. It's as if the tension between the metaphysical and physical worlds, between two orders of temporality, produces a glitch in the pictorial matrix" (9). This is most clearly marked in

Bastien-Lepage's painting through Joan of Arc's left hand, which seems to disappear into the background, that is, the "future saint" is being pulled into the metaphysical realm. The narrator doesn't comment on this, but the spatiality of this pulling is odd, for Joan appears to be pulled forward, or maybe sideways, whereas the three angels in the painting are behind her. In other words, Joan appears to irresistibly be pulled into a future to which her back is turned—a reading that reinforces the novel's "back to the future" leitmotiv,[27] as well as resonates with Walter Benjamin's presence in the novel and Benjamin's famous story about the angel of history, represented through Paul Klee's image that is reproduced in Lerner's novel with the caption: "The storm irresistibly propels him into the future to which his back is turned" (25).

In this case too, the issue is driven to a climax (twice) in the context of a discussion of a work of art. The first is the novel's discussion of Christian Marclay's *The Clock*, a twenty-four-hour video montage "of thousands of scenes from movies and a few from TV edited together so as to be shown in real time; each scene indicates the time with a shot of a timepiece or its mention in dialogue; time in and outside of the film is synchronized" (52). The narrator puts it very simply: "*The Clock* is a clock" (52), indicating the (impossible) co-incision of a representation with the reality it represents.

It's easy to see why *The Clock* would have been of interest to the author of *10:04*—and I don't just mean because of the fact that "Big Ben" appears in it several times (the novel's narrator, we learn, is also called Ben). Like Jorge Luis Borges's imaginary map that I alluded to in the introduction, Marclay's work seems to overcome the gap between reality and its representation—"the ultimate collapse of fictional time into real time, a work designed to obliterate the distance between art and life, fantasy and reality" (54). This gap plays an important role in Lerner's work, for example in *Leaving the Atocha Station*, which pitches poetry against prose on this count and suggests prose is no more than a pareidolic form that "arranges stimuli into a significant image or sound . . . faces in the moon, animals in clouds" (69).[28] Poetry, on the other hand, comes closer to real being, and it is in the novel's poetic undoing that a higher degree of realism is achieved.

However, it quickly turns out that *The Clock* does not really accomplish this, for the author finds himself checking his watch while watching *The Clock*—something that's obviously unnecessary, given that one is watching a clock that is synchronized with real time. It is that habitual gesture that makes the author conclude, at a more philosophical level, that while the video's minutes were "mathematically indistinguishable" from real time, "they were nevertheless minutes from different worlds"—and so *The Clock* ends up underlining precisely the difference between reality and its representation that it seems to overcome. It indicates that "a distance remained between art and the mundane," between a representation and the world. "*Everything will be as it is now*," the paragraph concludes, "*just a little different*."

It is at this point that the author decides "to write more fiction—something I'd promised my poet friends I wasn't going to do"—and it is that decision that leads to "The Golden Vanity," which leads to the contracted Novel and, ultimately, to *10:04* (which is not the contracted Novel). If the author was born as a poet thanks to Reagan, we are witnessing a kind of afterbirth here of the author as a second-time novelist. But the drama of the moment begs the question: why does he decide to write fiction at this time, rather than poetry? Doesn't *The Clock* show, precisely, that fiction will never be able to accomplish the representation of reality? Wouldn't it be more appropriate to give up on fiction at this point and throw oneself wholly into poetry? If Marclay's *The Clock* comes close to being the perfect representation, it does so not as a narrative but as something that's more like a poem.[29] Is the decision to write fiction, then, a moving away from that, into the realm of art rather than the realm of the real?

If Lerner's project in *Leaving the Atocha Station* could still be read as the novel's poetic undoing into the real,[30] in *10:04* the focus shifts toward rethinking the art of the novel. It's not about dissolving the novel into a poem but about asking how one can write novels otherwise.[31] As Lerner indicates in an interview with Karl Smith, "collapsing the border between art and life" is not his project; he is interested "in complicating that border—but only within the aesthetic form."[32] So there is a continued attachment to the aesthetic form here that has to be acknowledged. Again, Adorno's text on cultural criticism can be useful. Lerner is no Karl Ove Knausgård, in the sense that he does not write "anti-fiction";[33] one might characterize it, rather, as counter-fiction. On this particular point, Lerner has in an interview (critically) referenced Fredric Jameson, whose work plays an important role in this book: "Fredric Jameson talks about how Hollywood cinema offers imaginary solutions to real problems and that's like the traditional Marxist understanding of art; but there's also this idea that you can attempt to really present and bring into the domain of experience and criticism the contradictions of your moment. And contradictions can be really moving and beautiful in addition to really hilarious and disturbing, you know?"[34]

In *Leaving*, the novel's salvation is relegated to the realm of poetry. In *10:04*, that is no longer the case: poetry is contracted into the novel to remove it from that messianic promise, to liberate a kind of alternative messianism within *both* the novel and poetry—the messianism of everything will be as it is now, just a little different.

That is the overarching view of totaled art, whether fiction or poetry. *10:04* focuses on the novel in this context because it has a less marginal economic role—and the focus in *10:04* is quite clearly on finance. But a similar argument could be made about poetry. If it seemed in Lerner's first novel that some of what was going on was the pitching of poetry against the novel and vice versa in the project of writing reality, *10:04* moves away from that into a broader concern with art and finance. To write against finance means to undermine the promissory structure not only of the novel-on-contract but also of a virtual Realism that the novel promises to deliver one day. Perhaps that is why the realist novel, like poetry, has also accrued some hatred: because it can never deliver on that count.

It may be that there are better media for that purpose: photography, or film, for example. In general, *10:04* takes an art-oriented approach, showing how artists undermine the "reality" effect of those media. *10:04* does draw the Challenger disaster into the orbit of this conversation, pointing out that many remember watching the disaster "live" on TV. However, the narrator also claims that "almost nobody saw it live" (111). Most "major broadcast stations had cut away before the disaster" and what most Americans saw were "taped replays" (111). So as far as the "live" event goes, the Challenger disaster cannot be appropriated as such. What many people did watch live, however, "was Ronald Reagan's address to the country"—and this is what makes the author decide to become a poet. However, if Reagan's address is live, what is praised in the author's description of it, the moment when the address connects with poetry, is not so much its live-ness as the fact that Reagan, by mobilizing poetry, was able to draw the terrible disaster "back into a framework of meaning" (112): it is a moment of law-making ("poets were the unacknowledged legislators of the world") where the "live" event is in fact turned into "law," into art. Poetry, then, doesn't operate as a reality fetish but as a law-making practice—further justifying my reading of the final line of the novel as poetry's contraction into prose rather than prose's dissolution into poetry.

Ultimately, and after the debunking of finance and traditional messianism, *10:04* turns its energies toward realism, and how it is caught up between poetry and the novel. Thus, it takes realism out of a financial and traditional, messianic logic of promising the real. That is not, *10:04* seems to say, what the realist aesthetic does; it does not partake in the future in that way. Instead, realism writes the future otherwise, as a minimal difference of what is, according to which everything that is will be as it is now—just a little different. This has something to do with the totaling of realism, with realism's entering into the Institute for Totaled Art—as long as one doesn't imagine that entry as a literal destruction.

If such a totaling would mark realism's dissociation from finance, its becoming tied to a different sense of the future, it is important to point out that it would also insert a rift into realism's connection to capitalism, since it would seek to remove realism from the realm of the commodity. It is on that count that *10:04* takes on the "capitalist realism" of Margaret Thatcher's neoliberal mantra, "there is no alternative." In Lerner's words:

> David Graeber talks about how capitalism has been a total failure as an economic policy—most of us don't believe it can go on, we think it's going to destroy the planet if it hasn't already, that it depends on the immiseration of all these people, it doesn't deliver the shit it says it's going [to] deliver except for the very rich and so on and so forth. Graeber says it's an amazing failure as an economic system but it's an amazing triumph as an ideology: everything thinks it can't go on and nobody really believes it can be replaced, right?[35]

On that last count *10:04*, and the other kind of realism it advocates, seeks to intervene—but in a very particular way. Neither financial/neoliberal nor capitalist, realism would be able to begin to explore a future where it is just as it is now, although also a little different: totaled in that particular sense and all the more loved because of it.

No Future?

That leaves us with a nagging political question—a question that is very much present in *10:04*, given, for example, the part of the novel in which the narrator hosts an Occupy Wall Street protestor at his Brooklyn apartment—namely, what actual change does such an alternative, Benjaminian messianic approach ultimately bring? It's a nice way for Lerner to reason himself out of the complicities of his novel's financialization into a novelistic thinking of an alternative future, but what is its political translation? If Graeber is calling for the "replacing" of capitalist ideology by something else, can Benjamin's alternative messianism really bring such a change? Or is it, ultimately, too weak for that? Is *10:04* ultimately a revolutionary or a conservative novel? Does its conservatism ultimately come from its continued investment, however minimal, in the future? Should it have sought to find the utopian on the far side of the future, in a contemporaneity of change that claims to be postfuturist?

In her review of *10:04*, Maggie Nelson references Lee Edelman's book *No Future* when she discusses the subplot of how the novel's narrator impregnates his friend, Alex.[36] As she sees it, *10:04* can be seen to develop in relation to Edelman's book, which argues "against something [Edelman] calls 'reproductive futurism,' in which all politics are cast as taking place on behalf of the innocent child."[37] Although *10:04* continues the "reproductive futurism" that Edelman polemically rages against—note that Edelman characterizes such futurism early on in his book in economic terms, as a "Ponzi scheme"[38]—its particular version of it, albeit the same, is definitely also a little different: it's a reproductive futurism that has been effected by Benjamin's weak messianism. And those who are with Edelman may consider that a cop-out.

Nelson of course may have her own reasons for aligning Lerner with this particular stance: her book *The Argonauts*, which as far as genre goes can be associated with Lerner's *10:04*, also revolves around "reproductive futurism," even if it too is (as the title suggests) a reproductive futurism that is very much transformed—so much so that it might ultimately no longer look like what Edelman makes it out to be.[39] Nelson's (as well as Lerner's) futures have something decidedly queer to them, challenging Edelman's identification of the queer with "no future." It is probably worth noting in this context that *The Argonauts* was a critical success—leading to a *New Yorker* profile, a National Book Critics Award, and a MacArthur Fellowship. In other words, here is another autofiction (or a work of "auto-theory," as Nelson has referred to her own work) that, rather than rejecting the future, critically dabbles in it and finds success—including financial success, given the "genius grant." For Nelson, that's not a problem: part of what *10:04* teaches her is that one should "not [be] ashamed of the desire to make a living doing what we love, while also daring to imagine 'art before or after capital.'"[40] One might quibble about how "to make a living" matches up to "a strong six-figure advance" or a MacArthur Fellowship, but I won't.[41] My point is that this is not the radical position that there can be no poetry after Auschwitz; the question is, rather, how to write poetry otherwise. With respect to finance, then, or even capitalism for that matter, it seems the move would likely be the same: Nelson and Lerner are not raging against it, and calling for its end. They might imagine it; but ultimately, they are not ashamed to make their living within it. They might be reluctant entrepreneurs, but they are entrepreneurs nevertheless.

Edelman's book suggests there may be other options—indeed, *10:04* includes those other options when it has Alena smash the Jeff Koons artwork to pieces, or through its focus on the Challenger explosion. But Lerner (like Nelson) is no punk.[42] For the punk position, one may want to turn to Berardi's *After the Future*, which makes the case that with the financial crisis of 2008, the twentieth century's belief in the future came to an end. This belief, which Berardi ties to futurism and avant-garde politics in general, is in his view definitively shipwrecked with the 2008 collapse of housing market, at which point politics (as a result of a process that Berardi dates back to the 1970s) detaches itself from the future. "Life" has been accelerated or sped up, up to this destructive point at which Berardi feels compelled to declare the end of the future—and the end of accelerationism and speed. If futurism could, for the longest time, harbor the possibility of an alternate future, now that the future has arrived, we see that it is actually no different, or worse even.[43]

One might begin to wonder whether the continued investment in the future as one finds it in Lerner is not in part a consequence of a white, male subjectivity that hasn't suffered the same kind of catastrophe as its black, female, or queer counterparts; for whom things have, to put it simply, never looked quite as grim. Nelson makes Lerner's subjectivity—"young, white, Ivy League–educated American male"[44]—part of her discussion of *10:04*, but she argues that Lerner's awareness of it, of his being "on the winning end of an unjustifiable system,"[45] makes up for that. However, it may be that the two—Lerner's subjectivity and his continued investment in the future, albeit a different future—may have to be considered together, with that continued *investment* as linked to that subjectivity, and in the realization that both are tied to the "weak" understanding of totaling that one finds in *10:04*. Unlike the part of Koons's art that is smashed to pieces, both Lerner's subjectivity and the future survive their totaling in *10:04*, looking as they are now, just a little different. It may be, however, that such weak messianism is not enough when it comes to the economic and political tasks of today. In particular in view of the result of the 2016 presidential elections in the United States, which was read by many as a certain subjectivity's claim to the future, it seems that another response may be needed.

I am not sure what such a response would look like. Berardi calls for passivity, "refusal of participation": "Radical passivity means active withdrawal, and withdrawal means creation of spaces of autonomy where solidarity can be rebuilt, and where self-relying communities can start a process of proliferation, contagion, and eventually, of reversal of the trend."[46] For Berardi, that means abandoning "the illusion of the future."[47] At certain points, that withdrawal begins to sound a lot like the discussion of totaled art in *10:04*: "Let's withdraw our intelligence from the race of capitalist growth and national identity, let's withdraw our creativity and our time from productive competition."[48] Withdrawing creativity from capitalism: isn't that what totaled art is all about? The question then may have to be thrown back at Berardi: why does the withdrawal he advocates have to be completely severed from the future? As I already asked earlier: Wouldn't it mean to let neoliberalism and finance win if we let them destroy our future, hegemonize our future, scale it down until there is hardly anything left? Shouldn't the struggle take place on the terrain *of* the future, rather than "after it," as the title of Berardi's book proposes?

That last path seems to be the one Lerner has chosen, possibly in view of some of the conclusions that Berardi reaches, emphasizing from the opening pages of *10:04* the law-making rather than the law-breaking capacities of poetry, and thus poetic regulation rather than poetic deregulation. If Bifo associates experimentation with the latter, *10:04* seems to show that it can just as well be tied to the former, and that it is worth pursuing that association for the sake of the future—a future that, similarly, *can* but *doesn't have to be* a neoliberal or financial one. If Berardi is a kind of nostalgic proponent of postfuturism, Lerner refuses to leave the future behind; I would argue that he can be said to be writing or working *through* the future, in order to ultimately write *to* another kind of future (as the title of the book his narrator self-publishes with Roberto puts it).

Minimalist Realism

10:04 accomplishes a similar gesture with respect to realism, which it doesn't abandon but seeks to practice otherwise. One could recall here James Wood's infamous review of Zadie Smith's *White Teeth*, in which Wood launched the term "hysterical realism" to refer to the *recherché* postmodernism that characterizes a slew of information-heavy novels that he considers to be pathological reflections of the digital age. Those novels could be characterized as "maximalist" given the expansive approach they take to the information age's challenge to realist representation. Although *10:04* arguably includes traces of the information novels that Wood characterizes, it nevertheless feels like a very different kind of novel; compared to the door-stopping tomes that Stefano Ercolino writes about in *The Maximalist Novel*, *10:04* is rather slim.[49] If most of the novelists that Ercolino and Wood discuss are aligned with postmodernism, Lerner is generally situated at some distance from that, announcing the arrival of a new form of novel writing associated with, for example, Chris Kraus, W. G. Sebald, Teju Cole, Sheila Heti, Karl Ove Knausgård, or Geoff Dyer—all "realists," in a way, or authors who have taken on the problematic of realism in their post-postmodernist writings. In view of Lerner's extensive discussion of the work of Donald Judd in the fourth section of *10:04*, I am inclined to characterize the particular kind of realism that can be found in Lerner's novel as "minimalist"—partly in contrast to the novels that Wood and Ercolino discuss, but mostly in recognition of the transformed realism that, surprisingly, the narrator of *10:04* finds in Judd's work.[50]

The fourth part of Lerner's novel takes place in Marfa, Texas, where the narrator has traveled for an artist residency: he is supposed to be working on a poem, but the tension between poetry and prose traverses his entire stay there. When he is introduced as "a novelist" at a party, he adds that he is "more of a poet" (184), and the novel's prose several times takes on the layout of poetry (though as far as I can tell with no other significant differences that would clearly identify the text as "poetry," even if they may also have been published as such elsewhere). Given the importance of the tension between poetry and prose for Lerner's engagement with realism, it should probably come as no surprise that representation, reflection, and mimesis appear to be a key concern in this part of the novel as well.

Consider, for example, how, on his first night in Marfa, the narrator walks through the dark town, which has been "an 'art tourism' destination ever since Donald Judd established the Chinati Foundation in the eighties, a museum just outside of town that presents Judd's large-scale works in permanent installation, along with work by his contemporaries" (164). Walking up to an interesting-looking building, the narrator tries to look through one of its side windows and sees "a series of John Chamberlain sculptures, which are largely hewn from chrome-plated and painted steel, often the mangled bodies of cars"—"an art of the totaled," as the narrator explicitly points out (165). Stepping back from the window, the narrator "regarded his work through my own faint reflection in the window," a description that seems to anticipate the author's wish, in the fifth and final part of the book, to wake up in the Institute for Totaled Art.

The description recalls, through its very phrasing, a moment in W. G. Sebald's *Austerlitz*, where Jacques Austerlitz, looking at the objects collected behind the windows of a shop in Terezin (formerly the Theresienstadt camp), is able to recognize "my own faint shadow image barely perceptible among them."[51] When this meaningful moment of self-recognition occurs in *Austerlitz*, it is most directly in reference to the Holocaust, and less directly in reference to a broader history of destruction, the way in which time's all-consuming progress tends to ultimately ruin almost everything that is caught up in its dimension. In other words, the reference here is the past, and the question is how the present could have survived its destruction. Given the destructiveness of the past, how is it that the past allowed for any future—the future of our present? In more messianic terms, how is it that anything was saved from the past's destruction?

When Lerner sees his reflection in Chamberlain's totaled art, similar notions are in play, although Lerner's discussion of totaled art earlier in the novel evidently adds to Sebald's questions an economic dimension. That involves, I would argue, insisting more on the future: although Chamberlain usually worked with Oldsmobiles, and although his sculptures thus arguably represent a way of saving objects from the past—from time's forward-moving destruction—in my view the work also has a Futurist dimension, in that it flirts with that movement's aestheticization of violent, technologically driven destruction (the car plays an important role, for example, in Filippo Marinetti's "Manifesto of Futurism").

In *10:04*, the scene introduces the theme of reflection, which is picked up again immediately afterward when the narrator, upon turning into the garage of his Marfa residence, sees his "headlights reflected green off the eyes of a small animal." "The *tapetum lucidum*," he continues, "the 'bright tapestry' behind the eyes, bounces visible light back through the retina, making the pupils glow" (166). This then develops into a late-night confrontation with another Marfa resident, living in a house just like the narrator's across the street from him—or, as the narrator puts it, "in the reflection of my house across the street" (169)—whom he imagines to be the ghost of the dead poet Robert Creeley. It develops into the claim, now related to the tension between poetry and prose in *10:04*, that "what I loved about poetry was how the distinction between fiction and nonfiction didn't obtain, how the correspondence between text and world was less important than the intensities of the poem itself, what possibilities of feeling were opened up in the present tense of reading" (171). That seems to situate us beyond "reflection," which is the eternal problem of prose. At that point, prose slips into poetry, at first hesitantly, with lines of poetry rendered in prose (i.e., separated by slashes), to then adopt the fully poetic mode that will return at several moments throughout this part of the novel. Poetry takes over, and the novel, tellingly—the Novel-under-contract that is supposed to expand on the narrator's short story—is deferred until the next day: "Tomorrow I'd begin work on my novel," *10:04* goes, just before it slips back into poetry to say that "Tomorrow I'll see the Donald Judd/permanent installations in old hangars, but/now it's tomorrow and I didn't go" (174).

Interestingly, Judd appears to be associated with "the Novel" here, in the sense that both are put off into a future that at first doesn't arrive. When the narrator finally does go to see Judd's work, he notes that he "had never had a strong response to Judd's work . . . [his] desire to overcome the distinction between art and life," for example, was something the narrator "felt I could get . . . by walking through a Costco or a Home Depot or IKEA"

(178). But the work takes him by surprise: Judd's aluminum boxes, whose material features "were easy to enumerate" (179)—all the same on the outside, but each with a different, unique interior—devastate the narrator by their effect, namely, the constantly changing way in which they reflect the world. As the narrator notes, Judd's boxes were "set in time" (179)—his sculpture can be considered a time-based medium—and out in the desert, in the "refashioned artillery sheds" (178) (used as war prisoner camps during World War II—something that Sebald, no doubt, would have been interested in) whose "garage doors" Judd had replaced "with walls of continuous square and quartered windows," the boxes' "reflective surfaces" somehow manage to capture the living presence of the world: "the light was changing, the dry grasses going gold in it [Judd's work], and soon the sky was beginning to turn orange, tingeing the aluminum. . . . At one point I detected a moving blur on the surface of a box and I turned to the windows to see two pronghorn antelope rushing across the desert plain" (178–79).

At first, and probably due to the refurbished artillery shed setting, the narrator associates the boxes with the past, and notes that they have the quality of "a memorial," a term that strengthens Lerner's affinity with Sebald in this context. But he also quickly notes:

> [*M*]*emorial* wasn't really the right word: they didn't seem intended to focus my memory, they didn't feel addressed to me or any other individual. It was more like visiting Stonehenge, something I've never done, and encountering a structure that was clearly built by humans but inscrutable in human terms, as if the installation were waiting to be visited by an alien or god. The work was located in the immediate, physical present, registering fluctuations of presence and light, and located in the surpassing disasters of modern times . . . but it was also tuned to an inhuman, geological duration, lava flows and sills, aluminum expanding as the planet warms. . . . I thought of the "impossible mirror" of Bronk's poem. (180)

As opposed to only being associated with the past or with a realism of the present—their capacity to capture the world—the precise quality that the boxes project is their capacity to capture the world as if from the future in terms that exceed the human and operate in geological time. They mirror, but not for us; they mirror something that exceeds the human scale. If there is a realism that Judd's boxes accomplish, a world that they reflect, it is a reflection that partly operates in a time different than ours—a future time that might even reflect the absence of human beings altogether. "Feel the presence of absent human beings," as Brian Holmes in his work on the Chicago exchange has it.[52]

If realism is not abandoned here, it will be clear that it is very much transformed, pushed into ex-human regions that are not at all its traditional habitat. After realism's critical development into modernism and postmodernism (and taking into consideration the latter's association with science fiction, as Donna Haraway in her famous manifesto indicates[53]), realism makes a return here after postmodernism, having been affected by it, but reemerging from it not as dead but as something else altogether, as what one might characterize as a "speculative realism" that would be able to reflect the time before and after the human being—both the time of the Big Bang and the time after human extinction. Lerner gestures toward this kind of realism in his writing—I would suggest that the shiny, metallic cover of his novel seeks to mimic one of Judd's boxes—and his doing so opens up new ways of considering, for example, Sebald's work as well, as an oeuvre that, while generally associated with the past, might also operate as subtle kind of science fiction and speculative realism even. For that, one might have to redirect one's focus from World War II in Sebald's writing to his engagement with the Cold War, which marks the apocalyptic fulcrum of his art.

Upon entering the refurbished sheds where Judd's work is on show, and that "once held German prisoners of war," the narrator of *10:04* notes that "German-language messages were still painted on the brick: "DEN KOPF BENUTZEN IST BETTER ALS IHN VERLIEREN" (178; better to use your head than to lose it). A photograph of the message appears at the very end of this part of the novel. To lose one's head is the "no future" solution that I discussed earlier, the piece of the Jeff Koons artwork smashed to pieces, the Challenger explosion, punk. That's not, I think, the project of *10:04*. Rather, the novel advises us to use our heads toward another future. "Better to use the future than to lose it," one might rephrase the motto; "better to use realism than to lose it." As I indicated earlier, when it comes to finance that motto may begin to crumble: "better to use finance than to lose it"? Is *10:04* ultimately no more than a cynical novel about how a literary player was able to use the financial system to his benefit (and my apologies to everyone else who got screwed over)? Or might we be talking about another kind of "use" here—"use" not in the sense of "exploit for one's own benefit" but as a kind of emancipatory dismantling or profaning, as Giorgio Agamben theorizes it,[54] a removal of finance from its quasi-sacralized realm into a "wholly transformed" economy?[55]

Whatever the latter may look like, Lerner's *10:04* indicates, as Maggie Nelson already suggested, that to go forward means to go through: it just won't do to leave finance aside as a territory where the novel doesn't go. The example of *10:04* as a finance novel, then, is to take on what Tom Wolfe already imagined as "the beast" of financial reality, not so much to bring it to terms, as Wolfe proposed, but to hold up a kind of impossible mirror to it where the very limitations it poses to representation are exposed, explored, and turned into a new art of representation itself. If that new art cannot quite shake its attachment to finance, cannot quite "lose" finance, this is not something to be regretted, not something for which this new art should be hated, but an attachment that should be used for the continued exploration and transformation not only of art but also of the economic reality of our lives. *10:04* operates within that complicity and finds new life in it.

Conclusion

> [I]t seems to me worthwhile considering whether it is good to build fortresses and whether they are harmful or useful to those who build them.
>
> —NICCOLÒ MACHIAVELLI, *The Discourses*[1]

> [I]t is often our mightiest projects that most obviously betray the degree of our insecurity.
>
> —W. G. SEBALD, *Austerlitz*[2]

> The practice of speculation produces a world of potential, where uncertainty can no longer be analytically explained nor practically contained through calculative strategies.
>
> —VYJAYANTHI VENUTURUPALLI RAO, "*Speculation, Now*"[3]

In the Shadow of 9/11

Although this book has focused on financial fiction, I suggested in the introduction that it partly operates in the shadow of the terror attacks of September 11, 2001, and I want to return to that suggestion now to explore how, exactly, I consider this to be the case. Specifically, I want to suggest that our contemporary economic situation, as I sketched it out in the previous chapters, is the outgrowth of an economic defense system (EDS) that has produced what I call stock market fortification. Such fortification—a term that evokes a stability and rigidity that appear to be at odds with the perpetually moving liquidity of today's markets—names various strategies that seek to obtain financial immunity. Although such strategies intend to bring stability to the market by protecting profit from dwindling or disappearing altogether (in other words, by guaranteeing profit), they in fact contribute to its destabilization. *Fortification* is meant to name the ways in which such strategies of financial immunization freeze up markets in their destructive pursuit of perpetual profit.

The effects of EDS follow a logic familiar from other fields, and I propose (again, working within the shadow of the 9/11 events) to look at military theory as one such related field. In W. G. Sebald's novel *Austerlitz*, architectural historian Jacques Austerlitz analyses military fortifications—the star-shaped defense structures of the time when war still followed what theorist-of-war Carl von Clausewitz called "the geometrical principle"[4]—as operating according to a logic that is similar to that of financial immunity: the more fortifications seek to protect life, the more they put life at the risk of dying. This flip from biopolitics to thanatopolitics (as described in the opening pages of Roberto Esposito's *Bíos: Biopolitics and Philosophy*[5]) culminates in Sebald's novel in the architecture of the penal camp, a specific historical formation that was opened up for more general use when the Italian philosopher Giorgio Agamben theorized the camp as "the space that opens up when the state of exception starts to become the rule."

While the logic of fortification continues to be at work in the stock market today, the specific kind of fortification that can be found in the contemporary stock market is not that of the camp, in part because the reality it confronts is not the reality that the camp was confronting. Today, the stock market has become an absolutely contingent formation, with major crashes occurring ever more frequently and an ordinary day on the market playing itself out through various mini- or micro-crashes (considered the new normal—although it can hardly be described as a rule). That situation is due, as many have suggested, to the complex financial products that are being traded, as well as to the contemporary mode of trading: so-called high-frequency trading (HFT)—digitized, algorithmic trading at speeds that neither humans nor computers can record. A type of trading that was invented to fortify the market (an intention that is evident, for example, in the name of one successful HFT hedge fund: Kenneth Griffin's *Citadel*), it has in fact come to contribute to the market's destruction. Along the way, this has produced what some have begun to call an "ontology of finance" (Suhail Malik) defying the powers of a traditional, scientific realism: contemporary market philosophy takes recourse to a trend in contemporary philosophy called "speculative realism" in order to think the reality of the market today. Although a historical expression of the logic of fortification, the concept of the camp can nevertheless not capture this altered reality, which seeks new expressions.

Economic Defense Systems

I want to begin by noting that the term *economic defense system* is a pleonasm, since every economy is (however minimally) a defense system and every defense system follows an economic principle. If the term economy refers, as in the classical sense of the word, to the law or *nomos* according to which a house or *oikos* is governed, then certainly the term names a kind of organization that seeks to protect a community. (The managerial operations of modern governments have developed out of this, as both Michel Foucault and Giorgio Agamben have shown,[6] with the "MBA President" George W. Bush being the figurehead of such managerial politics.) Even if the term economy is taken in its modern sense, as referring to the wealth or resources of a region, nation-state, or group of nation-states (as in for example the Flemish, Belgian, or European economies), it too evokes a notion of defense: economies are supposed to be strong, both individually and in relation to each other (as part of a group system). Economies are defense systems and to talk about an economic defense system is in a way to merely state the obvious. On the other hand, defense systems are economic in nature: they count or determine who or what falls inside or outside of their protection. As Jacques Derrida has helped us see through his book *Politics of Friendship*,[7] they are military, political logics of counting (military-political economies), and for this reason too EDS is a pleonasm. The question is, of course: what kind of counting are we talking about, exactly? Strategies of defense have hardly remained the same from classical times to today.

In this general context, it should not come as a surprise that the term *financial immunity*, which crosses economic and defensive concerns, is an established notion in economic discourse. One is likely to know the notion of immunity from medical discourse, or—if one is interested in its extensions—from political or philosophical discourses that have also mobilized the term (with greater or lesser degrees of precision). Indeed, the medical strategy of incorporating a small dose of a life-threatening virus in order to trigger the body into the generation of antibodies that, when confronted with the full-blown virus, will be able to resist it, has had a rich afterlife in both the realm of politics (with immunity being used, for example, as a metaphor for how to deal with a political threat) and philosophy (where the notion of immunity, at the crossroads of poison and cure, as well as the notion of autoimmunity, or a defense system that comes to attack itself, have taken up prominent places). Although an economic logic, and in some instances also the term *economy* itself, has played an important role in immunity discourses, very few theories of immunity have brought the notion of immunity in direct conversation with the actual economy—say, with the ways in which the stock market has evolved in the last fifty or so years. And yet, in economic discourse, immunity is an important concept. Here too, however, the question would be: what kind of immunity, exactly? There are many different understandings of the notion that circulate.

In economic theory in particular, "financial immunity" names an investment strategy that guarantees profit: a strategy that protects profit from dwindling or disappearing entirely. Another way of saying this is that it protects profit against risk. To be financially immune means to ultimately be unaffected by the fluctuations of the market—it means to always be able to make up for your losses by your gains. Technically, "hedging" is probably closest to the medical practice of allowing a small dose of poison into one's system so as to be able to better resist a full-blown poison attack: it's a practice of calculating with loss rather than simply against it (probability versus predictability, as I have indicated in previous chapters). Unsurprisingly, the notion of financial immunity has become particularly meaningful in today's high-risk economy, in which complex financial products—rather than commodities or goods—are traded by algorithmic agents at speeds that defy both human and technological observation (and, by consequence, regulation). We now know that such products and such a way of trading are responsible for stock market crashes, ranging from the Black Monday crash on October 19, 1987 (which was caused by a collapsing system of portfolio insurance that was based on a flawed theorization of market risk, the Black-Scholes model) to the more recent "flash crash" on May 6, 2010 (the day when the Dow Jones Industrial Index made a historical drop, only to recover from it within minutes—but with stocks dramatically changing prices in the meantime, so drastically in fact that many of the trades made on that day needed to be canceled). Financial immunity is a strategy that seeks to protect investors against those risks. And as I have already indicated, everything depends here on one's notion of risk: many would probably agree that a risk that can be predicted, is no longer truly a risk. Indeed, if risk today is still considered calculable it marks a calculability that is of the order of the probable rather than the predictable. But what about a risk that escapes even that? Not mere probable (or improbable) risk, but risk as the absolute contingency of what happens on the market—outside of probability and improbability theory?

Today, we have a contemporary stock market that is highly compromised by both the "what" and the "how" of trading.[8] When it comes to the "what"—complex financial products such as CDOs that are generated through what is tellingly called the securitization of assets such as home mortgages—the situation can be compared to the dotcom bubble of the 1990s, where tremendous value was generated around online companies even before they existed and had proven their worth. Looking back on it now, it seems that those companies were created as financial instruments, for the sole purpose of accruing speculative value; as a practice, this is ultimately not so different from the Wells Fargo employees who were exposed in 2016 to have created fictitious accounts in order to collect fees and bonuses.[9]

But there is also the "how"—the algorithmic, high-frequency trading (HFT) that I have already discussed. The problems there are multiple: first of all, most high-frequency trading takes place in "dark pools," meaning, nonlit, nontransparent trading environments that have (until recently) largely remained outside of regulation. (It is, perhaps, for that reason that they have names such as "Island," marking their utopian reality beyond the law.) Secondly, HFT creates an unfair advantage: by having access to special high-speed fiber optic cables and locating their computers close to those of the stock exchange (so-called colocation) HFT firms can intercept orders of traders who do not have those advantages, steal what they are trying to buy away from under their noses, and offer it to them again at a slightly higher price. Thus, they collect fees related to buying and selling plus make a small profit; but they also slightly decrease the profit that the other trader would otherwise have made. Although we are talking about small gains here in terms of the immediate effect on pricing, doing this hundreds of thousands of times every day of the year adds up to a big profit in the long run—and without the trading bots ever having truly invested in the market. One final issue with HFT is that it has become so ingrained in the market that it is unlikely to disappear. It appears that the future of today's markets will have to involve HFT.

As one can already gather from the examples I gave earlier—I referred to portfolio insurance as being the key factor in the 1987 crash—from the perspective of financial immunity, the economic situation is a complex one because the very financial instruments that are being created to achieve immunity (such as portfolio insurance) end up contributing to the collapse of the market, thus effectively enhancing the risk of investment losses and (the cycle continues) further increasing the need for financial immunity. Recalling immunity's origin in medical discourse for a moment, this is a pathological, addictive situation that has produced, in the eyes of some, a market that is "rigged" (as Scott Patterson and Michael Lewis have suggested) or even "broken" (per Sal Arnuk and Joseph Saluzzi, heads of Themis Trading).[10]

Ultimately, and Patterson's account of the origins of algorithmic trading shows this, what we encounter with high-frequency trading is a fantasy of financial immunity based on artificial intelligence and mathematical models that provide a "probable" account of future reality and, as such, are expected to (in the long run) beat the market. As Brian Holmes (silently echoing the work of Michel Foucault on neoliberalism) points out, according to such a vision "the financial markets could therefore be presented as objective mechanisms of verification, or truthful speech."[11] There is a certain notion of financial realism at work here that undermines the stability of the market, because it promises that through its realism, it can turn a bet into a likely win (in the long run).

As my language suggests, this is an issue that cuts across mathematics and finance—and literature. Hari Kunzru arguably draws this out in *Gods Without Men*—which revolves around the psychotic finance man Jaz—when he describes the kind of mathematical model that is characterized in his novel as "an organism" rather than a computer program (something that felt "alive") only to ask: "It was as if Bachman [who created the model] was trying to fit the whole world into his model. What was external to [it]? Was there anything it *didn't* aim to comprehend?"[12] Jaz suspects, in fact, that it is this model—named Walter, a name that (given that its author has the

German-sounding name Bachman) may refer to the German *walten* (to prevail or reign), associated with the idea of a supreme rule—that may have caused the 2008 market crash, which is explicitly mentioned in the novel's closing pages.[13] Now, the interesting thing is that this description occurs in a dazzlingly ambitious novel that cuts across historical times with what some readers might perceive to be a similar aspiration to totality. In other words, there is a complicity between the novel's ambitious storytelling project and the mathematical model's attempt to comprehend the world.

The math-based fantasy of financial immunity thus has some kind of affinity with a certain ambitious form of storytelling—and in both cases, one would have to recognize how those fantasies of totality point to intelligences that exceed what is considered the normal human brain. They point, of course, to artificial intelligence (a transhistorical narrative voice, for example, would count as such an intelligence); but one doesn't need to move toward the artificial for this: as for example *The Big Short* reveals through the real-life character of Michael Burry (portrayed by Christian Bale), people with autism or Asperger syndrome appear to be particularly well-suited to develop the kind of strategies that are thought to enable us to "beat the market."[14]

The Military Logic of Fortification

> You can hedge against anything, and even hedge your hedges with reinsured insurance. But the frequency and severity of crises only seems to increase.[15]
>
> *Frank Pasquale*, The Black Box Society

I propose to call the strategies that inform the conviction that the market can be beaten yet produce the collapse of the market as a consequence *fortifications*, a term that due to the architectural stability and rigidity that it evokes appears to stand at odds with today's stock market, hooked on liquidity.[16] I initially propose this term on the basis of a surprising and perhaps contentious source, namely the analysis of fortifications that is provided by a novelistic character, the architectural historian Jacques Austerlitz in Sebald's *Austerlitz*. Indeed, Sebald's work can help us establish the relation between "bankers" and "bunkers" and "bunkers" and "bytes" that I want to consider.[17]

As I already summarized in *States of Exception*,[18] *Austerlitz* tells the jumbled life story of its titular character, Jacques Austerlitz, an architectural historian who was cut off from an idyllic childhood in Prague when his mother put him on a *Kindertransport* to London, in the hope that this would save him from the impending destruction of World War II. Austerlitz was saved: his adoptive parents never mention his origins, and his history lessons at school end long before the disasters of World War II. Even though he thus escapes from the war, and specifically from the concentration camps in which (as he later comes to suspect) both his parents may have died, the war and the camps haunt Austerlitz in his adult life: they turn into a trauma that prevents him from finishing his doctoral dissertation on nineteenth-century architecture. Nevertheless, architecture—and not only nineteenth-century architecture—is featured very prominently in the book, so prominently in fact that it makes one wonder whether there may perhaps be a relation between Austerlitz's obsession with architecture and the trauma of World War II.

I want to reconsider Austerlitz here as something like a financial historian who through his analysis of military fortification can provide insights into stock market architecture today. From the opening pages, architecture takes up a prominent place in the book. Much of the discussion at the beginning of the book revolves around early modern, star-shaped fortifications. Fortifications show, as Austerlitz explains, "how we feel obliged to keep surrounding ourselves with defenses built in successive phases as a precaution against any incursion by enemy powers, until the idea of concentric rings making their way steadily outward comes up against its natural limits."[19] As such, however, fortifications ultimately do not serve their purpose. There are three reasons, according to Austerlitz, why this is the case: first, because "the largest fortifications will naturally attract the largest enemy forces" so that "the more you entrench yourself, the more you must remain on the defensive"; second, because by fortifying yourself, you "[draw] attention to your weakest point, practically inviting the enemy to attack"; and, third, because the time to build fortifications increased (it took longer and longer to complete them) "and with it the probability that as soon as they were finished, if not before, they would have been overtaken by further developments, both in artillery and strategic planning."[20]

Such was the case, for example, with the city of Antwerp, Belgium, where the book begins. After Antwerp's fortifications had been reduced to rubble during an 1832 siege, "the only conclusion anyone drew from it, incredibly, was that the defenses surrounding the city must be rebuilt even more strongly than before."[21] The city's answer to the violence it had suffered was thus to repeat the very measure that, in Austerlitz's view, had attracted this violence. The new fortifications continued "the same old logic"[22] and were bound to lead to the same violent results. However, before these new fortifications were completed, artillery and strategic planning had already developed to such a degree that a new wall needed to be built even further away from the city center. The question was even raised at that point whether the line of forts should not be moved even further out to include Antwerp's "rapid industrial growth and development," thus "bringing it within the sight of the outskirts of Mechelen," a neighboring town.[23]

It then turns out that Austerlitz is particularly interested in the last link of this chain of fortifications around Antwerp, namely the fortress of Breendonk. Completed just before the outbreak of World War I, the fort was used as a "reception and penal camp"[24] during World War II. Whereas the fortifications were thus supposed to protect the city, and specifically the human life that resided within it, against enemy incursions, they actually ended up destroying it. For Austerlitz, the fortress of Breendonk thus marks the relation between the early modern practice of fortification and the destruction of life in the National-Socialist camps. The camp (not a death camp, to be precise, but a reception and penal camp) is presented in the book as the logical conclusion of the attempt to fortify life.

The logic of fortification, and its relation to the camp, will turn out to haunt almost all of the architectures that Austerlitz discusses—even buildings that one might, at first sight, be reluctant to associate with the camp, such as the French national library. I want to propose here, taking my cue from Austerlitz's analysis, that the same logic of fortification also haunts the contemporary development of the stock market, and ask whether we can conclude then that such a development has culminated today in a camp-like economy?

I have already laid out what I consider to be the fortification of the stock market in my discussion of financial immunity and its counterproductive strategies. In order to consider the provocative leap to the economy as camp, more is required. Of course, I do not mean an actual (penal or concentration) camp, even if my use of the term references this. Instead, the term *camp* seeks to abstract, to the degree it is possible (and some may argue that it is not) a theoretical notion of a camp from the highly particular, unique, and exceptional experience of the concentration camp in order to distill from it something like a theoretical paradigm that can be used to analyze other, "similar" situations. Such a provocative move has been accomplished in the work of Giorgio Agamben, the Italian philosopher who, in recent years, has emerged as an "economic" historian of sorts (adding impressive economic analyses to his already established work on sovereignty, biopolitics, and governmentality).[25] In a short essay titled "What is a camp?," published in his *Means Without End: Notes on Politics*, Agamben proposes to call a camp "*the space that is opened up when the state of exception starts to become the rule.*"[26]

Agamben defines a camp not as a physical place (even if most of us, when we think of camps, will think of actual places, with proper names, for example—Auschwitz) but as a space; there is a virtualization of the camp that ought to be taken into consideration when reviewing Agamben's definition. Agamben also mentions "the state of exception": this is a notion from legal and political theory that refers to a situation or state in which the normal rule of law is suspended in the name of a security threat or an emergency event. Such states of exception are supposed to be temporary: once the threat is over or the emergency has been dealt with, the law is put in place again. But a camp is not a state of exception. A camp is a situation in which the state of exception's temporary suspension of the law becomes permanent, and even the rule—in which a new way of doing things is established that is the way of the exception and its suspension of the law. The exception effectively becomes the new normal, and the term *camp* names that situation.

By abstracting a highly specific historical event such as Auschwitz into a theoretical notion, Agamben is asking us to consider that there may be a principle, (perverse) law, or what he calls (following Schmitt) "nomos" at work in the modern event of the concentration camp that can also be seen at work elsewhere, and that might continue in our contemporary societies, long after the concentration camps have ended. Today, he argues, we are still living in the matrix of the camp and if we want to undo the logic that was operative in Auschwitz, another effort is required.

What if the fortification of the stock market through strategies of financial immunity has rendered the economy into a space (a virtual entity rather than an actual physical location) in which the state of exception has become the rule, in which a suspension of stock market law has actually become the new, normal way of stock market operation? This would raise two important points.

First, by calling the economy "a virtual entity," one would have to clarify that this does not mean that it is not rooted in actual, material conditions—Michael Lewis's book *Flash Boys*, for example, has effectively demonstrated that although the reality of today's stock market might escape our full control, that reality is nevertheless produced through practices of HFT that are made possible by material constraints/enablers such as fiber optic cables and the practice of colocation.

Second, the claim about "the state of exception" can be expanded into different directions: for one, to explore the topic of regulation/deregulation, and to show how deregulation—the exceptional, suspension of the law—has become the new rule of the stock market. HFT's struggle with regulation is long and complex, has been challenged by a lack of understanding (those who were meant to regulate HFT did not understand how it worked), and has involved many conflicts of interest (with some regulators ending up working for HFT firms[27]). This would be the most obvious, legal and political track to pursue. When it comes to considering the well-being of those whose 401Ks are being traded by HFT firms, this argument could be extended all the way back to the principles that informed the Securities Exchange Act from 1934: the stock market is no longer the platform for fair trade that it was meant to be, and this has lead to the claims that I have already quoted about the stock market being "rigged" or even "broken."

However, at the more colloquial level of exception and norm, one could also focus on the typical security or emergency situation that we associate with the stock market, namely, a crash. Crashes used to be fairly rare; they are inseparable from the affect of panic, as Michael Lewis and others have shown.[28] Panic names the irrational component of the market, one of the reasons why—as some have argued—the market cannot be beaten: because one can never anticipate what will produce a panic, and what a panic will produce. (The market is not all numbers, people still decide whether to invest or withdraw their money—a straightforward and calculable example of this would be the periodically returning spectacle of the head of the US Federal Banking System talking about raising interest, and thereby potentially sending the bond market into decline, or keeping interest low so as to encourage people to take money out of their savings accounts and invest it in bonds.) Portfolio insurance, for example, was an immunization strategy that sought to protect investors from a crash. The problem was, however, that when the market appeared to be in decline, and no one was interested in buying, the portfolio insurance system—which relied on the possibility of selling—only contributed further to the market collapse. And some of these problems continue when humans are removed from the trading floor and replaced by algorithms, which don't panic: for example, on April 23, 2013, when the Associated Press twitter feed was hacked and a message was posted that the White House had been hit by two explosions that injured President Barack Obama, the tweet sent the Dow plunging because algorithms had picked up on this false information and had changed their trading patterns in response. Regulators who were interviewed about this situation said there was basically no way in which this kind of effect could be controlled—all one could do was to wait for the market to bounce back, or for the algorithms to get smarter.[29]

Exceptional, major market crashes like the one from 1987 caused by portfolio insurance have become more and more frequent. At the same time, economic analysts have observed that another kind of crash, a mini- or micro-crash, has come to characterize the economy's daily development, as if the crash were the economy's new norm. Shorting, the practice of betting against an asset, is probably one of the best indicators of how that is the case: it marks the extreme point where losing itself is turned into a strategy for profit-making. Generally, HFT has been thought responsible for those mini-crashes, which reveal a fundamental instability of the market—like small earthquakes that are an ongoing reminder of the "Big One"—that may one day (soon?) translate into what some (including some high-frequency traders) have been calling a "splash crash."[30]

This changed market reality—a reality that, as a rule, operates through mini-crashes, with the next "Big One" permanently just around the corner—at first sight may seem to qualify as what Agamben calls a camp: a space in which the state of exception has become the rule, and as a result a space in which anything cannot just happen but in which *anything is already happening*—right now.

Camp would need to refer here to a catastrophic, extreme loss-dealing reality that has come about through a progressive process of *market fortification*, a term I propose to capture the immunizing financial strategies that have sought to guarantee profit—a positivity that the market, quite simply, can *never* guarantee (in the sense of "predict"; and even "probability/improbability" theory, as suggested in chapter 4, is ultimately limited on this count). If it could, we would be dealing with a market that is rigged or broken, as critics of the contemporary stock market have suggested. Although my use of the term *fortification* may at first appear out of place, given the stability and rigidity that fortification evokes (versus the liquidity of the market), I have chosen this term specifically to suggest that the digital algorithms that practice high-frequency trading, for example, are today's fortifications of the market, supposedly providing liquidity but effectively sucking all liquidity out of the market as soon as the heat is on.[31] It is in part for this reason that today's markets have been characterized as black holes: although their characterization as a "cosmic vacuum cleaner" is exaggerated (see chapter 4), it is nevertheless the case that within the sphere of a black hole, on the inside of its horizon, everything moves toward the black hole's center—nothing can escape the pull of the "hole's" gravitational mass. When the heat is on, financial fortifications operate similarly. At that point, they become liquidity blockers, revealing that the liquidity that they claim to provide is more like a liquidity effect (or, as I will put it in anticipation of my discussion of Baudrillard, a liquidity illusion) rather than actual liquidity. I say this not to make the case for liquidity (the term doesn't really mean all that much anymore given today's markets), but to make the case against military-like, fortifying approaches to the market that seek to accomplish a positivity that goes contrary to the reality of the market, and of life.[32]

Going back to the two mottos that introduce this chapter, this would mean not only to turn Sebald into a theorist of finance but also to think of Machiavelli in a similar light. After all, he was interested in the taming of fortune which he infamously described as a lady—not unrelated, as scholars have indicated, to Lady Credit[33]—that should be beaten and struck into obedience.[34] The statement stands today as an accurate description of the attitude to the market that I have analyzed, especially since Machiavelli's association of this attitude with a boldness that exceeds total calculation or predictability. Given the state of the market, however, we must surely ask ourselves—as Machiavelli encourages us to do elsewhere—whether such a pursuit of mastery, even if it is a mastery of the probable or improbable rather than the predictable, is harmful or useful both to the market and to those—all of us—whose fortunes ultimately depend on them.

Welcome to the Economic Tsunami Hazard Zone

Can the concept of the camp—the culmination of military processes of fortification—really cover this new economic reality—the culmination of economic process of fortification? Can the camp travel from the military into the economic sphere? Is the camp an economico-political concept in that sense? Agamben's philosophy, which in spite of its weak points has proven so productive for theorizing the contemporary political state of exception, falls short when it comes to thinking the new ontology of the economic state of exception. Indeed, his philosophy does not truly think the ontology of perpetual exception that characterizes the contemporary economy: instead, the exception is ultimately eclipsed in his thought by the rule, with the exception becoming the new rule (as his definition of the camp as a permanent state of exception puts it). However, a more rigorous notion of the exception would arguably defy such a rule and retain a connection to an exception that does not become the rule (a negativity that is not subsumed by the dialectic).

In the case of the mini- or micro-crashes that have become the new norm of today's stock market operations, one can imagine an epistemology in which these would dialectically become the new rule, a situation in which one would ultimately learn to "calculate" with these crashes (again, think of the practice of "shorting"). However, the fact that these mini- or micro-crashes are merely minor indications of a bigger crash haunting the market reveals they are ultimately signs of a much bigger incalculable—a splash crash, as I have already indicated, that (tsunami-like) will wash away the global market. (Economically speaking, we are all in the Tsunami Hazard Zone.) Such a splash crash is not a new rule: it is a more radical mark of exception, and it is this mark that I am interested in here—not the "Big One," to keep the comparison to natural disasters going, but the "Really Big One," as a rather troubling 2015 *New Yorker* article put it.[35] Whereas a camp may be a space in which the exception becomes the rule, I am trying to think an even more extreme articulation of the camp that would simply be a state of perpetual exception—without that exception ever translating itself into a rule. *That* is the state that corresponds to the contemporary economic reality; not the state of "the big short," where a profit can still be made, but of "the really big short," when the market implodes.

I have described this reality in detail in chapter 4. Thinking the reality of the economy today means to adopt a mindset that would fit the reality of the economic universe—it would mean to adopt the mindset of a speculative, "cosmic" realism that would be able to account not just for what escapes the probable, but for the absolute contingency of the market.[36] In his work on what he calls (following thinkers such as Claude Lefort and Jacques Rancière) "the regimes of politics," political theorist Martín Plot distinguishes among a theological regime of politics (associated in this book with state of exception theory, and thinkers such as Walter Benjamin, Carl Schmitt, and Giorgio Agamben), an epistemic regime of politics (a rationalist, knowledge-driven, scientific approach to politics), and an "aesthetic regime of politics that is strictly identical with the regime of democracy."[37] With today's economic reality, which has been produced by an epistemic regime (the theory of financial immunity that thinks it can "scientifically" beat the market, all the time), we are at the limits of the epistemic regime, confronting an ontology that defies the flexing of the epistemic muscle. We are moving, instead, into the realm of the speculative, of a cosmos that can still be thought but that cannot be known, anticipated, or calculated outside of the particular moment in which it occurs (*contingere*). Epistemes need to be invented ("written," as Elie Ayache proposes) on the spot, in response to a reality that, although it has been generated by human activity, is at this point forever merely "happening" to us, setting the always contemporary stage over which we seek to desperately exercise control. This speculative regime—which I would add to Plot's threefold distinction among theological, epistemic, and aesthetic regimes—is a desperate, exhausting regime for it allows for no stability, certainty, or security other than the need to be on guard all the time and make reality as it offers itself to us. It is a desperate, exhausted regime of "scripting" in response to a reality generated by previous scripts. In today's economy, we are writing in response to the effects of our writing, trying to control our predecessors' attempts to control and thus adding to the problem.

To return to a term that has quite some traction in this book: if the camp ultimately remains with the psychoanalytic/epistemic model of neurosis, with speculative realism we move toward psychosis. There are two different theories of the exception that are at work in those two mindsets (one more radical than the other) and that is the difference that I am trying to theorize. In today's economy, it's as if we keep throwing epistemic solutions at an ontological problem, not realizing that the rules of the game have changed. We are using our neuroses to battle what is in reality a psychotic situation—and the more we fight, the more the psychosis is exacerbated. It is not surprising that in this tense state of the epistemic regime, the theological regime would reappear. One can think here—and the context for this thought is in part the reflection about "panic" that I developed in chapter 3—of the case of Sean Hyman, a former pastor, who claims to have discovered in the Bible a code for making money on the stock market, the "biblical money code," a biblical trading algorithm, combining the theological and the epistemic.[38]

Although it is yet to acknowledge the full consequences of such a conclusion, all of this means that speculative realism thus thinks the reality of the economy today—a complicity that conversations about this trend in philosophy in my view must confront. It is, I think, a new regime that has separated itself from the epistemic one, largely for philosophical reasons, but also—and perhaps outside of its own realization—in response to a contemporary economic situation that remains to be thought.

One of the more difficult issues that we have to confront in this context is the relation between the speculative regime and the aesthetic one, two regimes that exist not only in tension but also partly in overlap. In political terms, this would mean to think the tension and overlap between neoliberalism (speculative regime) and democracy (aesthetic regime, according to Rancière). Indeed, in Rancière's description of democracy—"a certain regime of politics, a regime based on the indetermination of identities, the delegitimation of positions of speech, the deregulation of partitions of space and time"[39]—one may find a resonance with the speculative regime, and its troubling of stability, certainty, and security. There are marked differences between the two regimes, of course, some of which I begin to sketch out here. However, such a project would involve thinking a rift between the aesthetic/democratic and the speculative/neoliberal that is beyond the scope of these final pages.[40]

Is There an Alternative?

> I mean, I know it's not the point of Occupy, but I'm telling you that now . . . I don't act like my cock weighs a ton.[41]
>
> *Ben Lerner,* 10:04

> [A]nd possibly being Karim-esque, although it is not confident or experienced or a strong negotiator or many other factors that make a skilled businessman, is still a positive class of being.[42]
>
> *Teddy Wayne,* Kapitoil

Those operating within the theory of financial immunity would undoubtedly argue that the appropriate response to this economic situation is more stock market fortification: we need to come up with better algorithms to continue turning a profit in a crash-based environment. This is what I have characterized earlier as an epistemic solution. According to this view, the crash is considered a negativity to which the positivity of the fortification is opposed. However, it is evident from what I have shown that today's crashing economy was produced by too much fortification, by too much positivity—that stock market fortification and market crashes are related. It is the scripting—and more precisely the coding—of stock market fortification that produces the crashes and the desperate, exhausting writing they require. The solution can therefore not be to add more positivity to it, as such a move would merely reinforce the problem.

Others may also argue for more fortification, and for precisely that reason, to reinforce the problem: one imagines that accelerationism,[43] closely associated with speculative realism, would propose to speed up stock market fortification so as to bring about the dreaded splash crash. Let's have even more fortification to bring down the entire economy! I am not sure that even accelerationists can foresee the catastrophe that such a strategy may produce. As a political parallel, one might consider here Julian Assange and his threats in October 2016 to bring down Hillary Clinton's presidential campaign through revelations about Clinton's e-mail traffic: as an accelerationist strategy that perhaps sought to put Donald Trump in power and bring about the end of the United States, it makes sense. But can Assange really foresee the consequences of such an ending? What alternatives does he, or anyone else for that matter, have to offer?

One obvious response to accelerationism might be decelerationism.[44] Let's slow down, perhaps go back even to how the stock market used to be (economic nostalgia, if you will, and all of the problems it entails). This deceleration seems to be the response that can be found in W. G. Sebald's work, which offers a gloomy, melancholic kind of writing that couldn't possibly be more inimical to the accelerated tweet (one of Sebald's sentences, in which the horrors of the Theresienstadt concentration camp are revealed, amounts to multiple pages). Sebald is by signature a slow writer, steeped in the nineteenth century (the world of capitalism, commodities, and colonialism) rather than in the twentieth and twenty-first centuries (the world of finance, digital trading, and neoliberalism)—even if, of course, that doesn't mean he is "nostalgic" for capitalism. Indeed, it is the premodern where his nostalgia tends—an era when the world somehow still made sense. In one of the rare occasions when Sebald describes an architecture that seems to go against fortification and provide refuge for life, he offers the cabinet of wonder that appears to be hopelessly out of date in our time. Packed full of dead insects and animals, as one should note in objection to its all too romantic representation, its glass is also cracked,[45] perhaps indicating that the fantasy that Austerlitz projects about the cabinet of wonder is fissured—at least for the careful observer. (In other words, no *pre* will do as the utopian realm when the world still made sense.) The cabinet of wonder may return in object-oriented ontology (OOO) approaches which, although they relate to speculative realism, appear to be more on a decelerationist rather than accelerationist track and thus harbor a different political potential, one that I associate with ecology. One of the things OOO writing and Sebald's writing share is certainly the experimental form of the list whose attempt to "record" the impossible totality of everything must probably be put in dialogue with the digital era of too-much-information.[46] There is a way in which the decelerated observation of OOO approaches (and even Sebald) echoes the accelerated generation of stuff (objects and information) in the contemporary moment. If in Sebald, one arguably sees the decelerated, descriptive approach collapse in response to the contemporary, OOO seems to have taken the contemporary in stride and happily embraced its opening up onto the infinity of the universe. There is none of Sebald's gloom in OOO, only tremendous excitement about the infinite variety of the world. OOO's ecology may be dark, but its darkness shares very little with that of Sebald's and its allusions to the Holocaust.

How to respond to the logic of fortification and the problems it has produced, both politically and economically? I don't mean to be defeatist, but there may be some value in realizing that death cannot be overcome, that the market cannot be beaten, and that human endeavors will always be limited in response to the reality that they not only confront but also cogenerate. There might be a positive investment in our limitations that should be valued—a lesson in utopianism that, as per Anahid Nersessian's remarkable reading,[47] the romantics already passed on to us. *Investment in limitation* doesn't mean one should give up, take one's life, throw in the towel. It means one shouldn't live or invest in the expectation that immortality and perpetual profit are out there, somewhere, for those who try hard enough to find it. It's about adjusting our hopes and ambitions, those that inform our mightiest projects (which are shaped, Sebald suggests, in response to our greatest insecurities). It would mean to reorient our practices of self-determination, and of what I wouldn't hesitate to continue calling sovereignty, whether in life or the economy, starting from the basic and inescapable fact of a negativity or loss (in that sense, the adjustment would actually yield us more than we currently have). Surely, if we operated in this way, outside of the fantasy of positivity as well as these other forms of negation, we would avoid the types of fortifications, military or economic, that I have criticized. It may be even that some of the most common psychopathologies of our time—depression or burnout—would be avoided as soon as the obsessive focus on positivity is broken.[48]

Toward the end of his life, Jean Baudrillard—whose work on semiocapitalism and hyperreality resonates with the analyses I presented in this book—took on this fantasy of positivity in a couple of texts published in *The Vital Illusion*. Granted, he was writing first and foremost about cloning—but some of what he has to say about the fantasy of immortality matters in this context. The question of cloning, for Baudrillard (who takes on a certain kind of "scientific" regime in his text), is the question of immortality. Cloning aims to make us forget death, a possibility that, as Baudrillard explains, already lies occluded within our very cells, for our cells can, and this is beyond the phantasmatic, forget to die: when they do so, they become cancerous. A cell that forgets to die "goes on to clone itself again and again, making thousands of identical copies of itself, thus forming a tumor."[49] It is in response to this cancerous multiplication of "life" that Baudrillard takes it up for death in this text. "We must struggle," he writes, "against the possibility that we will not die."[50] This is a struggle against "pathological immortality," a cancerous positivity that in Baudrillard's apocalyptic view risks to threaten the continued existence of the human species.

There are problems with Baudrillard's text,[51] but read in light of the argument I have laid out here about stock market fortification, it becomes possible to read it as an analysis of the cancer of the market, and the illusion of liquidity that HFT projects as a kind of "final solution" (a reference that Baudrillard himself makes in the text) for a market in which profit can never be guaranteed. With the intensification of economic defense systems and ever more powerful strategies of stock market fortification, we are witnessing an extermination of the market due to the fantasies of immunity—of immortality. Again, the practice of shorting—betting on the negative—appears particularly problematic in this context.

In her discussion of Bret Easton Ellis's *American Psycho*, Leigh Claire La Berge argues that the novel "emplots" the violent "metaphorical language of finance," the financial talk about making a killing on Wall Street or "hostile takeovers" and "takeover defenses."[52] In line with the argument I am developing here, La Berge suggests that the language of finance is a certain kind of military talk: the kind that is associated with "war," "battles," and "weapons."[53] She adds that in *The Art of the Deal*, Donald Trump "includes a picture of himself as a military school teenager marching down New York City's Fifth Avenue in full military regalia with the caption: 'This was my first real glimpse of prime fifth avenue property.'"[54] In this context, she suggests that to finance is "to go to the end (*finir*), but of life itself."[55] However, death may not be finance's end for everyone: the financier might bring death for the ones he closes a deal with, but the deal is often driven, I have suggested, by an aversion to death—by an obsession with immortality. That too is part of the military logic and my discussion of fortification in relation to the 9/11 event has enabled me to draw this out.[56]

But some nuance must be added here, partly in view of how military defense has developed after 9/11. For we are not so much dealing with old-school military violence here (territorial war between nation-states) but terror. Bateman is arguably not so much a figure of military violence but of terror. This has produced a different kind of military activity that operates not so much within the order of prediction but of probability; one that ultimately realizes that even the probable cannot account for the absolute contingency of reality. In that sense, there will always be terror. Contemporary markets even include the practice of betting on it.[57]

In architecture, and to come back to my discussion of Sebald, deconstructivist architecture has most consistently pursued the project of building around negativity or loss.[58] Parametricism, the more recent algorithmic trend in architecture, is openly (at least in the case of Patrik Schumacher, one of its major proponents) in line with the neoliberal, "positive" paradigm and is received very critically for that reason.[59] We know, of course, the parodies of negativity to which deconstructivist architecture or the ethics of the gift have lead: no buildings at all (as with Daniel Libeskind's early work, for example) or dysfunctional buildings that are hard to distinguish from ruins—bad architecture. That is of course not what I intend to promote, in the same way that I am not promoting a market that would bring only loss. But a rethinking of attempts at self-determination from the perspective of the precarious, the vulnerable, and the disposable may also trigger other, more successful types of living, counting, and building for our time.

In short, I think there is an alternative, or rather that there are alternatives, if by alternative we do not mean the ill-conceived speeding up of what is already there, the slowing down of what's already there and the nostalgic return to the past, or the immediate destruction of what is already there. We must rather break with the fantasy of immunity and immortality, and rethink our economic and political forms of life from there. I don't think (as I have explained elsewhere[60]) that this means, for example, getting rid of sovereignty altogether; if sovereignty may be traditionally opposed to damage or hurt, to loss, pain, or death, in the sense that it is supposed to protect its subjects from those (even if it sometimes may inflict death upon its subjects to protect itself), its true dismantling will only arrive if another sovereignty is thought (and practiced): a sovereignty that would be committed otherwise to the protection that it is supposed to provide. Sovereignty thus conceived would always exist *in spite of* its impossibility—and such a reconceptualization of sovereignty, of a sovereignty limited or adjusted, would likely mark a different behavior of sovereign states upon the international political scene. In the economy also, the fantasy of immunity—of guaranteed profit—needs to be abandoned, as a normal and healthy market in which people do not take extreme risks is a market in which everyone occasionally loses. No one should be allowed to bet on those losses. It is, in that sense, negativity—the fundamental fact of loss—that would keep risk-taking in check. This is partly a question of abandoning a technocratic fantasy of sovereignty over the market (through algorithmic trading) because it blocks fair exchange by rigging and even breaking the market. Why would one put one's money in the market if those doing one's trading systematically have the best trades stolen away from them by bots using computers and fiber optic cables to move faster than a trader can? Even if HFT supposedly increases liquidity in the market overall, thus creating a better market that is to the benefit of all, this unfair form of trading still creates much greater forms of risk setting the stage for a crash that is much greater even than what we have experienced in recent times. It is also a question of going beyond that and tackling those market practices that seek to profit from the market insecurity that the technocratic model has produced.

Bradley Katsuyama's experiment with IEX—the new stock exchange he and his team created (approved by the SEC in 2016[61]—even though *Citadel*'s Kenneth Griffin furiously resisted the approval[62]) as per Michael Lewis's account in *Flash Boys*—is worth noting in this context as an alternative. Although it does not seek to crash the economy, capitalism, or electronic trading, it takes on some of their most problematic aspects.

Going back to psychotic theories of money and ultimately finance that I focused on in the introduction and chapter 2, theories that argue that money originates not in the positive value of cattle or shells but the negative value of credit or debt, one should no doubt consider the liberating, even emancipative consequences of such a conclusion: if it is indeed the case not only that the gold standard has been dropped but also that money was always merely symbolic and never held any intrinsic value, then the solution to many of our problems—which seem to originate from a rather ill-guided continued attachment to a gold standard or some variant of it—would seem to lie in the forgiveness of credit or debt.

The neoliberal economies of the West have profited tremendously from the abolition of the gold standard, speculation, the creation of complex financial instruments, and the rise of high-frequency trading—even though those same developments have obviously also brought tremendous losses. Why then, when the chips are down, do they appear to resort to an attachment to a (nonexisting) gold standard that allows them to enforce austerity or the payment of debts?[63] There appears to be a double measure that enables tremendous greed on the one hand, and relentless nonforgiveness on the other, with the former based in the abolition of the gold standard and the latter on an anachronistic holding-on to it.[64]

As J. M. Coetzee in his rewriting of Plato's allegory for the financial age—which I used as a motto for this book[65]—indicates, it might ultimately be our salvation that finance, unlike commodity capitalism, is really mere numbers flickering on the screen: value generated around obscure financial artifacts that, when it comes down to it, are worth nothing.[66] If this is the case, why is it so difficult to redraw the numbers and to let go of what wasn't worth anything in the first place? If one were giving up things of real material value, the situation would appear to be different. But in our psychotic situation, in which we are governed by fictitious values of our own creation, what is stopping us from decreating or refictionalizing such values whenever and however we need to? From rewriting the finance fictions that, all too often, appear to be writing us?

Of course, and this has only become clearer since Tom Wolfe's *The Bonfire of the Vanities* was published, finance is a tremendous fictioning force, and to be sure there are complex powers in place—not only outside of us, but within us even, when it comes to our desire—that prevent any simple intervention in this realm. At the same time, doesn't the creation and approval of IEX show that it can be done? For many of course, IEX won't go far enough—it is still an exchange, after all; it still has algorithmic, high-frequency trading (albeit under different conditions). But it seems that an intervention was made there in the realm of finance and its fictions that is worth noting. David Graeber's *Debt*, which discusses a history of the periodic forgiving of debt in society, was a major inspiration for the Occupy Wall Street movement, and its attempt to live otherwise. Continuing the work of the Black Panthers, Black Lives Matter seeks to reclaim the power of black life to "draw its own picture," as Bigger in *Native Son* puts it, rather than have a picture be drawn for it. Granted, the kind of drawing that Bigger is doing is probably not the one we want; but still, and as his lawyer explains during his trial, it marks a moment of freedom and self-determination that resonates through Wolfe's *Bonfire* as well—now in the context of a finance novel—all the way to the contemporary moment that once again combines finance and issues of race and class.

It seems defeatist to simply give up on autonomy—on our capacity to write our own lives—in the face of finance's complexity or the powers that determine our racial or economic situation. That complexity and those determinations are psychotic fictions that are often forced onto us—or into which we are lured—and disavow the realities of our lives, substituting other ones for them. I am not so naïve as to suggest they should be exposed by a return to reality; but I do think that they must be fought with other, non-psychotic fictions, expressions of autonomy that challenge the determinations of class and race, as well as finance. This is not simple, but that doesn't mean it can't be done. As I see it, it would be a way of putting a certain kind of philosophical and literary realism into action.

ACKNOWLEDGMENTS

I started thinking about this project around 2008. I first spoke publicly about some of the ideas that informed it in 2012, at an event at the California Institute of the Arts organized by Tom Leeser. My work on the project was greatly accelerated by the "Psychopathologies of Cognitive Capitalism" conference that I organized with Warren Neidich and Jason Smith in Los Angeles in 2012. I presented the first writing that would become central to the project at the second cognitive capitalism conference in Berlin, in 2013. On that occasion, Armen Avanessian also invited me to workshop my books, including the beginnings of *Finance Fictions*, at the Haus der Kulturen der Welt in Berlin. Armen and Hannah Wallenfels invited me back to Berlin in 2015 to present "Financial Realism" at Merve publishing—I can't thank them enough for their hospitality. Also in 2015, I presented parts of the project at the University of Notre Dame, Gallery 400 (University of Illinois, Chicago), the Universitat Pompeu Fabro (Barcelona) and the University of Leuven (Belgium): thank you to my friends Kate Marshall, Anna Kornbluh, Santiago Zabala, and Stijn De Cauwer for the invitations. Thank you Brian Kim Stefans for inviting me to present chapter 3 at M/ELT (Modernist/Experimental Literature and Text-Art; UCLA). Speaking invitations by Holly Brown and Stef Craps (Ghent University, Belgium) and Liam Connell (University of Brighton) provided incentive to finish the project. Support for those speaking engagements was provided by the Faculty Development Funds of the California Institute of the Arts and the School of Critical Studies. The project was completed during my Spring 2016 CalArts Creative Leave.

Earlier versions of chapter 3 were published as “Modern Creatures,” *European Journal of English Studies* 19, no. 1 (2015) and in *The Psychopathologies of Cognitive Capitalism*, vol. 2 (Berlin: Archive Books, 2015). Excerpts from chapter 2 were published in *The Psychopathologies of Cognitive Capitalism*, ed. Arne De Boever and Warren Neidich (Berlin: Archive Books, 2013). Excerpts from chapter 4 appeared in *Genealogies of Speculation: Materialism and Subjectivity Since Structuralism*, ed. Armen Avanessian and Suhail Malik (New York: Bloomsbury, 2016) and *Rancière and Literature*, ed. Grace Hellyer and Julian Murphet (Edinburgh: Edinburgh University Press, 2016).

Pascal Gielen, Dennis Duncan, Suhail Malik, Julian Murphet, Grace Hellyer, Evan Kindley, Jonathan Hahn, and Pieter Vermeulen edited publications related to this project and greatly sharpened my thinking. I did my best to address the generous feedback I received from Anthony Curtis Adler and Dominic Pettman, as well as one reviewer who preferred to stay anonymous. Every day I benefit from my involvement in *Parrhesia*, the *Los Angeles Review of Books*, and *boundary* 2. Thank you Paul Bové for supporting my work and sending on articles; thank you David Golumbia for sharing your work on the politics of bitcoin and high-frequency trading; thank you Stathis Gourgouris, Efraín Kristal, and Bruce Robbins for comments on the project summary and support with fellowship applications; thank you Tricia Dailey for the Los Feliz dinner parties, where some of this work was informally discussed; thank you Martin Woessner for the conversations about Coetzee and realism.

At CalArts, Claire Phillips found a project outline in the department’s copy machine and provided enthusiastic and useful feedback. Janet Sarbanes had the patience to hear me out about Michel Houellebecq. Some of my weirdest references for this book can be traced back to James Wiltgen. Thank you, Martín Plot for the playground conversations about political epistemology. The remarkable intelligence of Reza Negarestani and Stephen Wright guided some of my reading on high-frequency trading. My research assistants Geoff Derven, Christopher Brown, Nathaniel Deines, Emily Womack-Donnini, and—at the eleventh hour—Ryan Green and Rhana Tabrizi dug up many of my secondary sources and had the patience to talk through parts of the argument with me even though they had their own theses to write. My former student Ryan Jeffery and Boaz Levin made a film titled *All That Is Solid Melts into Data* that deals with some of what’s in this book—it's required viewing, really. Asmund Havsteen-Mikkelsen allowed me to use his painting *Directing the Economy* in this book; to my eyes, the painting (from his Blue Devils series) shows the empty throne of finance and captures the connections between sovereignty, the economy, and the absence of humanity that I am interested in here. The artwork on the cover is by my friend Dan Davis.

Finally, I'd like to express my warmest thanks to my parents, for their support; Céline, Koen, Lily, and Olivia, for their hospitality; Kathy, for setting the example; Anneleen, for helping out in a time of acute crisis; and Dieter and Pieter, my oldest friends.

To Olivia, Ada, and Louise: I know debt is not the right term of relation, but once again, I owe you—for drastically reducing my work time.

—*Los Angeles, January 2017*

NOTES

INTRODUCTION

1. Meg Wolitzer, *The Interestings* (New York: Riverhead, 2013), 331.

2. Don DeLillo, *Cosmopolis* (New York: Scribner, 2003).

3. Michael Naas, "Autonomy, Autoimmunity, and the Stretch Limo: From Derrida's Rogue State to DeLillo's *Cosmopolis*," in *Derrida From Now On* (New York: Fordham University Press, 2008), 147–66. Randy Laist has suggested in this context that Eric Packer is himself "a kind of third Twin Tower, a monolithic symbol of global economic hegemony"; see Laist, "The Concept of Disappearance in Don DeLillo's *Cosmopolis*," *Critique*, no. 51 (2010): 258.

4. Note here that *Cosmopolis* is not usually considered DeLillo's "9/11 novel"; that would be *Falling Man*. See, for example, Anne Longmuir, "'This Was the World Now': *Falling Man* and the Role of the Artist after 9/11," *Modern Language Studies* 41, no. 1 (2011): 42–57. As for the relevance of *Cosmopolis* in the context of my book, Cornel Bonca has indicated in an essay about the novel published in the *Los Angeles Review of Books* (and picked up by *Salon*) that the novel, while "widely dismissed upon release," was "prophetic" in its treatment of digitized finance, among other matters; see Bonca, "Rethinking *Cosmopolis*," www.salon.com/2012/09/14/rethinking_cosmopolis/.

5. Giovanna Borradori, *Philosophy in a Time of Terror: Dialogues with Jürgen Habermas and Jacques Derrida* (Chicago: University of Chicago Press, 2003).

6. I have analyzed the absurdity of this in a chapter on W. G. Sebald's *Austerlitz* in my *States of Exception in the Contemporary Novel: Martel, Eugenides, Coetzee, Sebald* (New York: Continuum, 2012), 101–36. I will return to my analysis of Sebald in the conclusion of this book.

7. DeLillo, *Cosmopolis*, 54.

8. Ibid., 58.

9. Ibid., 77.

10. Ibid., 78.

11. Ibid., 80.

12. Ibid., 85.

13. I borrow the term *pre-9/11 novel* from Teddy Wayne, whose novel *Kapitoil* (New York: Harper Perennial, 2010) is itself situated within these various connections.

14. Chuck Palahniuk, *Fight Club* (New York: Henry Holt, 1996), 206.

15. Ibid., 206–7.

16. I have experimented, perhaps a little irresponsibly, with this aesthetic similarity in my courses, where I have started playing the ending of Fincher's *Fight Club* only to gradually replace the image (but not the song "Where is My Mind?" by The Pixies) to recordings of the Twin Towers collapsing. Students have found the effect profoundly disturbing.

17. *The Big Short* (directed by Adam McKay; Paramount, 2015) includes a reminder of the 9/11 attacks when it has some CDO managers at the American Securitization Forum in Las Vegas unload their guns at the shooting ramp at images of Osama Bin-Laden.

18. Cristina Alger, *The Darlings* (New York: Penguin, 2012).

19. I suggested this in a review of Alger's novel: Arne De Boever, "It's Not All Rotten Apples on Wall Street," https://lareviewofbooks.org/review/its-not-all-rotten-apples-on-wall-street. See also Annie McClanahan, *Dead Pledges: Debt, Crisis, and Twenty-First-Century Culture* (Stanford, CA: Stanford University Press, 2017), 30–33.

20. Jess Walter, *The Zero* (New York: Harper, 2006), 229.

21. Ibid.

22. As for the reversal of that chronology, and its suggestion that finance—or something else—may have "caused" 9/11: Walter states in a conversation published at the end of his novel: "I don't personally subscribe to the belief that we were in any way to blame for the attacks of 9/11, that American policy somehow led to a terrorist response. I think that's insane. These were irrational and criminal attacks, entirely unprovoked" (ibid., 6). "In any way," "irrational," and "entirely unprovoked": for Walter, the attacks came, then, "out of the blue," as one critic of 9/11 fiction has suggested; see Kristiaan Versluys, *Out of the Blue: September 11 and the Novel* (New York: Columbia University Press, 2009). One might wonder here, not simply about the naïveté of this position (as an American position) but also about its extreme limitations when it comes to understanding "the terrorists."

23. Leerom Medovoi has read the novel in this context as "belonging to a current mode of world literature engaged by the transitional moment associated with Giovanni Arrighi's sense of the 'terminal crisis' in American world-system hegemony"; see Medovoi, "'Terminal Crisis?': From the Worlding of American Literature to World-System Literature," *American*

Literary History 23, no. 3 (2011): 643–59. Mohsin Hamid's finance novel *How to Get Filthy Rich in Rising Asia* (New York: Riverhead, 2014) is also worth mentioning here.

24. Most of the critical work (and most of the best critical work) about the finance novel focuses on the Victorian period. There is plenty of work on the contemporary finance novel (in particular novels from the 1980s)—and its volume has been growing since the 2008 financial crisis—but at the time when I pursued the research for this book it was well eclipsed by scholarship about earlier periods.

25. Karl Marx, *Capital*, vol. 1, *A Critique of Political Economy*, trans. Ben Fowkes (London: Penguin, 1990), 247–57.

26. For a good discussion of finance and financialization, see Randy Martin, "The Twin Towers of Financialization: Entanglements of Political and Cultural Economies," *The Global South* 3, no. 1 (2009): 108–25. A CDO, as I understand it, is a very large group of mortgages that, while they are by themselves not top-rated, become top-rated when they are part of a very large group. A CDS is a financial instrument that was invented so traders could "short" or "bet against" the housing market with the goal of collecting a profit when homeowners start defaulting on their mortgages and CDOs collapse.

27. Randy Martin, *The Financialization of Daily Life* (Philadelphia: Temple University Press, 2002), 12.

28. See, for example, Luc Boltanski and Eve Chiapello, *The New Spirit of Capitalism*, trans. Gregory Elliott (New York: Verso, 2007); Pascal Gielen, *The Murmuring of the Artistic Multitude: Global Art, Memory and Postfordism* (Amsterdam: Valiz, 2009); Catherine Malabou, *What Should We Do with Our Brain?*, trans. Sebastian Rand (New York: Fordham, 2008).

29. One can find the term *cognitariat* in the works of Franco Berardi and Bernard Stiegler, among others; I will return to Berardi and Stiegler in chapters 2 and 3.

30. The language of shock is certainly appropriate here given the research presented in Naomi Klein, *The Shock Doctrine: The Rise of Disaster Capitalism* (New York: Picador, 2007).

31. Fredric Jameson, "Culture and Finance Capital," in *The Cultural Turn: Selected Writings on the Postmodern, 1983–1998* (New York: Verso, 2009), 138; Arjun Appadurai, *Banking on Words: The Failure of Language in the Age of Derivative Finance* (Chicago: Chicago University Press, 2016), 2–3.

32. Jameson, "Culture," 154.

33. Felix Martin, *Money: The Unauthorized Biography—From Coinage to Cryptocurrencies* (New York: Vintage, 2015); David Graeber, *Debt: The First 5,000 Years* (New York: Melville House, 2011).

34. It would be important to note here though that the role of debt/credit has changed: whereas they used to create a society of "balanced obligation and mutuality," as Annie McClanahan points out, that role has been destroyed by contemporary forms of debt/credit or what McClanahan summarizes as the "regime of securitization and exploitable risk, of expropriation and eviction" (McClanahan, *Dead Pledges*, 183).

35. Graeber, *Debt*, 40. I will return to this general point at length in chapter 2.

36. Ole Bjerg, *Making Money: The Philosophy of Crisis Capitalism* (New York: Verso, 2014), 149.

37. The link to literature and some of the questions about realism (and, by extension, naturalism) that I will be interested in in this context has been established by other scholars, see, for example, Walter Benn Michaels, *The Gold Standard and the Logic of Naturalism* (Berkeley: University of California Press, 1987).

38. Leigh Claire La Berge, *Scandals and Abstraction: Financial Fiction of the Long 1980s* (New York: Oxford University Press, 2015), 73.

39. Palahniuk, *Fight Club*, 168 and 173.

40. This is my particular engagement with the debates about "masculine identity" in financial culture.

41. It's beyond the scope of this introduction to review all the psychoanalytic approaches to money, capital, and finance. I take the novels that I discuss in this book as my starting point for my development of the psychoanalytic terms and will let my general argument develop from there.

42. Sigmund Freud, "Neurosis and Psychosis," in *The Ego and the Id and Other Works*, trans. James Strachey (London: Hogarth, 1975), 149–53, and "The Loss of Reality in Neurosis and Psychosis," in ibid., 183–87.

43. Klaus Biesenbach, "Sympathy for the Devil," in *Timeline*, ed. Douglas Gordon and Klaus Biesenbach (New York: Museum of Modern Art, 2006), 16.

44. Readers interested in thinking along the lines I develop in the following paragraphs may also benefit from Benjamin Kunkel, "Politicopsychopathology: Neurotocrats vs. the Grand Old Psychosis," https://nplusonemag.com/issue-15/politics/politicopsychopathology/.

45. Marx, *Capital*, 1:163.

46. Karl Marx, *Capital*, vol. 3, trans. David Fernbach (London: Penguin, 1991), 596–97. Marx doesn't define "fictitious capital" in these pages; I take the definition here from the online *Marxists Internet Archive Encyclopedia*, www.marxists.org/glossary/index.htm.

47. Jameson of course already makes this point in "Culture and Finance Capital"; see Jameson, "Culture," 143.

48. I focus on the 2010 "flash crash" in chapter 3.

49. Scurati launches this term in a discussion about realism, based on his own work in media studies; but I think it can gain traction in the study of the finance novel as well. I owe this reference to Monica Jansen.

50. See my *Narrative Care: Biopolitics and the Novel* (New York: Bloomsbury, 2013).

51. 1971 is again a key date here as it marks the invention of the microprocessor. See Brian Holmes, "Information's Metropolis: Chicago and the New Nature of Global Finance," in *Volatile Smile*, ed. Beate Geissler, Oliver Sann, and Brian Holmes (Nuremberg: Moderne Kunst Nürnberg, 2014), 36.

52. Walter Wriston, quoted in Holmes, "Information's Metropolis," 31–32. According to Holmes, Wriston "portrayed with brutal clarity . . . the transition to a highly integrated financial governance, with no popular mandate, no elected representatives and no responsibility to anything but profit. This was a cyborg system, integrating human beings and machines in an improvised and rapidly changing network" (ibid., 36).

53. See Kate Marshall's new book project, *Novels by Aliens*.

54. A good example in this context could be John Lanchester, *Capital* (New York: Norton, 2012).

55. See, for example, Teju Cole, "Seven Short Stories About Drones," https://storify.com/joshbegley/teju-cole-seven-short-stories-about-drones. Particularly interesting in the context of how I am framing this book is Joshua Clover, "How I Quit Spin," https://storify.com/bradshoup/how-i-quit-spin.

56. I am currently planning to treat these developments in more detail in a future book about the novel and information. It's interesting to ask in this context, as Quentin Tarantino has done, why the double-feature film is unthinkable in the era of binge-watching: why does the contemporary mode of attention accommodate the latter, but not the former?

57. Paul Virilio, *Speed and Politics: An Essay on Dromology*, trans. Mark Polizzotti (Los Angeles: Semiotext(e), 2006).

58. The most prominent reference is probably Fredric Jameson's work.

59. While completing this book, I became aware that Alison Shonkwiler would publish a book focusing on the same issue—literary realism and finance—but the book was set to be published too late for me to consider it here. See Alison Shonkwiler, *The Financial Imaginary: Economic Mystification and the Limits of Realist Fiction* (Minneapolis: University of Minnesota Press, 2017).

60. Anna Kornbluh, *Realizing Capital: Financial and Psychic Economies in Victorian Form* (New York: Fordham University Press, 2015), 4.

61. Kornbluh, *Realizing Capital*, 4.

62. Jameson's work is somewhat of a vanishing mediator in this book.

63. I am building here in part on a point that Leigh Claire La Berge makes in her reading of *American Psycho*, namely, that the novel destroys the very genre of the finance novel that it creates; see La Berge, *Scandals*, 114.

64. See, for example, *Bernard Stiegler: Amateur Philosophy*, ed. Arne De Boever, *boundary* 2 44, no. 1 (February 2017).

65. Joseph Vogl, *The Specter of Capital*, trans. Joachim Redner and Robert Savage (Stanford, CA: Stanford University Press, 2015). Vogl borrows the title of his book from DeLillo's *Cosmopolis*. It is worth noting, given the connections that I am establishing in this introduction between the question of sovereignty and that of finance, that Vogl has written about sovereignty in this context as well.

66. DeLillo, *Cosmopolis*, 96.

67. Karl Marx, *The Communist Manifesto* (New York: Norton, 1988), 54.

68. Jameson also makes Derrida part of this particular conversation; see Jameson, "Culture," 142. Cristina Alger accomplishes this point beautifully at the end of her realist novel *The Darlings*, with an epilogue that brings back from the dead the hedge fund manager/Ponzi scheme operator whose ghost haunts the pages of her book.

69. See, for example, Jonathan Roffe, *Abstract Market Theory* (London: Palgrave MacMillan, 2015).

70. Ute Schütte, "Out of the Shadows," *Times Higher Education*, September 22, 2011, www.timeshighereducation.com/features/out-of-the-shadows/417486.article.

71. Alex Palmer, "The Fall of Xu Xiang," *New York Times Magazine*, April 3, 2016, 48–49.

72. Holmes, "Information's Metropolis," 29.

73. In this, it is very different from McClanahan's *Dead Pledges*, which focuses on the other side.

1. REVISITING *THE BONFIRE OF THE VANITIES*

1. Tom Wolfe, "Stalking the Billion-Footed Beast: A Literary Manifesto for the New Social Novel," *Harper's Magazine* (November 1989), 52.

2. Wolfe, "Stalking," 45.

3. Literary postmodernism arrives on the US critical scene with the first issue of *boundary* 2, in 1972.

4. Wolfe, "Stalking," 55.

5. Michelle Chihara, "What We Talk About When We Talk About Finance," *Los Angeles Review of Books*, September 18, 2015, https://lareviewofbooks.org/article/what-we-talk-about-when-we-talk-about-finance/.

6. Leigh Claire La Berge, *Scandals and Abstraction: Financial Fiction of the Long 1980s* (New York: Oxford University Press, 2015), 82.

7. Kenneth Goldsmith, *Capital: New York, Capital of the 20th Century* (New York: Verso, 2016).

8. Tom Wolfe, *The Bonfire of the Vanities* (New York: Picador, 1987), 11. Hereafter cited in text by page number.

9. While this economic history gives two highly valuable points of reference, not mentioned here is the use or abuse of bonds to create complex financial products to be traded, the collateralized debt obligations mentioned in the introduction. It would seem that the opening up of the era of speculation (high-risk financial action) to make greater (obscene, even) profits, necessitated the intensification of economic defense systems (designed to prevent risk) that I will discuss in the conclusion.

10. Anticipating my argument about economic defense systems and stock market fortification in the conclusion, it is helpful that Leigh Claire La Berge characterizes this narrative as one of "narcissistic fortification and its loss"; La Berge, "The Men Who Make the Killings: *American Psycho*, Financial Masculinity, and 1980s Financial Print Culture," *Studies in American Fiction* 37, no. 2 (2010): 277.

11. While "jungle" appears to be a (racist) reference here to the Bronx, it may also refer to New York City at large. More specifically, and beyond the obvious racist reference, it also resonates with the figuration of the finance world as a "jungle" ("the financial jungle," as one reviewer of Oliver Stone's *Wall Street* put it; John Smith, quoted in John Stone, "Evil in the Early Cinema of Oliver Stone: *Platoon* and *Wall Street* as Modern Morality Plays," *Journal of Popular Film and Television* 28, no. 2 (2000): 80–87. Maria Ruskin also makes this connection to the financial jungle in *Bonfire*: Wolfe, "Stalking," 272.

12. Their panic is anticipated early on in *Bonfire*, when the novel references "that deep worry that lives in the base of the skull of every resident of Park Avenue south of Ninety-sixth Street" (16)—a worry that arises, on this count, when Sherman is about to cross a black youth in the street. Panic returns later on in the novel (459, 479), when Sherman ends up in jail. I will discuss this affect in detail in chapter 3.

13. Wolfe, "Stalking," 54.

14. Ibid., 55.

15. Ibid.

16. Ibid. 55, 56.

17. Ibid.

18. Ibid. I'm not sure what to make of this Marlboro-man novelist figure, and this *ars poetica* that promises to tame reality into submission. If it may have still held water at the time, part of what I intend to show in the following chapters is that it is shipwrecked irreparably on the shores of contemporary finance.

19. Ibid., 54.
20. Ibid., 45.
21. Ibid., 47.
22. Ibid.
23. Ibid.
24. Ibid., 48.
25. Ibid., 49.
26. Ibid., 50. Of course, with journalists like *Bonfire*'s Peter Fallow, who are really writing fiction, it's no surprise that the novelist would want to step in and offer reality.
27. Ibid., 51.
28. Ibid., 52.
29. See, for example, Liam Kennedy, "'It's the third world down there!': Urban decline and (post)national mythologies in *Bonfire of the Vanities*," *Modern Fiction Studies* 43, no. 1 (1997): 93–111; Joshua J. Masters, "Race and the Infernal City in Tom Wolfe's *Bonfire of the Vanities*," *Journal of Narrative Theory* 29, no. 2 (1999): 208–27.
30. Tom Wolfe, "Radical Chic," *New York Magazine*, July 8, 1970, http://nymag.com/news/features/46170/.
31. Ibid.
32. Ibid.
33. Ibid. Note that the support included anti-Semitic propaganda.
34. Ibid.
35. Ibid.
36. Ibid.
37. Ibid.
38. Ibid.
39. Ibid.
40. Ibid.
41. Karl Marx, *Capital*, 1:247–57.
42. Peter Sloterdijk, *Rage and Time: A Psychopolitical Investigation*, trans. Mario Wenning (New York: Columbia University Press, 2010). I discuss the figure of the rage bank in my review of Sloterdijk's book: "From Erotic Rage Bank to Thymotic World Culture," *boundary* 2 41, no. 3 (2014): 179–201.
43. A version of such a bank that has a prominent role in Wolfe's book is the so-called favor bank, where one will deposit a favor only to later reclaim it with interest.
44. Wolfe, "Stalking," 54.
45. Ibid.
46. Ibid., 54–55.

47. Lester K. Spence, "The Neoliberal Turn in Black Politics," *Souls* 14, nos. 3–4 (2012): 139–59. See also Spence, *Knocking the Hustle: Against the Neoliberal Turn in Black Politics* (New York: Punctum Books, 2015). Unsurprisingly, Spence dates this turn back to the 1970s.

48. Wolfe, "Radical," 36.

49. Richard Wright, *Native Son* (New York: Harper Perennial, 2005), 158.

50. Ibid., 396.

51. Ibid., 412.

52. Cristina Alger, *The Darlings* (New York: Penguin, 2012), 259.

53. Boris Groys, *Art Power* (Cambridge, MA: MIT Press, 2008), 124.

54. Paul Krugman points out in a 2002 article in the *New York Times* that "the America of *Wall Street* and *The Bonfire of the Vanities* was positively egalitarian compared with the country we live in today"; Krugman, "For Richer," *New York Times* October 20, 2002, www.nytimes.com/2002/10/20/magazine/for-richer.html.

55. Alger thanks Wolfe in her acknowledgments. The novel also includes a reference to Gordon Gekko from Oliver Stone's *Wall Street* (20th Century Fox, 1987). See Alger, *Darlings*, 87.

56. Alger, *Darlings*, 149.

57. Ibid., 174.

58. Suskind, quoted in Mark Danner, "Rumsfeld: Why We Live in His Ruins," *New York Review of Books*, February 6, 2014, 40.

59. Franco Berardi, *Heroes: Mass Murder and Suicide* (New York: Verso, 2015), 23.

60. See Nathaniel Popper, "Computerized Trading Firm to Take Over Barclay's NYSE Seats," www.nytimes.com/2016/01/27/business/dealbook/computerized-trading-firm-to-take-over-barclayss-nyse-seats.html.

61. Greif, "Bonfire," 55.

2. PSYCHOTIC REALISM IN (*AMERICAN*) *PSYCHO*

1. Frédéric Neyrat, "From Libidinal Economy to the Ecology of the Spirit: An Interview with Bernard Stiegler," trans. Arne De Boever, *Parrhesia*, no. 14 (2012): 9–15.

2. Richard Godden's suggestion that Bateman's activities are allegorical of finance capital during the presidency of Ronald Reagan is fairly typical of how Ellis's novel is made out to discuss finance indirectly. See Godden, "Fictions of Fictitious Capital: *American Psycho* and the Poetics of Deregulation," *Textual Practice* 25, no. 5 (2011): 853–66. Leigh Claire La Berge has made the best argument for the presence of finance in *American Psycho*; with the exception of her discussion of the presence of ATMs in the novel, though, La

Berge draws out finance's presence in the novel through a discussion of the novel's intertextual references to financier's biographies (Ivan Boesky's *Merger Mania*, Donald Trump's *The Art of the Deal*, and T. Boone Pickens's *Boone*) and its use of finance as a "frame"; in short, even in the work of as incisive a reader as La Berge, finance's direct presence in the novel is under some pressure. See La Berge, *Scandals and Abstraction: Financial Fiction of the Long 1980s* (New York: Oxford University Press, 2015), in particular 132–33.

3. In this context, it is worth noting that Aaron Chandler, in a discussion of the psychotic Eric Packer in Don DeLillo's novel *Cosmopolis*, compares Packer to a series of existentialist heroes, including, for example, Albert Camus's Meursault. Packer, who owes something to Bateman, also continues the existentialist dimension of that character. See Chandler, "'An Unsettling, Alternative Self': Benno Levin, Emmanuel Levinas, and Don DeLillo's *Cosmopolis*," *Critique* 50, no. 3 (2009): 243.

4. I will get to those histories later in this chapter. See also Simon Critchley and Tom McCarthy, "Of Chrematology: Joyce and Money," *Hypermedia Joyce Studies* 4, no. 1 (2003), http://hjs.ff.cuni.cz/archives/v3/critchley_mccarthy.html.

5. David W. Price, "Bakthinian Prosaics, Grotesque Realism, and the Question of the Carnivalesque in Bret Easton Ellis's *American Psycho*," *Southern Humanities Review* 32, no. 4 (1998): 321–46.

6. I am building here on La Berge's analysis of the novel's "realist and autobiographical modes of financial representation." Leigh Claire La Berge, "The Men Who Make the Killings: *American Psycho*, Financial Masculinity, and 1980s Financial Print Culture," *Studies in American Fiction* 37, no. 2 (2010): 274. In the article, La Berge contrasts Ellis's "postmodern" mode of narration to Wolfe's "realist one," insisting on *American Psycho*'s "detachment from reality" (277). La Berge's article is included in a revised version in her book *Scandals and Abstraction*, where some of the oppositions are nuanced—the novel is now presented as a "patchwork of what might be categorized as capitalist realist, postmodern, and autobiographical styles of financial representation" (La Berge, *Scandals*, 114).

7. Gein also makes an appearance in *American Psycho*: Patrick Bateman seems to mention him appreciatively in conversation, noting he was "an interesting guy"; Bret Easton Ellis, *American Psycho* (New York: Vintage, 1991), 92.

8. I mention this rich afterlife of *Psycho* because I think the financial aspect of these horror films ought to be pursued. Annie McClanahan has done some fascinating work on horror in this context; see, for example, "Dead Pledges: Debt, Horror, and the Credit Crisis," Post45 (website), May 7, 2012, http://post45.research.yale.edu/2012/05/dead-pledges-debt-horror-and-the-credit-crisis/.

9. Robert Bloch, *Psycho* (New York: Overlook, 2010), 170–71.
10. Ibid., 172.
11. All of this explaining has lead some to characterize Michelangelo Antonioni's *L'Avventura* (Cino Del Duca, 1960—the same year as Hitchcock's film) as the narratively more disturbing version of *Psycho*: although in *L'Avventura* a woman protagonist also disappears early on in the film (just as in Hitchcock's *Psycho* Janet Leigh), *L'Avventura* never answers the questions that that disappearance raises. Hitchcock does answer them, and answers them with psychosis.
12. Bloch, *Psycho*, 174–75.
13. Ibid., 172.
14. Ibid., 36.
15. Ibid.
16. Ibid.
17. Ibid., 38.
18. I am trying to restore attention here to Marion in Hitchcock's film. When Marion is killed off early on into Hitchcock's feature, the money theme is also killed off—but in a sense the film's challenge is to read the theme of psychosis, around which the bulk of the film revolves, back into its opening half hour.
19. Cynthia Erb's reading of Hitchcock's film goes in this direction, focusing on Marion for her discussion of "the meaning of money" in the film. Erb, "'Have You Ever Seen the Inside of One of Those Places?': *Psycho*, Foucault, and the Postwar Context of Madness," *Cinema Journal* 45, no. 4 (2006): 60.
20. "Neuroeconomics" and "behavioral finance" are fields that are driven in part by this realization. Part of what they focus on is the irrational component of the market, namely panic (which I discuss in chapter 3).
21. I would suggest that this connection of gazes also be extended to Mary Harron's *American Psycho* (Lionsgate, 2000) and Adam McKay's *The Big Short* (Paramount, 2015). See for example John Thomason's comparative discussion of Christian Bale's gaze as Patrick Bateman in *American Psycho* and as Michael Burry in *The Big Short* in "'We Would Prefer Not To': 'The Big Short' and Liberalism's Myths," *Los Angeles Review of Books*, February 27, 2016, https://lareviewofbooks.org/article/we-would-prefer-not-to-the-big-short-and-liberalisms-myths/.
22. Patrick McGilligan, "Fact-checking Hitchcock: The Man, the Movie, and the Myth," *NPR*, December 24, 2012, www.npr.org/2012/12/24/167539437/fact-checking-hitchcock-the-man-the-movie-and-the-myth.
23. William Gaddis, *J R* (Champaign, IL: Dalkey Archive, 2012), 3.
24. Ellis, *American Psycho*, 108.
25. La Berge, *Scandals*, 73.

26. Bloch, *Psycho*, 17–18.

27. Needless to say, this is an evolution that has effected "real estate" as well, as evidenced by the 2008 crash. For an excellent overview of bitcoin and a provocative discussion of its politics, see David Golumbia, *The Politics of Bitcoin: Software as Rightwing Extremism* (Minneapolis: University of Minnesota Press, 2016).

28. La Berge points out that the Chemical Bank, which is mentioned on the novel's first page, "was the first bank to have a functioning ATM in 1971" (*Scandals*, 134).

29. The *Monopoly* board game was rather popular in the 1970s, with the first international *Monopoly* tournaments being held. See also the references to "Monopoly Capital" in Fredric Jameson, "Culture and Finance Capital," in *The Cultural Turn: Selected Writings on the Postmodern, 1983–1998* (New York: Verso, 2009), 136–61.

30. Marc Jongen, ed., *Der Göttliche Kapitalismus: Ein Gespräch über Geld, Konsum, Kunst und Zerstörung mit Boris Groys, Jochen Hörisch, Thomas Macho, Peter Sloterdijk und Peter Weibel* (Paderborn, Germany: Wilhelm Fink, 2007).

31. On this count, see A. Kiarina Kordela, "Political Metaphysics: God in Global Capitalism (the Slave, the Masters, Lacan, and the Surplus)," *Political Theory* 27, no. 2 (1999): 789–839.

32. Anna Kornbluh, *Realizing Capital: Financial and Psychic Economies in Victorian Form* (New York: Fordham University Press, 2015), 12.

33. Adam Smith, *The Wealth of Nations* (New York: Modern Library, 2000).

34. Ibid., 25.

35. Ibid., 27.

36. Ibid., 30.

37. Ibid.

38. Felix Martin, *Money: The Unauthorized Biography—From Coinage to Cryptocurrencies* (New York: Vintage, 2015).

39. David Graeber, *Debt: The First 5,000 Years* (New York: Melville House, 2011).

40. Ole Bjerg, *Making Money: The Philosophy of Crisis Capitalism* (New York: Verso, 2014), in particular chs. 3 and 4.

41. On the psychotic economic culture, see also Frédéric Kaplan, "Quand les mots valent l'or," *Le Monde diplomatique* (November 2011), www.monde-diplomatique.fr/2011/11/KAPLAN/46925.

42. Cristina Alger evokes this other reading of financial performance as well when she indicates that the feigned suicide of hedge fund manager/Ponzi scheme operator Morty Reis "had been . . . his best performance." Alger, *The Darlings* (New York: Penguin, 2012), 318.

43. Christian Marazzi, *Capital and Language: From the New Economy to the War Economy*, trans. Gregory Conti (Los Angeles: Semiotext(e), 2008), 33–36;

Bernard Stiegler, *For a New Critique of Political Economy*, trans. Daniel Ross (Cambridge: Polity, 2013), 67.

44. Karl Marx, *Capital: Volume 1*, trans. Ben Fowkes (London: Penguin, 1990), 257.

45. *Capitalism: A Love Story*, directed by Michael Moore (Overture, 2009).

46. Stiegler, *New Critique*, 47.

47. Marx quoted in Stiegler, *New Critique*, 39. When in Robert Harris's *The Fear Index* (discussed in chapter 3) the quants working at a hedge fund need to dismantle a risky market position that their algorithm has taken up, none of them know how to do any actual trading—technology, as Hugo Quarry puts it, had "enfeebled" them, had "proletarianized" them, in Stiegler's language. Harris, *The Fear Index* (New York: Knopf, 2012), 192.

48. Franco Berardi, *The Uprising: Poetry and Finance* (Los Angeles: Semiotext(e), 2012), 134.

49. Marx, *Capital*, 3:596–97. I take the definition from the online *Encyclopedia of Marxism*, www.marxists.org/glossary/terms/f/i.htm.

50. Andrea Fumagalli and Sandro Mezzadra, *Crisis in the Global Economy: Financial Markets, Social Struggles, and New Political Scenarios*, trans. Jason Francis Mc Gimsey (Los Angeles: Semiotext(e), 2010).

51. Arjun Appadurai, *Banking on Words: The Failure of Language in the Age of Derivative Finance* (Chicago: Chicago University Press, 2016), 4.

52. Appadurai, *Banking*, 4.

53. Ibid.

54. Ibid., 5.

55. See, for example, Nathan Heller, "Cashing Out: Are There Costs to Getting Rid of Paper Money?," *New Yorker*, October 10, 2016, 48–55. See also Bill Maurer, *How Would You Like to Pay? How Technology is Changing the Future of Money* (Durham, NC: Duke University Press, 2015).

56. Ellis, *American Psycho*, 7.

57. Heller, "Cashing Out," 54.

58. Ellis, *American Psycho*, 44–45.

59. Mark Hansen, "The Time of Affect, or Bearing Witness to Life." *Critical Inquiry* 30, no. 3 (2004): 591–92.

60. Michael Fried, *Four Honest Outlaws: Sala, Ray, Marioni, Gordon* (New Haven, CT: Yale University Press, 2011), 188.

61. Christine Ross, "The Insufficiency of the Performative: Video Art at the Turn of the Millennium," *Art Journal* 60, no. 1 (2001): 31.

62. Jeff Gordinier, quoted in Scott Timberg, "Reassessment: The Gen X Poster Boy's Endless Ennui; Bret Easton Ellis Won't Care, but Colleagues See New Respect Coming" (*Los Angeles Times*, March 23, 2008, F1).

63. See the introduction.

64. Ayn Rand's obsession with the serial killer William Edward Hickman is worth noting in this context, even if Lisa Duggan may have made too much of it in her "Optimistic Cruelty," *Social Text Online*, January 15, 2013, http://socialtextjournal.org/periscope_article/optimistic-cruelty/.

65. See, for example, John N. Berry III, "American Psycho Is Not the Problem," *Library Journal* 116, no. 1 (1991): 6.

66. Ellis, *American Psycho*, 4.

67. Ibid., 36.

68. Ibid., 37.

69. Ibid., 38.

70. Ibid., 15–16.

71. Bateman is, on this count, certainly more confusing than one of his heroes, Donald Trump, who when he was running for president clearly came down on the racist side of Bateman's seemingly split personally.

72. Ellis, *American*, 18.

73. Ibid.

74. Ibid., 207–8.

75. Ibid., 387.

76. Theodore Martin has drawn out this connection in "The Privilege of Contemporary Life: Periodization in the Bret Easton Ellis Decades," *Modern Language Quarterly* 71, no. 2 (2010): 153–74.

77. Bernard Stiegler, *The Decadence of Industrial Democracies: Disbelief and Discredit*, vol. 1., trans. Daniel Ross and Suzanne Arnold (Cambridge, UK: Polity, 2011), 62–63.

78. Ibid., 81–82.

79. Stiegler, *New Critique*, 64.

80. Ellis, *American*, 377.

81. Bernard Stiegler, *Uncontrollable Societies of Disaffected Individuals: Disbelief and Discredit*, vol. 2, trans. Daniel Ross (Cambridge, UK: Polity, 2013), 49–50.

82. Stiegler, *Uncontrollable*, 50.

83. Bernard Stiegler, *Acting Out*, trans. David Barison, Daniel Ross, and Patrick Crogan (Stanford, CA: Stanford University Press, 2009), 38.

84. Martin Scorsese pictures Belfort's life, as described in his books, in *The Wolf of Wall Street* (Paramount, 2013).

85. See also Franco "Bifo" Berardi, *Heroes: Mass Murder and Suicide* (New York: Verso, 2015).

86. The reference is to Jean-Paul Sartre's play *Huis Clos* (1944), translated as *No Exit*, which includes the famous line "l'enfer, c'est les autres" (Hell is other people). The novel's reference to the hellish "no exit" thus brings *American Psycho* full circle, given that the text begins with a reference to Dante's *Inferno*.

87. Ellis, *American Psycho*, 137, 143, 148, and 177.

88. Carla Freccero recalls this fact in "Historical Violence, Censorship, and the Serial Killer: The Case of 'American Psycho,'" *Diacritics* 27, no. 2 (1997): 54.

89. Thomas Heise notes that "Bateman is best understood not as a misogynist or a racist or even a serial killer but as Ellis's fantasy of the quintessential neoliberal subject or, as Barry Keith Grant has suggested, as 'merely the logical end of human relations under capitalism.'" Heise, "*American Psycho*: Neoliberal Fantasies and the Death of Downtown," *Arizona Quarterly* 67, no. 1 (2011): 144.

90. Ellis, *American Psycho*, 376–77.

91. Ibid., 377.

92. Ibid.

93. In other words, there is something about Bateman that exceeds what Reza Negarestani has called "the labor of the inhuman." Negarestani, "The Labor of the Inhuman, Part I: Human," *e-flux journal*, no. 52 (2014), www.e-flux.com/journal/52/59920/the-labor-of-the-inhuman-part-i-human/.

94. In a review of Mary Harron's cinematic rendering of the novel, Linda S. Kauffman writes of Bateman's "robotic consumption." Kauffman, review of *American Psycho*, *Film Quarterly* 54, no. 2 (2000–2001): 42; another reviewer of the film speaks of Ellis's "bland, almost mechanical prose." Richard Porton, review of *American Psycho*, *Cineaste* 25, no. 3 (2000): 44. Leigh Claire La Berge characterizes Bateman's narration as that of an "automated teller" (*Scandals*, 136).

95. Stiegler, *New Critique*, 45.

96. Dominic Pettman, *Look at the Bunny: Totem, Taboo, Technology* (Winchester: Zero Books, 2013), 66.

97. Ibid., 66–67.

98. See Brian Holmes, "Information's Metropolis: Chicago and the New Nature of Global Finance," in *Volatile Smile*, ed. Beate Geissler, Oliver Sann, and Brian Holmes (Nuremberg: Moderne Kunst Nürnberg, 2014), 32.

3. FINANCIAL REALISM IN *THE FEAR INDEX*

1. Karin Knorr Cetina, "What If the Screens Went Black?," in *Volatile Smile*, ed. Beate Geissler, Oliver Sann, and Brian Holmes (Nuremberg: Moderne Kunst Nürnberg, 2014), 113.

2. Robert Harris, *The Fear Index* (New York: Knopf, 2012), 3. Hereafter cited in text by page number.

3. Something similar will happen later in the novel when records indicate that he bought all of his wife's art at her gallery opening—but he is quite certain that he never did such a thing.

4. I began to discuss the relevance of this (specifically, the autoimmunizing effects of such attempts at immunization/fortification) in the introduction, in my reading of Don DeLillo's *Cosmopolis*; I will come back to it at length in the conclusion. That the problematic here is one of intense sovereignty is made clear on page 53 of *The Fear Index*, where the building floor that is occupied by Alex's company is described as "a kingdom within a kingdom."

5. The novel repeatedly casts Alex as the algorithm's father (149, 215, 232, 262), even if Alex is also referred to as "babyish" in its opening and closing pages (16, 286). This suggests that the novel is about the creator's transformation into a creature. This is further reinforced by the information that Alex's wife Gabrielle has had several miscarriages: VIXAL-4 is like a child to Alex (89); the novel suggests the same thing about Gabi's relation to her art. The vulnerable side of Alex, and by extension of human beings in general, is evoked in the novel through Gabi's art. Modeled after the real artwork of Angela Palmer (www.angelaspalmer.com), the work suggests the precariousness of human life that stands in stark contrast with Alex's math-based attempt to beat the market. On this, see also the conclusion.

6. Ibid., 73.

7. Hoffmann is involved in the study of particle acceleration and is associated with acceleration at several points in the novel (for example, ibid., 247). One might think of him as an "accelerationist" who moved from physics into the realm of finance.

8. Panic is of course an important category in economy theory. See, for example, Paul Krugman's review of Timothy Geithner's book *The Stress Test*, "Does He Pass the Test?," *New York Review of Books*, July 10, 2014, www.nybooks.com/articles/2014/07/10/geithner-does-he-pass-test/. For an overview of panic in literature, see David Zimmerman, *Panic! Markets, Crises, and Crowds in American Fiction* (Chapel Hill: University of North Carolina Press, 2012).

9. One of the field's most important figures, Richard Thaler, makes an appearance in Adam McKay's *The Big Short* (Paramount, 2015) to explain (with Selena Gomez) what a synthetic CDO is.

10. In the terms suggested by Donald MacKenzie, it's not just a camera but an engine; see MacKenzie, *An Engine, Not a Camera: How Financial Models Shape Markets* (Cambridge, MA: MIT Press, 2006).

11. The novel's general background is the austerity crisis in Europe, in particular in Greece. See ibid., 49.

12. Cetina, "What If," in Geissler et al., *Volatile Smile*, 114.

13. Importantly, it is automation that will lie at the root of Alex's downfall, as it is the key enabler for his destruction in the novel.

14. Throughout, the novel plays with the suggestion that it is Alex himself who is the agent of his destruction. When Alex asks the man who appears to be after him why he wants to kill him, he replies: "Because you invited me" (160). This recalls the problematic of autoimmunization as I discussed in the introduction.

15. For my characterization of Pan, I rely on *Wikipedia*, https://en.wikipedia.org/wiki/Pan_%28god%29.

16. Franco Berardi, *Precarious Rhapsody: Semiocapitalism and the Pathologies of the Post-Alpha Generation* (London: Minor Compositions, 2009), 44.

17. Ibid., 44.

18. Ibid., 45

19. Franco Berardi, *After the Future*, trans. Arianna Bove et al. (Edinburgh: AK Press, 2011), 94–95.

20. Franco Berardi, *The Soul at Work: From Alienation to Autonomy*, trans. Francesca Cadel and Giuseppina Mecchia (London: Minor Compositions, 2009), 98.

21. Berardi, *Soul*, 101.

22. Ibid.

23. Ibid.

24. Ibid.

25. One contemporary philosopher who has developed a sustained analysis of this situation is Bernard Stiegler. See in particular Stiegler's three-volume "Disbelief and Discredit" series: *The Decadence of Industrial Democracies* (*Disbelief and Discredit*, vol. 1), trans. Daniel Ross and Suzanne Arnold (Cambridge, UK: Polity, 2011); *Uncontrollable Societies of Disaffected Individuals* (*Disbelief and Discredit*, vol. 2), trans. Daniel Ross (Cambridge, UK: Polity, 2013); and *The Lost Spirit of Capitalism* (*Disbelief and Discredit*, vol. 3), trans. Daniel Ross (Cambridge, UK: Polity, 2014). Two other references, more closely related to Berardi's work, that are helpful in this context are: Christian Marazzi, *Capital and Language: From the New Economy to the War Economy*, trans. Gregory Conti (Los Angeles: Semiotext(e), 2008); Andrea Fumagalli and Sandra Mezzadra, eds., *Crisis in the Global Economy: Financial Markets, Social Struggles, and New Political Scenarios*, trans. Jason Francis McGimsey (Los Angeles: Semiotext(e), 2010).

26. Dominic Pettman, *After the Orgy: Toward a Politics of Exhaustion* (Albany: State University of New York Press, 2002), 25.

27. Pettman, *Orgy*, 32.

28. VIXAL-4 is an example of what has been called an "autonomous artificial agent"; Chopra and White, quoted in Frank Pasquale, *The Black Box Society: The Secret Algorithms That Govern Money and Information* (Cambridge, MA: Harvard University Press, 2015), 193.

29. Like Eric Packer's body in DeLillo's *Cosmopolis*, Alex's body is both a body politic and a body economic in this situation, marking both the political invasion of his home fortress and the imminent collapse of his fort-like business.

30. Bernard Stiegler, *Dans la disruption: Comment ne pas devenir fou?* (Paris: Les Liens Qui Libèrent, 2015).

31. Hannah Arendt, *The Life of the Mind* (New York: Harcourt, 1978).

32. Of course, the trope includes degrees of madness, ranging from the mild, generalized psychosis by which Mary Crane is overcome in Robert Bloch's *Psycho* (1959) when she is faced with $40,000 in cash, to the more extreme financial psychosis of Bret Easton Ellis's Patrick Bateman in *American Psycho* (1991), to name just two examples. For more details, see chapter 2.

33. Ibid., acknowledgments.

34. See "Death and the Machine," *Economist*, October 1, 2011, www.economist.com/node/21530936.

35. Pettman humorously stages this difference in: "Love in the Time of Tamagotchi," in *Look at the Bunny: Totem, Taboo, Technology* (Washington, DC: Zero Books, 2013), 99–119.

36. Alex himself in fact explicitly warns against this, saying that it is a mistake to think that artificial intelligence research seeks to imitate the human mind (38).

37. This "aesthetic" problem also marks the key ethical issue of the book, which is whether human beings should interfere with the extremely risky market position that the algorithm is taking up, for example when it turns out the algorithm is removing the hedge of its fund—thus taking away the funds' protection against loss.

38. Ian Bogost, *Alien Phenomenology, Or What It's Like to Be a Thing* (Minneapolis: University of Minnesota Press, 2012), 40.

39. Ibid.

40. This may in part be why others have been able to argue that more experimental literary forms are better equipped to capture the reality of algorithmic life. See Brian Kim Stefans, "Terrible Engines: A Speculative Turn in Recent Poetry and Fiction," *Comparative Literature Studies* 51, no. 1 (2014): 159–83.

41. Cetina, "What If," in Geissler, *Volatile Smile*, 123.

42. Pettman, *Look*, 76.

43. Alison Shonkwiler and Leigh Claire La Berge, eds. *Reading Capitalist Realism* (Iowa City: University of Iowa Press, 2014), 1.

44. Ibid., 11.

45. Ibid., 15.

46. Ibid., 16.

47. Jameson, quoted in ibid., 17.

48. Anna Kornbluh, *Realizing Capital: Financial and Psychic Economies in Victorian Form* (New York: Fordham University Press, 2014), 4.

49. I take the definition here from the online *Marxists Internet Archive Encyclopedia*, www.marxists.org/glossary/index.htm.

50. Leigh Claire La Berge, *Scandals and Abstraction: Financial Fiction of the Long 1980s* (Oxford: Oxford University Press, 2015).

51. Shonkwiler and La Berge, *Reading*, 9.

52. Kluge, quoted in ibid., 252.

53. Julia Breitbach, *Analog Fictions for the Digital Age: Literary Realism and Photographic Discourses in Novels after 2000* (Rochester, NY: Camden House, 2012), 6.

54. Ibid., 7–8.

55. Ibid., 8.

56. Ibid., 9–10.

57. Ibid., 10.

58. La Berge, *Scandals*, 82: "there is something wonderfully postmodern about Wolfe's project."

59. Jeffrey Nealon, *Post-Postmodernism, Or, the Cultural Logic of Just-In-Time Capitalism* (Stanford: Stanford University Press, 2012).

60. See Shonkwiler and La Berge, *Reading*, 2 and 4, for example.

4. THE FINANCIAL UNIVERSE (AFTER MEILLASSOUX)

1. Mark Fisher, *Capitalist Realism: Is There No Alternative?* (Winchester, UK: Zero Books, 2009).

2. Jodi Dean and Mark Fisher, "We Can't Afford to Be Realists: A Conversation," in *Reading Capitalist Realism*, ed. Leigh Claire La Berge and Alison Shonkwiler (Iowa City: University of Iowa Press, 2014), 28.

3. The fact that we are dealing with an ontological shift here demands that we develop a philosophical approach to it, as Ole Bjerg (following Heidegger) has argued. See Ole Bjerg, *Making Money: The Philosophy of Crisis Capitalism* (New York: Verso, 2014).

4. Brian Holmes, "Information's Metropolis: Chicago and the New Nature of Global Finance," in *Volatile Smile*, ed. Beate Geissler, Oliver Sann, and Brian Holmes (Nuremberg: Moderne Kunst Nürnberg, 2014), 49.

5. Scott Patterson, *Dark Pools: The Rise of the Machine Traders and the Rigging of the US Stock Market* (New York: Crown Business, 2012).

6. Suhail Malik, "The Ontology of Finance: Price, Power, and the Arkhéderivative," in *Collapse VIII: Casino Real* (Falmouth, UK: Urbanomic, 2014), 686.

7. Frank Pasquale, *The Black Box Society: The Secret Algorithms That Govern Money and Information* (Cambridge, MA: Harvard University Press, 2015),

171. The term *black hole* appears elsewhere in Pasquale's book as well, for example on page 175.

8. Bret Easton Ellis, *American Psycho* (New York: Vintage, 1992), 276.

9. Ibid., 275.

10. See, for example, *The Fear Index*, which represents such "black box" trading: Robert Harris, *The Fear Index* (New York: Knopf, 2012), 100.

11. For example, Michael Lewis, *Flash Boys: A Wall Street Revolt* (New York: Norton, 2014), 165.

12. Cristina Alger, *The Darlings* (New York: Penguin, 2012), 82. Alger also twice uses the term *black hole*, on pages 142 and 281.

13. See Pasquale, *Black Box Society.*

14. Bernard Stiegler, *La société automatique 1: Le futur du travail* (Paris: Fayard, 2015).

15. See in particular Lewis, *Flash*, ch. 3.

16. Vincent Bontems and Roland Lehoucq, *Les idées noires de la physique* (Paris: Les Belles Lettres, 2016), 13. For their discussion of "phenomenotechnics," a neologism coined by Gaston Bachelard, see ibid., 11. All translations from the French are mine. The book's title translates as "black ideas in physics," but the authors point out in the book's final chapter that to translate "noires" as "black" does not fully work in English as many of the phenomena that are called "noir" in French are translated by "dark" in English.

17. Scott Patterson uses the phrase "money grid" to refer to what I have in mind; see Scott Patterson, *The Quants: How a New Breed of Math Whizzes Conquered Wall Street and Nearly Destroyed It* (New York: Crown Business, 2010), 118.

18. Leigh Claire La Berge, *Scandals and Abstraction: Financial Fiction of the Long 1980s* (Oxford: Oxford University Press, 2015), 130.

19. Renaissance Technologies is credited in *The Fear Index* as "the daddy of all algorithmic hedge funds" (Harris, *Fear Index*, 181).

20. Patterson, *Quants*, 112.

21. Brian Holmes also mentions this in "The Philosophy of Finance," Continental Drift (blog), August 12, 2011, https://brianholmes.wordpress.com/2011/08/12/the-philosophy-of-finance/.

22. See *New York Review of Books*, March 10, 2016, www.nybooks.com/issues/2016/03/10/.

23. James Owen Weatherall, *The Physics of Wall Street* (New York: Houghton Miflin Harcourt, 2013). Once one starts looking, the universe is suddenly everywhere in accounts of finance. In his account of the fall of China's hedge fund king Xu Xiang, for example, Alex Palmer notes that Xiang's career started at the "Galaxy Securities trading hall." See Alex Palmer, "The Fall of Xu Xiang," *New York Times Magazine*, April 3, 2016, 48.

24. Bontems, *Idées*, 85. The chapter on which I am relying was written by Roland Lehoucq. Because of its gravitational pull, it is difficult to see a black hole—all surrounding information is pulled back to its center.

25. Ibid., 91.

26. Ibid., 88.

27. This is a key element of the plot of Christopher Nolan's film about black holes, *Interstellar* (Paramount Pictures, 2014). When Joseph Cooper travels into a black hole, he can communicate with earth only by using gravity to sign through messages in binary code and morse. One of the many interesting things about *Interstellar* is that it operates in a realist mode for its representation of this most psychotic of subjects, the black hole. Consider, for example, the hyperrealistic testimonies with which Nolan opens the film—Nolan in fact sets up a realist challenge here, for we will see the testimonies again at the end of the film when they turn out to be video materials that are presented as part of a space station museum exhibit; Nolan appears to be asking whether the testimonies' realism is undermined by their setting—as well as the fact that Nolan for his narrative and representation of black holes worked closely with scientists from the California Institute of Technology.

28. Ibid., 89.

29. The year 1971, of course, is a crucial date in this book for other reasons: it is the year when Nixon abolishes the gold standard, causing, as I have suggested, the foundations for the financial markets as we know them today to be laid; the date also marks postmodernism's takeover of realism as per Tom Wolfe's account, discussed in chapter 1; the date turned out to be significant for the history of black power as well—both for the history of the Black Panther Party (which split up in 1971), and for the neoliberalization of black power (as documented by Lester Spence).

30. Ibid.

31. Ibid., 99.

32. Elie Ayache, *The Blank Swan: The End of Probability* (Chichester, UK: John Wiley, 2010).

33. Nassim Nicholas Taleb, *The Black Swan: The Impact of the Highly Improbable* (New York: Random House, 2010).

34. One would be forgiven here if one heard an echo of "black holes" in "Black Scholes." I thank Jonathan Arac for bringing this to my attention. The name "Black Scholes" refers to the scholars Fischer Black and Myron Scholes, who came up with the formula. It is also often referenced as the Black-Scholes-Merton formula to include Robert Merton, who expanded it using "Japanese rocket science." See Holmes, "Information's Metropolis," in *Volatile Smile*, 35.

35. This is, as I see it, the "wild" randomness (as opposed to merely "mild" randomness) that Benoit Mandelbrot theorizes. See Bjerg, *Making Money*, 224.

36. Jon Roffe, "The Writing of the Market: Interview with Elie Ayache," in *Collapse VIII: Casino Real* (Falmouth, UK: Urbanomic, 2014), 517–602. What Ayache has in mind is "pricing" in particular. My own understanding of "writing" exceeds that to include modeling and coding.

37. Elie Ayache, *The Medium of Contingency: An Inverse View of the Market* (New York: Palgrave, 2015).

38. See, for example, Gordon Haber, "The Biblical Money Code," Religion Dispatches (online), August 23, 2013, http://religiondispatches.org/the-biblical-money-code/. I will return to this in the conclusion.

39. Quentin Meillassoux, *After Finitude: An Essay on the Necessity of Contingency*, trans. Ray Brassier (New York: Continuum, 2008), 7.

40. Quentin Meillassoux, *The Number and the Siren: A Decipherment of Mallarmé's* Coup de dés, trans. Robin MacKay (Falmouth, UK: Urbanomic, 2011), 216.

41. See also Armen Avanessian and Gerald Nestler, eds., *Making of Finance* (Berlin: Merve, 2015).

42. Michel Houellebecq, *H. P. Lovecraft: Against the World, Against Life*, trans. Dorna Khazeni (San Francisco: McSweeney's Believer Books, 2005).

43. Tom Wolfe, "Stalking the Billion-Footed Beast: A Literary Manifesto for the New Social Novel," *Harper's Magazine* (November 1989), 45.

44. Ibid., 48.

45. Ibid., 50.

46. Ibid., 51.

47. Ibid., 55.

48. Arne De Boever, *Narrative Care: Biopolitics and the Novel* (New York: Bloomsbury, 2013).

49. Julia Breitbach summarizes "certain die-hard characteristics" of realism, "such as the focus on what the reader deems to be ordinary people leading ordinary lives, a particular attention to quotidian detail, or the shunning of unheard-of incidents and improbabilities. Realism, as David Lodge has aptly summarized it, deals in 'the representation of experience in a manner which approximates closely to the descriptions of similar experiences in nonliterary [discourses] of the same culture.'" Julia Breitbach, *Analog Fictions for the Digital Age: Literary Realism and Photographic Discourses in Novels after 2000* (Rochester, NY: Camden House, 2012), 9–10.

50. Ian Watt, *The Rise of the Novel: Studies in Defoe, Richardson and Fielding* (Harmondsworth, UK: Penguin, 1970), 25.

51. Daniel Defoe, *Robinson Crusoe* (New York: Random House, 2001).

52. Yann Martel, *Life of Pi* (Orlando, FL: Harcourt, 2001), viii.

53. Michel Foucault, "The Right of Death and Power over Life," in *The History of Sexuality: An Introduction*, vol. 1, trans. Robert Hurley (New York: Vintage, 1990), 135–59.

54. Peter Sloterdijk, "Rules for the Human Zoo: A Response to the *Letter on Humanism*," *Environment and Planning D: Society and Space*, no. 27 (2009): 23.

55. The word *taming* occurs multiple times in Ole Bjerg's philosophical approach to finance (which does not mention Wolfe). Bjerg associates the term with the trader's desire (Bjerg, *Making Money*, 45); Bjerg also mentions in his discussion of predictability versus probability Ian Hacking's book *The Taming of Chance* (ibid., 65). There are obviously different modalities of taming—predictability versus probability name two of them—and while a desire to tame continues to inform market approaches today, it will nevertheless be important to consider a shift in the modalities of taming that has to do with the ontological shift that I am diagnosing here.

56. Claude Lévi-Strauss, *Structural Anthropology*, trans. Claire Jacobson and Brooke Grundfest Schoepf (New York: Basic Books, 1974), 206–31.

57. Fredric Jameson, *The Political Unconscious: Narrative as a Socially Symbolic Act* (Ithaca, NY: Cornell University Press, 1982), 77.

58. Roland Barthes, *S/Z*, trans. Richard Miller (New York: Hill and Wang, 1974), 217.

59. Jeffrey Nealon, *Post-Postmodernism, Or, the Cultural Logic of Just-In-Time Capitalism* (Stanford: Stanford University Press, 2012). Nealon writes that "there's probably no better description of the notoriously complex financial device known as the 'derivative' than what Derrida called, after Benjamin, a 'messianism without messianism'" and insists that "the dominant logic of economics in the neoliberal revolution years has in many ways been isomorphic—how could it not be?—with the cultural logic of the humanities and the rise of theory" (173).

60. See James Wood, "Human, All Too Human," *New Republic* (online), July 23, 2000, www.newrepublic.com/article/books-and-arts/human-all-too-inhuman.

61. See Zadie Smith, "This Is How It Feels to Me," *Guardian*, October 13, 2001, www.theguardian.com/books/2001/oct/13/fiction.afghanistan.

62. Quentin Meillassoux, "Metaphysics and Extro-Science Fiction," trans. Robin MacKay, Florian Hecker, *Speculative Solution*, Urbanomic, 2010, compact disc, liner notes, 25–60. All references here are to this essay. For the book, see Quentin Meillassoux, *Science Fiction and Extro-Science Fiction*, trans. Alyosha Edlebi (Minneapolis: Univocal, 2015).

63. Meillassoux, "Metaphysics," 27.

64. Ibid.

65. Ibid., 30.

66. Ibid., 31.

67. Ibid.

68. Ibid., 35.

69. Ibid., 36.
70. Ibid., 50.
71. Ibid., 52.
72. Ibid., 56–57.
73. Ibid., 60.
74. Ibid.
75. Ibid., 58.
76. Michelle Chihara, "What We Talk About When We Talk About Finance," *Los Angeles Review of Books*, September 18, 2015, https://lareviewofbooks.org/article/what-we-talk-about-when-we-talk-about-finance/.
77. Ian Bogost, *Alien Phenomenology, Or What It's Like to Be a Thing* (Minneapolis: University of Minnesota Press, 2012), 40. The reference to Ben Marcus is on page 82. I am taking the descriptions of Marcus's work from the book's cover.
78. Bogost, *Alien*, 82.
79. Katherine N. Hayles, "Cognition Everywhere: The Rise of the Cognitive Nonconcious and the Costs of Consciousness," *New Literary History* 45, no. 2 (2014): 199–220.
80. Brian Kim Stefans, "Terrible Engines: A Speculative Turn in Recent Poetry and Fiction," *Comparative Literature Studies* 51, no. 1 (2014): 159–83.
81. Mathew Timmons, *Credit* (Los Angeles: Blanc Press, 2009). See also the publisher's website at www.insertblancpress.net/products/credit-by-mathew-timmons. For a different perspective on *Credit*, see Annie McClanahan, *Dead Pledges: Debt, Crisis, and Twenty-First-Century Culture* (Stanford: Stanford University Press, 2016).
82. Brian Kim Stefans, *Conceptual Writing: The L.A. Brand* (Los Angeles: Area Sneaks, 2014), 9.
83. Ibid.

5. MICHEL HOUELLEBECQ, FINANCE NOVELIST

1. John McCann, *Michel Houellebecq: Author of Our Times* (Bern: Peter Lang, 2010), 5.
2. Not everyone appreciates what Houellebecq does with realism in this context. James Wood panned *The Map and the Territory*'s engagement with realism; see Wood, "Off the Map," *New Yorker*, January 2012, 78. Laura Kipnis's negative review also focuses on the issue of realism in the novel; see Kipnis, "Death by Self-Parody," *Bookforum* (December–January 2012), 22. A more accurate description would probably be that Houellebecq brings together realist and postmodernist aesthetics in his work.
3. Ben Jeffery, *Anti-Matter: Michel Houellebecq and Depressive Realism* (Winchester, UK: Zero Books, 2011), 68.

4. Bernard Maris, *Houellebecq Economiste* (Paris: Flammarion, 2014).

5. See Nurit Buchweitz, *An Officer of Civilization: The Poetics of Michel Houellebecq* (Bern: Peter Lang, 2015), in particular 97–118.

6. In the next chapter, I will look at a novelist who does put the novel at the center of such an investigation.

7. Carole Sweeney, "'And yet some free time remains . . .': Post-Fordism and Writing in Michel Houellebecq's *Whatever*," *Journal of Modern Literature* 33, no. 4 (2010): 41–56.

8. See, for example, Michael Hardt and Antonio Negri, *Empire* (Cambridge, MA: Harvard University Press, 2000).

9. Luc Boltanski and Eve Chiapello, *The New Spirit of Capitalism* (London: Verso, 2007). I have also learned much in this context from Pascal Gielen, *The Murmuring of the Artistic Multitude: Global Art, Memory and Post-Fordism* (Amsterdam: Valiz, 2010).

10. See Karl Marx, *Capital*, vol. 3, trans. David Fernbach (London: Penguin, 1991), 596–97. I take the definition from the glossary on Marxists .org, www.marxists.org/glossary/terms/f/i.htm.

11. Bernard Stiegler, with Frédéric Neyrat, "Interview: From Libidinal Economy to the Ecology of the Spirit," trans. Arne De Boever, *Parrhesia*, no. 14 (2012): 9–15.

12. Franco Berardi, *Precarious Rhapsody: Semiocapitalism and the Pathologies of the Post-Alpha Generation* (London: Minor Compositions, 2009).

13. Bernard Stiegler, *For a New Critique of Political Economy*, trans. Daniel Ross (Cambridge, UK: Polity, 2010), 47. Several years after Houellebecq's novel was published, Alan Greenspan published a book titled *The Map and the Territory: Risk, Human Nature, and The Future of Forecasting* (New York: Penguin, 2013), in which he looks back at the 2008 crash—asking how it was possible that the financial models that were being used at the time were wrong—and tries to figure out how we can better predict the future. I return to this problematic in the conclusion.

14. Bret Easton Ellis, *American Psycho* (New York: Vintage, 1991).

15. Van Wesemael points out that many of Houellebecq's characters "lose touch with reality." See Sabine van Wesemael, "Post-Realism and Anti-Realism," in Yra van Dijk and Thomas Vaessens, *Reconsidering the Postmodern: European Literature Beyond Relativism* (Amsterdam: Amsterdam University Press, 2014), 100. At some point in the novel, Houellebecq's narrator provides his revoltingly ugly colleague Raphaël Tisserand with a knife to kill a couple they meet at a club in one of the towns where they have traveled for work; Tisserand, however, doesn't go through with the murder and is killed in a car accident that same night. See Michel Houellebecq, *Whatever*, trans. Paul Hammond (London: Serpent's Tail, 2011), 116–20.

16. Biron, quoted in Sweeney, "And yet, 42.
17. Ibid., 43.
18. Ibid.; "vital exhaustion" is a quote from *Whatever.*
19. Houellebecq, quoted in ibid.
20. Ibid.
21. Ibid., 49; the quotes are again from *Whatever.*
22. Ibid.
23. Wood, "Off the Map," 78.
24. Ibid.
25. Ibid.
26. See, for example, Thomas Klinkert, *Epistemologische Fiktionen: Zur Interferenz von Literatur und Wissenschaft seit der Aufklärung* (Berlin: De Gruyter, 2010). Delphine Grass writes in this context of "Houellebecq and the Novel as Site of Epistemic Rebellion," www.ucl.ac.uk/opticon1826/archive/issue1/VfPHoullebecqPDF.pdf.
27. I have made this argument in Arne De Boever, "The Politics of Realism in Rancière and Houellebecq," in *Rancière and Literature*, ed. Grace Hellyer and Julian Murphet (Edinburgh: Edinburgh University Press, 2016), 226–48.
28. Houellebecq, *Whatever*, 155.
29. Michel Houellebecq, *The Map and the Territory*, trans. Gavin Bowd (New York: Kopf, 2012), 3. Hereafter cited in text by page number.
30. The joke is there in the original French as well, although I think it works better in translation. In French, Jed's confusion feels a little forced. Michel Houellebecq, *La carte et le territoire* (Paris: J'ai Lu, 2013).
31. When asked whether Houellebecq would be interested in writing such an essay, Beigbeder suggests that "money" might convince him (79).
32. See also Houellebecq, *Carte*, 150.
33. Ibid.
34. A separate chapter could be written about the role of Pollock in some of the sources that I worked with for this book. In Teddy Wayne's novel *Kapitoil* (New York: Harper Perennial, 2010), Karim Issar, a financial programmer from Qatar, visits the Museum of Modern Art in New York and sees a Pollock exhibition. At first, he does not enjoy the work, "but then I see some quotations by Pollock about his painting, such as 'I don't use the accident—'cause I deny the accident.' And I reevaluate that possibly Pollock's paintings have more value, because he has a philosophy similar to mine, which is that life is ultimately predictable" (17); that and another Pollock quote—"My paintings do not have a center, but depend on the same amount of interest throughout" (19)—will form the basis for Issar's stock market program, the algorithm he writes to predict the fluctuations in oil prices. Pollock's

"automatic art"—an art that is made without thinking but in which everything appears to be thought out—is also referenced in Alex Garland's *Ex Machina* (Universal, 2015), but to think a different kind of automated life than the one that Issar early on in *Kapitoil* alludes to: one that, precisely, would act nonautomatically, without thinking. I think the latter reading of Pollock is closer to the mark.

35. "Epistemology Noir" was the title of a talk MacKay delivered at the West Hollywood Public Library, at the invitation of the MA Aesthetics and Politics program at the California Institute of the Arts, on Thursday, November 10, 2016.

36. Negarestani presented "Requiem for the Detective Novel" in a talk at the Bijou theater at the California Institute of the Arts, on Monday, November 14, 2016. As will be clear, such a critique of the detective novel far exceeds what Ben Parker in a perceptive reading of the Sherlock Holmes stories calls "the method effect": if, as per Parker's argument, none of the clues provided in a Holmes story enable Holmes's deductive method—they merely create the method effect, whereas the method in fact always relies on some outside clue not available to the reader or to Holmes's assistant, Watson—the critique of the detective novel I pursue here radicalizes that "outside." Had the realism been more realist in a Holmes story—that is, had it represented all the details that Holmes saw—then the stories would really have been illustrations of the deductive method. The situation I am interested in, rather, is one in which all the details would have been provided, but without success for the deductive method. Reality escapes deduction. See Ben Parker, "The Method Effect," *Novel* 49, no. 3 (2016): 449–66.

37. Houellebecq, *Carte*, 365.

38. A more obvious translation for "couilles en or" would seem to be "brass balls." Although it is currently used to refer to an audacious person, it used to have an economic meaning (to drive a hard bargain). However, that sense is not appropriate in this context.

39. Tom Emerson, "Michel Houellebecq" (interview), *Art Review* (Summer 2016): 99.

40. Houellebecq, *Carte*, 374.

41. Ibid.

42. "There's a striking similarity between our oceanfront residences and the Jeff Koons sculptures we have on site," the real estate ad on the back of my *New York Times Magazine* (January 17, 2016) says. "Both are remarkably contemporary and highly sought after." Koons's *Pluto and Proserpina* is featured in the accompanying photograph.

43. I take this term from: Yuk Hui, *On the Existence of Digital Objects* (Minneapolis: University of Minnesota Press, 2016).

6. FINANCING THE NOVEL: BEN LERNER'S *10:04*

1. Hari Kunzru, "Impossible Mirrors," review of Ben Lerner, *10:04*, *New York Times Sunday Book Review*, September 7, 2014, 12.

2. Ben Lerner, *10:04* (New York: Faber and Faber, 2014), 112. Hereafter cited in text by page number.

3. Karl Smith, "Time Is a Flat Circle: Ben Lerner Interviewed," Quietus.com, February 8, 2015, http://thequietus.com/articles/17190-ben-lerner-interview-1004-leaving-atocha-station-poetry-time-knausgaard.

4. Franco Berardi, *After the Future*, ed. Gary Genosko and Nicholas Thoburn, trans. Arianna Bove et al. (Edinburgh: AK Press, 2011), 34.

5. Kunzru, "Impossible," 12.

6. See, for example, Pieter Vermeulen, "How Should a Person Be (Transpersonal)? Ben Lerner, Roberto Esposito, and the Biopolitics of the Future." *Political Theory* 1, no. 23 (2016): 1–23. I would like to thank Pieter for his helpful comments on an earlier version of this chapter.

7. The sentence is repeated on 109.

8. Sarah Chihaya, Joshua Kotin, and Kinoshi Nishikawa. "'The Contemporary' by the Numbers," Post45 (website), February 29, 2016, http://post45.research.yale.edu/2016/02/the-contemporary-by-the-numbers/.

9. Tao Lin, "Interview with Ben Lerner," *Believer* (Fall 2015), www.believermag.com/exclusives/?read=interview_lerner_2.

10. Maggie Nelson, "Slipping the Surly Bonds of Earth: On Ben Lerner's Latest," *Los Angeles Review of Books*, August 24, 2014, https://lareviewofbooks.org/article/95063/.

11. When it comes to considering the novel as a thing of value, it is mostly the Novel-on-contract to which our attention turns—not the actual novel. With artworks, that situation seems to be different: their value crucially depends on their actuality (not their virtuality). It may be the novel, then, that is the financial instrument *par excellence*—much more so than the artwork, which generates speculative value after its actualization rather than before.

12. Marx, Karl. *Capital*, vol. 1, trans. Ben Fowkes (London: Penguin, 1976), 163–77.

13. Walter Benjamin, "The Work of Art in the Age of Mechanical Reproduction," in *Illuminations*, ed. Hannah Arendt, trans. Harry Zohn (New York: Schocken, 1968), 217–51.

14. Ben Lerner, *The Hatred of Poetry* (New York: Farrar, Straus and Giroux, 2016), 6–7. Lerner published what seems to have been a trial run for *Hatred of Poetry* in "Diary," *London Review of Books* 37, no. 12 (2015): 42–43.

15. Ben Lerner, *Leaving the Atocha Station* (Minneapolis: Coffee House Press, 2011), 58.

16. Lerner, *Hatred*, 8–9.

17. Ibid., 38.

18. Ibid.

19. Giorgio Agamben, *The Coming Community*, trans. Michael Hardt (Minneapolis: University of Minnesota Press, 2003), 89.

20. On this, see Wendy Brown, *Undoing the Demos: Neoliberalism's Stealth Revolution* (New York: Zone Books, 2015). I learned a thing or two on this count from Pieter Vermeulen's lecture "Downscaling the Future: Literature after the Space Program," delivered at the international conference *Questions of Scale in Contemporary Literature and Criticism*, Ghent University, March 23–25, 2016.

21. Ben Lerner, "The Polish Rider," *New Yorker*, June 6–13, 2016, www.newyorker.com/magazine/2016/06/06/the-polish-rider-by-ben-lerner.

22. Nicholas Brown, "Art After Art After Art," Nonsite.org, no. 18 (2016), http://nonsite.org/feature/art-after-art-after-art.

23. Kunzru associates this with the novel's criticism of neoliberalism. See Kunzru, "Impossible," 12.

24. See also Lerner, *10:04*, 81, 93, 99, 108, 148.

25. Vermeulen makes this point as well, suggesting that by the end of *10:04*, the novel has "earned its way back to a different future" ("How," 17).

26. See the introduction.

27. Joan's hand is in fact connected to and contrasted with Marty's disappearing hand in *Back to the Future*—in Joan's case her hand disappears because the future is present, in Marty's case it disappears because the future is absent, due to his traveling back into the past.

28. This quotation is taken from the narrator's *New Yorker* short story "The Golden Vanity," which is reproduced in *10:04*. In other words, it is taken from the narrator's prose, not his poetry. As if to underline the point that is made here about representational realism, the text is accompanied by an image.

29. Maggie Nelson has characterized the novel as a concept novel, which evokes its proximity to conceptual art. See Nelson, "Slipping."

30. I intend to explore this claim in detail in a future project.

31. On this count, Lerner's work has been associated with that of W. G. Sebald, Teju Cole, Chris Kraus, Sheila Heti, and Geoff Dyer for the ways in which it dissolves "plot and character . . . in a series of passages, held together by occasional photographs and a subjectivity that hovers close to (but is never quite identical with) the subjectivity of the writer" (Kunzru, "Impossible," 12). In the words of another reviewer, Lerner's work reveals a "distaste for the clunky machinery of traditional narrative fiction" that can also be found in the work of Jenny Offill or Karl Ove Knausgård: "Maybe the realistic novel has outlived its usefulness. . . . Maybe it's time to wean ourselves off plot and character and scenes and conflict and all the rest, just leave those things for television. Maybe the most we can hope for on the page is a pinpoint of focus

on the writer in front of us, the adventures of a single consciousness at play." Tom Perrotta, "Fall From Grace," review of Kate Atkinson, *A God In Ruins*, *New York Times*, May 10, 2015, 30.

32. Smith, "Time."

33. Ibid.

34. Ibid., 9.

35. Smith, "Time."

36. Lee Edelman, *No Future: Queer Theory and the Death Drive* (Durham: Duke University Press, 2004).

37. Nelson, "Slipping."

38. Edelman, *No Future*, 4.

39. Maggie Nelson, *The Argonauts* (Minneapolis: Graywolf Press, 2016).

40. Nelson, "Slipping."

41. It is worth pointing out that Michael Lewis, the financial journalist on whose work I've relied throughout this book, "declines to take advances, which he calls 'corrupting,' even though he could easily earn seven figures." Alexandra Alter, "The Men Who Shaped 'Moneyball,'" review of Michael Lewis, *The Undoing Project*, *New York Times*, December 4, 2016, 5. It may be that Lewis is in a position to decline such advances because, unlike Lerner or Nelson, he had a career in bonds trading before he became a writer.

42. See Tanya Agathocleous, "Life (Narrative) in the End Times," *Los Angeles Review of Books*, November 29, 2016, https://lareviewofbooks.org/article/life-narrative-end-times/.

43. See Berardi, *After the Future*.

44. Nelson, "Slipping."

45. Ibid.

46. Berardi, *After the Future*, 177.

47. Ibid., 166.

48. Ibid., 120.

49. Ercolino uses the term "the maximalist novel" to characterize works by some of the novelists that Wood mentions, even though (as Katherine Hayles in a review of Ercolino notes) the term *information* does not play a key role in his study of such novels. Stefano Ercolino, *The Maximalist Novel: From Thomas Pynchon's* Gravity's Rainbow *to Roberto Bolaño's* 2666 (New York: Bloomsbury, 2014). See also Katherine N. Hayles, "Maxing Out the Novel," review of Stefano Ercolino, *The Maximalist Novel*, *Novel* 49, no. 3 (2016): 519–21.

50. I write "surprisingly" because "minimalism" in art usually "describes a movement . . . that rejected representational content, even in its abstracted form, while foregrounding materials and construction"; in short, it wasn't realist at all. See Emily Zubernis, "Henry James' Minimalist Novel," *Novel* 49, no. 3 (2016): 467.

51. W. G. Sebald, *Austerlitz*, trans. Anthea Bell (New York: Modern Library, 2001), 197.

52. Brian Holmes, "Information's Metropolis: Chicago and the New Nature of Global Finance," in *Volatile Smile*, ed. Beate Geissler, Oliver Sann, and Brian Holmes (Nuremberg: Moderne Kunst Nürnberg, 2014), 52.

53. Donna Haraway, *Simians, Cyborgs, and Women: The Reinvention of Nature* (New York: Routledge, 1991).

54. Giorgio Agamben, "In Praise of Profanation," in *Profanations*, trans. Jeff Fort (New York: Zone Books, 2007), 73–92.

55. By "wholly transformed" I mean to echo Benjamin's notion of a "wholly transformed" work. Walter Benjamin, "Critique of Violence," in *Selected Writings*, vol. 1, *1913–1926*, ed. Marcus Bullock and Michael W. Jennings (Cambridge, MA: Harvard University Press, 1996), 246.

CONCLUSION

1. Niccolò Machiavelli, *The Discourses*, trans. Leslie Walker and Brian Richardson (New York: Penguin, 2003), 352.

2. W. G. Sebald, *Austerlitz*, trans. Anthea Bell (New York: Modern Library, 2001), 14.

3. Vyjayanthi Venuturupalli Rao, "Speculation, Now," in *Speculation, Now: Essays and Artwork*, ed. Vyjayanthi Venuturupalli Rao, Prem Krishnamurthy, and Carin Kuoni (Durham, NC: Duke University Press, 2014), 19.

4. See Anders Engberg-Pedersen, *Empire of Chance: The Napoleonic Wars and the Disorder of Things* (Cambridge, MA: Harvard University Press, 2015). See also Engberg-Pedersen, "Governed by Chance: On War, Disorder, and Representation," *boundary2*, September 29, 2015, www.boundary2.org/2015/09/governed-by-chance-on-war-disorder-and-representation/. The author recalls Laurence Sterne's satire of star-shaped fortifications and the geometrical principle, indicating the author's position—in line with his criticism of realism—that war as a phenomenon "could [not] be rationalized and brought under control . . . with the aid of the rules of geometry."

5. Roberto Esposito, *Bíos: Biopolitics and Philosophy*, trans. Timothy Campbell (Minneapolis: University of Minnesota Press, 2008).

6. Michel Foucault, *The Birth of Biopolitics: Lectures at the Collège de France 1975–1976*, ed. Arnold Davidson, trans. David Macey (New York: Picador, 2001); Giorgio Agamben, *The Kingdom and the Glory: For a Theological Genealogy of Economy and Government*, trans. Lorenzo Chiesa, with Matteo Mandarini (Stanford, CA: Stanford University Press, 2011).

7. Jacques Derrida, "Oligarchies: Naming, Enumerating, Counting," in *Politics of Friendship*, trans. George Collins (New York: Verso, 1997), 1–25.

8. One might point out that those two are not the same, and not necessarily related. But at least one of the novels I have discussed in this book suggests a connection. When Hugo Quarry starts to become nervous about the algorithm's trading pattern in *The Fear Index*, he associates his sinking feeling with the nervousness he felt "when I was . . . selling collateralized debt." Robert Harris, *The Fear Index* (New York: Knopf, 2012), 106.

9. One could argue in this context that indulgences were an early version of this kind of practice; this would, not entirely incorrectly, cast my book as a "protestant" response to such practices, evident in part in the distinction I have sought to trace here between finance and capitalism.

10. See Scott Patterson, *The Quants: How A New Breed of Math Whizzes Conquered Wall Street and Nearly Destroyed It* (New York: Crown Business, 2010); Scott Patterson, *Dark Pools: The Rise of the Machine Traders and the Rigging of the US Stock Market* (New York: Crown Business, 2012); Michael Lewis, *Flash Boys: A Wall Street Revolt* (New York: Norton, 2014); and Sal Arnuk and Joseph Saluzzi, *Broken Markets: How High Frequency Trading and Predatory Practices on Wall Street Are Destroying Investor Confidence and Your Portfolio* (Upper Saddle River, NJ: FT Press, 2012).

11. Brian Holmes, "Information's Metropolis: Chicago and the New Nature of Global Finance," in *Volatile Smile*, ed. Beate Geissler, Oliver Sann, and Brian Holmes (Nuremberg: Moderne Kunst Nürnberg, 2014), 37.

12. Hari Kunzru, *Gods Without Men* (New York: Vintage, 2013), 163.

13. Kunzru, *Gods*, 406.

14. Berthold Schoene already suggested in a reading of *American Psycho* that Patrick Bateman (whom Christian Bale will later portray in Mary Harron's film based on the novel) suffered from Asperger syndrome. See Berthold Schoene, "Serial Masculinity: Psychopathology and Oedipal Violence in Bret Easton Ellis' *American Psycho*," *Modern Fiction Studies* 54, no. 2 (2008): 378–97.

15. Frank Pasquale, *The Black Box Society: The Secret Algorithms That Control Money and Information* (Cambridge, MA: Harvard University Press, 2015), 137.

16. Normally, fortification would be associated with stability and security, whereas liquidity would be associated with instability and insecurity—dry land versus high seas, if you will. In the case of the stock market, however, liquidity is good and fortification is bad. You want the market to really flow—not just flow through the addition of hollow volume such as the volume created by high-frequency trading. When it comes to the stock market, fluidity is associated with stability and security, whereas fortification tends to mark a blockage of liquidity—a stop in the flow—and a frustration to the market. Economic defense systems, while claiming to add liquidity to the market, in fact contribute to its fortification.

17. I want to thank Ryan Jeffery for alerting me to Switzerland's reappropriation of what he (in a proposal for a video project that he shared in personal correspondence) refers to as "Switzerland's infrastructure of military bunkers and fortresses" to store data. Built during World War II and the Cold War, and designed to "withstand even nuclear attack" (Jeffery), these bunkers mark the way in which a nation of bankers seeks to turn data into gold today. I am refracturing that development here to think the way in which various forms of digitized trading mark a bunker-like fortification of the markets that, while claiming to bring more stability and security, in fact render the market less stable and less secure. I thank Ryan for the following references: Cornelius Rahn, Carolyn Bandel, and Hans Nichols, "Switzerland Shifting from Bankers to Bunkers in Data Push," Bloomberg Business, February 25, 2014, www.bloomberg.com/news/articles/2014-02-25/switzerland-shifting-from-bankers-to-bunkers-in-data-push; Jeremy Luedi, "Switzerland's Alpine Fortresses Spur Start-Up Boom," Global Risk Insights, December 20, 2015, http://globalriskinsights.com/2015/12/switzerlands-alpine-fortresses-spur-start-up-boom/.

18. The following three paragraphs are taken (with some minor adjustments) from my book *States of Exception in the Contemporary Novel: Martel, Eugenides, Coetzee, Sebald* (New York: Continuum, 2012).

19. W. G. Sebald, *Austerlitz*, trans. Anthea Bell (New York: Modern Library, 2001), 14.

20. Ibid., 15.

21. Ibid., 17.

22. Ibid.

23. Ibid., 18.

24. Ibid., 19.

25. I am not the only one to have turned to Agamben for a philosophical analysis of contemporary finance. See, for example, Bjerg, *Making Money*, 181–83. Bjerg uses Agamben's theory of the state of exception to refer to the peculiar status of the US Federal Reserve, both inside and outside government.

26. Giorgio Agamben, "What Is a Camp?," in *Means Without End: Notes on Politics*, trans. Vincenzo Binetti and Cesare Casarino (Minneapolis: University of Minnesota Press, 2000), 39.

27. This is briefly alluded to in Adam McKay's film *The Big Short* (Paramount, 2015), but it constitutes a key part of Cristina Alger's plot in *The Darlings*, as discussed in chapter 1.

28. Michael Lewis, ed., *Panic: The Story of Modern Financial Insanity* (New York: Norton, 2009).

29. The latter is the approach of Paul Willimott, who argues that mathematical models need to become more street smart and need to learn to distinguish, for example, between true and false information.

30. See, for example, Jeff Cox, "Ready for 'Splash Crash,' the Ultimate Market Meltdown?," CNBC, February 3, 2011, www.cnbc.com/id/41408510. Mark Gorton, for example, is one high-frequency trader who has warned of the imminent collapse of the market due to electronic trading. See "High-frequency Trader Warns of potential Market 'Catastrophe,'" *Financial Times* (online), February 4, 2016, www.ft.com/content/29919a66-cb28-11e5-be0b-b7ece4e953a0.

31. One can think here of the mortgage bond "Jenga" tower in McKay's *The Big Short*, which I already discussed in the introduction. The tower is construed to guarantee profit by providing liquidity. But as soon as the sub-prime mortgages fail, the collapsing tower sucks all liquidity out of the market, thus effectively operating as a liquidity blocker and revealing that the liquidity the tower provided was merely an effect or illusion.

32. There are two novels that have drawn out this complicity between fortification and contemporary finance very well: Don DeLillo's *Cosmopolis*, which operates in tandem with his defense strategy novel, *Point Omega*, and Robert Harris's novel *The Fear Index* (see the introduction and chapter 3, respectively).

33. As Leigh Claire La Berge points out in a footnote to her book, Marieke de Goede has indicated that "Lady Credit is not unlike [the] ancient goddess, Fortuna, who ruled capriciously over the affairs of men." Goede, quoted in Leigh Claire La Berge, *Scandals and Abstraction: Financial Fiction of the Long 1980s* (Oxford: Oxford University Press, 2015), 212n69.

34. Niccolò Machiavelli, *The Prince*, trans. David Wootton (Indianapolis: Hackett, 1995), 76.

35. Kathryn Schultz, "The Really Big One," *New Yorker*, July 20, 2015, www.newyorker.com/magazine/2015/07/20/the-really-big-one.

36. The term *cosmic realism* has been used before; see, for example, Francesca Mari, "Cosmic Realism," *New Republic*, May 27, 2008, https://newrepublic.com/article/62425/cosmic-realism.

37. Rancière quoted in Martín Plot, *The Aesthetico-Political: The Question of Democracy in Merleau-Ponty, Arendt, and Rancière* (New York: Bloomsbury, 2014), 9.

38. Also worth noting in this context is the possible importance of psychosis for religious history. See E. D. Murray, M. G. Cunningham, and B. H. Price, "The Role of Psychotic Disorders in Religious History Reconsidered," *Journal of Neuropsychiatry and Clinical Neuroscience* 24, no. 4 (2012): 410–26. The article focuses on Abraham, Moses, Jesus, and Saint Paul.

39. Rancière quoted in Plot, *Aesthetico-Political*, 9.

40. Vyjayanthi Venuturupalli Rao raises precisely these questions through a reference to Rancière as a different kind of speculator at the end of her

article "Speculation, Now," in Rao, Krishnamurthy, and Kuoni, eds, *Speculation, Now*, 14–25.

41. Ben Lerner, *10:04* (New York: Faber and Faber, 2014), 50.

42. Teddy Wayne, *Kapitoil* (New York: Harper Perennial, 2010), 281.

43. Nick Srnicek and Alex Williams, "#ACCELERATE MANIFESTO for an accelerationist politics," http://criticallegalthinking.com/2013/05/14/accelerate-manifesto-for-an-accelerationist-politics/. For a more nuanced account, see Nick Srnicek and Alex Williams, *Inventing the Future: Postcapitalism and a World Without Work* (New York: Verso, 2015).

44. The term *decelerationism* has many manifestations, but most relevant in this context is probably the work of Paul Virilio, in which it occurs; Virilio is a theorist of speed who also writes about military fortifications. See Paul Virilio, *Speed and Politics: An Essay on Dromology*, trans. Mark Polizzotti (Los Angeles: Semiotext(e), 2006).

45. See my *States of Exception.*

46. Nothing is beyond OOO approaches, not even nothing; OOO scholars are interested in the interconnectedness of everything. I am thinking, for example, of the use of lists in Ian Bogost's work; see, for example, the opening pages of Ian Bogost, *Alien Phenomenology, Or What It's Like to Be a Thing* (Minneapolis: University of Minnesota Press, 2012). Tim Morton in his *The Ecological Thought* (Cambridge, MA: Harvard University Press, 2010) insists on the interconnectedness of everything. I intend to come back to this in a future book project.

47. Anahid Nersessian, *Utopia, Limited: Romanticism and Adjustment* (Cambridge, MA: Harvard University Press, 2015).

48. See, for example Byung-Chul Han, *The Burnout Society*, trans. Erik Butler (Stanford, CA: Stanford University Press, 2015). However, I do not endorse Han's plea for "secrecy" that he has developed in his *The Transparency Society*, trans. Erik Butler (Stanford, CA: Stanford University Press, 2015).

49. Jean Baudrillard, *The Vital Illusion*, ed. Julia Witwer (New York: Columbia University Press, 2000), 5.

50. Ibid.

51. See, for example, Lee Edelman, *No Future: Queer Theory and the Death Drive* (Durham: Duke University Press, 2004), 60–64.

52. Berge, *Scandals*, 124.

53. Ibid., 125.

54. Ibid., 125–26.

55. Ibid., 126. Michelangelo Antonioni can be said to evoke this idea in his film *Eclipse* (Times Film Corporation, 1962), when he shows how trading on the exchange in Rome is interrupted for a minute to mark the death (heart attack, what else?) of a fellow trader.

56. The attention to architecture in Antonioni's *Eclipse*—and architecture is of course a key theme throughout his oeuvre—needs to be read in relation to that film's representation of the trading floor, and the inhuman aspects of both. To continue what I mentioned in the previous note: death, then, marks the intrusion of a human element in the uninhabitable environment of the market. Although it is a death that may have been produced by trading, as a negativity it also marks the interruption of trading's cancerous form of life that goes on even during a respectful minute of silence (the phones keep ringing, for example; they have no respect for death).

57. Pasquale has drawn out an interesting comparison in this context, namely, that although the terror attacks of 9/11 triggered a huge upgrade of the government's "surveillance capabilities in the search for terrorists," the 2008 financial crash did not produce "a similar level of restructuring, reinvestment, and fortification of surveillance in the financial realm" (*Black Box Society*, 186). I am adding some philosophical nuance to the term *fortification* here.

58. See my *States of Exception*.

59. See, for example, Matthew Poole and Manuel Shvartzberg, eds, *The Politics of Parametricism: Digital Technologies in Architecture* (New York: Bloomsbury, 2015).

60. Arne De Boever, *Plastic Sovereignties: Agamben and the Politics of Aesthetics* (Edinburgh: Edinburgh University Press, 2016).

61. See "SEC Approves IEX Proposal to Launch National Exchange, Issues Interpretation on Automated Securities Prices," press release, www.sec.gov/news/pressrelease/2016-123.html.

62. See, for example, Bourree Lam, "A New Stock Exchange?," *Atlantic*, November 18, 2011, www.theatlantic.com/business/archive/2015/11/iex-high-frequency-trading/416439/; and "'Flash Boys' Hero Is Picking a Fight With Hedge Fund Citadel," Bloomberg, January 29, 2016, www.bloomberg.com/news/articles/2016-01-21/iex-s-exchange-quest-spurs-a-flash-boys-fight-with-citadel.

63. Many countries have been repatriating their gold reserves, which, for example, Germany had stored in the United States due to the Russian threat. In 2013, however, Germany asked for its gold back, following a move started by Hugo Chavez, who repatriated gold to Venezuela. Many European nation-states followed, and the gold price was pushed up. So there appears to be a reinvestment in the gold standard that is taking place, a continued belief in the old saying that he who owns the gold, makes the rules (as Nico Pantelis has pointed out). See, for example Nico Pantelis, "Geef ons ons goud terug," *Standaard*, January 22, 2013, www.standaard.be/cnt/blnpa_20130122_001.

64. Bifo has suggested that in the face of this, the people should claim their "right to insolvency": Franco Berardi, *The Uprising: On Poetry and Finance* (Los Angeles, Semiotext(e), 2012), 55.

65. Pasquale also references Plato's allegory in his discussion of financial algorithms. See Pasquale, *Black Box Society*, 190.

66. In an interview about his film *Wall Street*, Oliver Stone points out: "Profit is only justifiable with real production. Profit based on speculation is not healthy for any society." "Interview: Oliver Stone," *New Statesman*, October 04, 2010, 73.

INDEX